RESOURCE COMMUNITIES

This book provides an innovative approach to understanding the governance of resource communities, by showcasing how the past and present informs the future.

Resource communities have complicated relationships with the past, and this makes their relationship with the future, and the future itself, also complicated. The book digs deeply into the myriad legacies left by a history of resource extraction in a community and makes use of interdisciplinary and transdisciplinary perspectives to understand the complex issues being faced by a range of different communities that are reliant on different types of resources across the world. From coal and gold mining, to fishing towns and logging communities, the book explores the legacies of boom and bust economies, social memory, trauma and identity, the interactions between power and knowledge and the implications for adaptive governance. Balancing conceptual and theoretical understandings with empirical and practical knowledge of resource communities, natural resource use and social-ecological relationships, the book argues that solutions for individual communities need to be embraced in the community and not just in the perspectives of visiting experts. Linking the past, present and futures of resource communities in a new way, the book concludes by providing practical recommendations for breaking open dependencies on the past, including deepening awareness of the social, economic and environmental contexts, establishing strong governance and developing community strategies, plans and policies for the future.

This book will be of great interest to students and scholars of natural resource governance and management, extractive industries, environmental policy, community planning and development, environmental geography and sustainable development, as well as policymakers involved in supporting community development in natural resource-dependent communities across the world.

Kristof Van Assche is a Professor of Planning, Governance and Development at the University of Alberta, Canada, and a Senior Fellow at the Centre for Development Research (ZEF) at Bonn University, Germany.

Monica Gruezmacher is a Research Associate in the Department of Earth and Atmospheric Sciences at the University of Alberta, Canada, and a Teaching Assistant Professor at the School of Science and the Environment at Memorial University of Newfoundland, Canada.

Lochner Marais is a Professor in the Centre for Development Support at the University of the Free State, South Africa, and an Honorary Professor at the Sustainable Minerals Institute at the University of Queensland, Australia.

Xaquin Perez-Sindin is an Assistant Professor in the Faculty of Economic Sciences at the University of Warsaw, Poland.

Earthscan Studies in Natural Resource Management

For more information about this series, please visit: www.routledge.com/books/series/ECNRM/

RESOURCE COMMUNITIES

Past Legacies and Future Pathways

Kristof Van Assche, Monica Gruezmacher,
Lochner Marais, and Xaquin Perez-Sindin

Routledge
Taylor & Francis Group
LONDON AND NEW YORK

earthscan
from Routledge

Designed cover image: © Getty Images

First published 2024
by Routledge
4 Park Square, Milton Park, Abingdon, Oxon OX14 4RN

and by Routledge
605 Third Avenue, New York, NY 10158

Routledge is an imprint of the Taylor & Francis Group, an informa business

© 2024 Kristof Van Assche, Monica Gruezmacher, Lochner Marais, and
Xaquin Perez-Sindin

The right of Kristof Van Assche, Monica Gruezmacher, Lochner Marais, and
Xaquin Perez-Sindin to be identified as authors of this work has been asserted
in accordance with sections 77 and 78 of the Copyright, Designs and Patents
Act 1988.

All rights reserved. No part of this book may be reprinted or reproduced or
utilised in any form or by any electronic, mechanical, or other means, now known
or hereafter invented, including photocopying and recording, or in any
information storage or retrieval system, without permission in writing from
the publishers.

Trademark notice: Product or corporate names may be trademarks or registered
trademarks, and are used only for identification and explanation without intent to
infringe.

British Library Cataloguing-in-Publication Data
A catalogue record for this book is available from the British Library

ISBN: 978-1-032-36474-2 (hbk)
ISBN: 978-1-032-36472-8 (pbk)
ISBN: 978-1-003-33214-5 (ebk)

DOI: 10.4324/9781003332145

Typeset in Times New Roman
by MPS Limited, Dehradun

CONTENTS

1

INTRODUCTION

Resource communities in the imperfect
grip of the past

Key questions

Resource communities have complicated relationships with the past. This makes their relationship with the future and their future itself complicated as well. The past is remembered in a continuous process of reconstruction and reinterpretation. Some versions of the past are codified and become history and that history can play a role in the formation of policies, plans, and future strategies. Other versions circulate as local knowledge and as institutional knowledge in governmental and other organizations. This knowledge of the past, this version of memory, is also likely to play a role.

Besides history and memory, the past leaves traces and creates legacies, both at personal level and at the level of communities. Legacies are broader and more numerous than memories. Such legacies can take different forms in the present and they can shape the future of a community. Discerning these legacies can help us understand how communities organize themselves, how they look at the future and how they can or cannot organize themselves for the future.

This book argues that resource communities are marked by a particular set of legacies that tends to create difficulties in envisioning and organizing alternative futures – social memory can play tricks. In many cases, communities lack the governance tools to move the community in a different direction, even when this is sorely needed. The need can be immediate, as when the industry already left or collapsed. It can also be less visible, as when a resource-based future looks very doubtful and very risky. Thus, we tackle two important questions.

DOI: 10.4324/9781003332145-1

How does the past shape resource communities and their functioning?

How does it shape the thinking about and organizing for the future?

In the next chapters, we will slowly unpack these questions and try to answer them using a variety of empirical and theoretical work. After answering them, we can try to address a third question, relevant for the resource communities themselves, but also for nations trying to move away from fossil fuel dependence, unsustainable extraction of minerals and irresponsible management of forests and seas:

How can resource communities extricate themselves from the past and choose more freely how to navigate the future?

Resource towns and their problems

Before we start unpacking these questions, we would like to visit a resource town. What kind of place are we talking about? Resource towns are found in almost every nation both north and south, in developing and developed countries, and in recent times as well as in the distant past. These are places usually in rural or natural landscapes that are dedicated to the extraction of a particular resource and whose life is to a large extent revolving around the extraction of this resource. Tight couplings between life and work contribute to the consolidation of a strong identity, one shared by most of the community (Fraser & Larmer, 2010; Halseth & Sullivan, 2002; Loayza & Rigolini, 2016; Marais et al., 2018). People in the resource town know about the resource itself, the risks and opportunities of its extraction and about the myriad technicalities associated with the entire process, even if they don't directly work in the industry.

When discussing resource towns, it is important to understand them beyond the physical footprint of the infrastructure or limit the concept to the administrative unit. When we refer to a resource town, we are referring to the people who live together and aspire to certain things. It can be understood as the idealized or perceived community from the point of view of those living in it and should not be confused with the interpretation of community from an outsider's perspective. As outsiders, we cannot assume that everyone living in a resource town feels part of a community or that they feel a part of that specific community. If the place is perceived by most to be a temporary arrangement, a means to make some money and move on, then investments in maintaining the community at all costs will amount to squandered resources. In contrast, if there is an aspiration to live together, to share a common future, then vicious circles need to be turned into virtuous circles and alternative ways forward need to be sought.

Resource towns are often lingering somewhere in-between being a community and being just a workplace, a camp or industry town. Resource towns constantly battle between short-term perspectives, forces that pull the community into divestment and longer-term forces that tend to push towards community identity. It is not necessarily a battle between good and evil (Freudenburg & Gramling, 1994; Hessing et al., 2014). Short-term perspectives and transient relationships with the place and the people have real implications on how a place responds to change. We will show that both transience and overly stable identities come with problems for observation of and response to changes in the environment.

We can distinguish two types of social networks present in any community: bonding networks (those that connect individuals within a group) and bridging networks (those that connect individuals between groups). If bridging networks unravel, chances for new ideas to enter are limited and new solutions become less visible and accessible. The tendency for similar individuals to "stick together" begins to take over resulting in a very homogenized community, as described below. We will speak in Chapter 7 of the concentration problem, as a tendency in resource communities to simplify discourse and simplify institutions in governance, to reduce diversity in voices and tie imagined futures to a repetition of the past.

Not all municipalities can be considered communities and not all communities are municipalities or have a form of self-organization equivalent to a municipality. They can be unincorporated, they can be settlements mostly governed by a county or regional government, they can be subjected to mostly private governance, and there can be special linkages with a federal government for which the resource might have a special significance (High, 2021; Maher et al., 2019; Menkhaus, 2007). In the following chapters, we allow for this diversity and provide examples drawn from many geographies which acknowledge such diversity in organizational forms and in forms of identification with group, place and activity.

The weak ties in workcamps are not always weak in every respect. Social bonds might in fact be strong, camaraderie might be real and mutual support significant. Even so, the ties with the place and the involvement in its organization, the thinking about its future might be weak (Marais & Cloete, 2013; Markey et al., 2012). In more chaotic goldrush-type situations, less controlled by corporate actors, anarchy might prevail at times, a more singly minded and selfish pursuit of the resource, but what is similar with the work camp is the lack of interest in the place itself, its quality of life, its governance, and its future (Umbeck, 1977). Certainly, there is little interest in articulating alternative futures, beyond the resource.

It usually takes time and an environment which becomes attractive enough for partners and families before the future imposes itself. When not all family members can find work in the industry, because it is in decline, or modernizing, or when all other activities are marginalized by the high salaries in the resource sector, then families start to ask questions. When the quality of schools, services, leisure and cultural activities is not great, questions of quality of life emerge. Those questions can lead to an active involvement in community life, in local government, in the hope of changing the community, or they can lead to disillusionment and possibly to a move (Shandro et al., 2011; Stedman et al., 2004; Storey, 2001).

Yet, time and social ties, we will see, can be a problem as well as an asset. If families stayed in the same village and the same resource activity for centuries, if people identify with the place and the resource and not much else happened, this creates deep legacies which might be hard to overcome when the need for adaptation arises. Resources are not limitless, certainly not in one locale, and markets can be volatile. A strong social identity upheld by a strong and unified social memory has many benefits, celebrated in many literatures, yet it also comes with problems (Larsen, 2004). It might create networks of mutual support, a cultural identity that works and feels like an enlarged home or a big family, yet it can also create pressures to be the same and stay the same. Such pressures can be felt by individuals, but they also apply to entire communities, where local governance tends to be ill-equipped to think differently, test alternative futures and organize for them (Freudenburg, 1992; Van Assche et al., 2017).

Governance is thus a key concept in this book, as it is in governance that stories about past, present and future are distilled and translated into collectively binding decisions. It is there that policies, plans, and laws can be enacted. If there is also a form of local government, that can put the community on a different track. If there is no local government, governance is still likely to occur, except maybe in the anarchic goldrush camp referred to earlier. Such governance might have to rely more on informal institutions, as in unwritten and/or parallel systems of rules and tools of coordination and they might have to rely more on regional or national-level policies, plans and laws and on lobbying at those higher levels. In each case, it has to be in governance that alternative futures have to be agreed upon and then, moved towards implementation, either through the creation of new policies, plans or other institutions, or through the judicious and combined use of existing tools (Maher et al., 2019; Van Assche et al., 2016). We will make the case for community strategy as a type of tool and approach to move beyond the resource, or to rethink the form of extraction, its impacts, the redistribution of benefits and risks.

Boom and bust

Community strategy is not an easy task. Change for resource communities is hard, both for the transient types and for the ones where tradition and local ties hold a grip on local imagination and on governance. Many resource communities are trapped in feedback loops that reinforce patterns, behaviors and perspectives that ultimately lead to their further decline and sometimes demise. Dependence on one economic activity makes communities vulnerable, a vulnerability which will be analyzed from different angles in the rest of this book. If that activity relies on a natural resource and, as is often the case, on one form of extraction, the risks amplify. The resource extraction, if profitable, tends to overtake other activities, pro-resource factions will take a hold of politics and both past and future will be simplified, while the tools for collective action, the institutions, which could forge a new path, tend to erode (Collier, 2007; D'Apice & Ferri, 2016; Van Assche et al., 2017). These processes, too, will be analyzed in detail in later chapters.

The rigidities that come with an increasing dependence on and identification with the resource are usually not softened by the shocks that come from volatile resource markets. Many resource communities are marked by violent swings between exceedingly good and terrible times. We speak of boom and bust episodes (Adalid & Detken, 2007; Collier, 2007; Loayza & Rigolini, 2016; Tornell & Westermann, 2002). When resource extraction is going well a boom starts gaining momentum. There is a growing interest to profit, to make money. Enjoying other things the place has to offer becomes less important. The motivation to invest in services and infrastructure, arts and culture, education, dwindles. Companies are not interested, have no time to lose, workers try to maximize their income, especially if they know a bust will follow. Local governance is dealing with the immediate needs of the day: housing for new workers, basic infrastructure serving the industry, maintaining law and order (Halseth et al., 2017; Halseth & Ryser, 2016; Marais et al., 2018).

When the boom loses momentum, things start to slow down, there is even less motivation to invest in the place. People begin to look for a better life elsewhere, if they are not tied down by now worthless real estate or family ties. A decline in population means a diminishing tax base, which in turn reduces even more available services, which then deteriorates the living environment and local businesses, discouraging the educated labor force from staying and investing. Those who stay, wait for the next boom, if they can afford it. A welfare state can alleviate suffering and increase individual options, through education, training, mobility, yet can also contribute to the problems by keeping people and activities in place where moving and adapting might be better strategies (Tornell & Westermann, 2002).

The difference between more rooted and more transient communities can be felt here, yet violent dramatic cycles of boom and bust tend to reinforce transience. Boom periods for a resource can engender exploration of new areas, establishment of new camps, or towns, while in existing resource towns, a sudden large influx of people new to the place, its culture, its governance, will direct attention towards temporary solutions, in terms of housing, health care and services. Incoming people will not expect to stay forever. The receiving community and its administration will not expect them to do so and this shared expectation tends to foster non-attachment, non-involvement and in short, transience. In camps, the transience is embraced and more manageable, also because expectations are lower on all sides, yet the camp model closes the door for other development paths, for a different, maybe more vibrant future as a self-governing community (Marais, 2022).

In resource towns with deep and solid roots, chances are relatively slim that they will be rocked by waves of boom and bust. In newer settlements, development can head in a more dramatic direction, with phases of shrink and growth and with scores of newcomers unsettling local culture and unable to be assimilated into it quickly enough. When waves of boom or bust do occur in the older communities, they are likely to be mitigated by processes of selection and boundary maintenance: newcomers are not allowed, they can't get to the place, or they are gently or less gently kicked out. Paperwork, technical skills, language, ethnicity, religion, strong local or regional autonomy, can all be used to keep resource communities rooted, stable and culturally homogeneous, through booms and bust. Of course, this will mean that the boom is less of a boom and, luckily, the bust less of a bust.

The shocks of boom and bust therefore trigger change, yet not necessarily dramatic change. They typically do not break the dependence of a place on the resource, the identification with the resource. We will argue throughout this book that it takes a dramatic shock, the closure of a formerly central industry, to make a community rethink its dependence and identity. And even then, it can take generations to realize that the industry is not likely to come back and not inclined to save the community. If young people leave town and do not come back, memories can linger, without any real interrogation of the past, while a slow decline can mask the downfall (Freudenburg et al., 1982; Keeling, A & Sandlos, J, 2017; Ryser et al., 2016). A revival of the industry elsewhere can keep hopes high. A quick and dramatic collapse, an unavoidable observation that a return to the past is impossible, can be enough of a shock to open the minds, but by then, it can be too late, as the options to respond are narrow indeed.

All this to say that 'diversification' would, in the abstract, make a lot of sense for many resource communities, but that, in the course of their history the obstacles for such diversification accumulate. Legacies accumulate and keep each other in place. The prospect of a return of the 'good times', the next boom, traps people's mindset, holds life on pause. A bust could be a time for reflection, reconsideration, yet one can observe that local governments in both boom and bust times cling to short time horizons. When things are busy, one cannot look into the future and time is money, while in slow periods, the future looks so bleak and local governance feels so weak that not much is expected for the future. Moreover, the attention might be directed toward urgent needs created by the collapse of services and the proliferation of social problems (Conde & Le Billon, 2017; Freudenburg & Jones, 1991; Shandro et al., 2011).

When and if investment arrives again, things need to start moving once more. People will come. The weakened infrastructure and capacity are under great pressure. Investments made are once again targeting the industry's needs rather than those of the society. When the economy is booming, reinforcing feedback loops lead to the aforementioned concentration problem. Capital is concentrated in one sector, power and expertise in turn are also focused on those sectors, bringing in people with similar expectations and a similar outlook on life (Collier, 2007; Hessing et al., 2014). Alternative voices might have existed in the community, in governance circles, yet boom periods put pressure on alternatives as all must be coordinated towards supporting the growth of the main engine. If a sizeable population stays, through ups and downs, homophily will occur, as similar people will tend to flock to the community and as new arrivals will assimilate to survive in the high-pressure environment of the boomtown. A spiraling self-selection process is set in motion, attracting people with similar interests who believe in similar stories of success and who slowly become invested in and dependent on that success story (High, 2021; Lewis, 1983; Marais et al., 2018).

In the next chapters and especially in Chapters 5, 6, 7 and 8, these patterns of feedback loops will be explored and tied to the idea of a risky simplification of the resource community, a simplification which makes it harder and harder for a place to rethink and reinvent itself. We will also further ground our analyses in diverse literatures in planning, community development, resource management, environment policy and economic development.

Resource towns can be monofunctional from the beginning and even if they are nominally a self-organizing entity, say a municipality early on, this can still be a rudimentary, simplified municipality, unprepared to receive families, to offer a rich social life, unable to even consider alternative futures, as its identity is closely tied to the fulfilling of one function for larger society, that is, resource extraction. Such a start tends to have implications for its later evolution. Where the town is economically and culturally diverse, rooted in place, when resources are discovered, the path tends to be different.

Going back to the Renaissance and to political theorist Niccolò Machiavelli, we can make a connection with the limited nature of socialization in many resource communities, the limited options for layered identification. If family does not exist, then family is not a point of reference and a source of identification; if cultural and social life is limited, the associated clubs and organizations are not much to identify with. If the set of professions is limited, if educational opportunities are limited or not valued, if environmentalism is seen as a threat, all those sources of identification are not there. If political life is reduced to a de facto one-party system, there is no other ideology to realistically identify with. For Machiavelli and for us, such layered identities and diverse sources of identification can be crucial both to overcome differences and to *create* difference, contrasting perspectives on past, present and future (Machiavelli et al., 1988).

It is not strange, therefore, that under the influence of these reinforcing feedback loops the meaning of 'community' is locally contested. Is this a place to identify with, a place worth investing in or is it a simply a workplace, where money can be made? The distinction becomes important for understanding which type of social networks dominate. If there is a predominance of bonding or connections within groups of like-minded individuals we are likely to observe homophily, a symptom of the concentration problem. A lack of connections between different groups in the society, in other words weak bridging connections, makes deliberation difficult and as we mentioned, closes the possibility to explore different paths forward. We will explore the danger of polarization in Chapters 3–5. A more extreme stage of the concentration problem, as we discuss in Chapter 7, will see a shriveling of political and community life to such an extent that bridging is not an issue anymore, as the resource identity captures all social life.

The shocks facing resource communities are more diverse than those emanating from a volatile economy. Especially in less prosperous countries and regions and in areas with imperfect rule of law and weak governance, the promise of prosperity can easily attract unwanted attention and create intractable conflicts. Factions, parties and armies might want to get rich quick or use the resource flows to improve their position of power. Violence might erupt and that violence cannot easily be addressed, either locally or by the centers of power (Bainton & Holcombe, 2018; Berger, 2019; Marais & Cloete, 2013). We discuss this in Chapters 5 and 6 but indicate that war and other exceptional events are not the focus of this book. Indeed, migration and forced migration, natural disasters, climate change all conspire to make life in resource communities even harder but will not be at the center of our attention. Our perspective does have clear implications for the way resource communities face disaster, as the patterns of feedback loops analyzed, their hauntings by the past, leave them less resilient, with a weak capacity to deal with exceptional circumstances.

Many resource towns have gone through dramatic periods of change, rapid growth and deep decline. Some have survived, some became ghost towns and others have reinvented themselves and found a new lease on life. Geography, the materiality and technical requirements of the resource, the identities constructed as well as the hardships and traumas endured by these communities makes each one unique. Which brings us to another key point this book intends to make: *despite the similarities between resource communities, the solutions to their problems will have to be unique.*

Blueprint solutions for reinvention, innovation or diversification will not work. The concentration problem or the presence of trauma might be shared features between two resource communities but each concentration problem and each trauma is unique, as each therapy has to be unique (Antze & Lambek, 2016; Freud et al., 2005). What is possible in terms of livelihoods under diversification, population size, hinges on unique paths of development, unique assets and, alas, *unique forms of damage* done by a history of resource extraction and identification. Even comparison with other places dependent on the same resource will not generate the required answers (Gourevitch & Gourevitch, 1986).

If, against all odds, locally a shared desire emerges to leave the past behind, it often overlooks the legacies still prevalent in the community. Recognizing and understanding these legacies can help communities to discriminate opportunities for a different future. Those legacies can mark individual identities, groups, the whole community and they can mold governance and its tools in ways that are hard to observe from within the system. The legacies explored in this book were observed in mining communities of different sorts, fishing towns, oil-producing areas, logging communities and others in different political, social and ecological contexts.

Strategy in governance

Deepening awareness of legacies for us requires the cultivation of reflexivity. In some resource communities, this might not be enough and a thorough self-analysis, beyond forms of reflexivity which can be routinized, might be necessary. In Chapters 10–12, we detail how such self-analysis can be structured and how it can be rooted in the insights of the previous chapters, insights in legacies, memories, in trauma and the myriad manifestations of the concentration problem. Whereas reflexivity might be a continuous conversation about the past and how it shaped the community and its current governance, in many resource communities, such conversations might need to be deep and broad and take on the character of a collective self-analysis. Such analysis can shift the perspective on the past and restructure social memory; it can shake up the shared understanding of past glories and problems and on the dangers of expecting a return to the past or eternal repetition of the present as the best way forward.

Such self-analysis might also shift the perspective towards the physical environment, often simplified in the observation and social memory of resource communities and reduced to the distinction between a useful or useless environment for the resource extraction. A new perspective on the relation between community and environment can illuminate features of the embedding social-ecological system which were not observed before, rather usefully, as those systems are likely limited in their resilience by the history of resource extraction and selective neglect. Alternative futures will have to find a basis in new understandings of both assets and the scars in the landscape, in carefully assessed opportunities and risks stemming from altered social-ecological systems. Finding new ways of observing those systems, through a process of self-analysis, which might take the character of self-therapy, will be part and parcel of such groundwork for future strategy.

In our view *strategy* should be marked as the way forward for resource communities. That is, collective strategy, at community level. Such strategy needs to be located in governance, as it is there that collectively binding decisions have to be taken. If not, if the future is still in the hands of companies or higher-level governments, then the potential for self-organization and self-transformation as a way out of the collective pickle is diminished (Bradbury, 1979; Ellis, 2000). If the future is officially in local hands, but the locals are not aware of this, or do not trust their own potential to navigate the future, or if local governance is fragmented and missing legitimacy, a unified and unifying strategy is less likely to emerge. In local governance, possibly a reinforced form of local governance, social memory has to be interrogated, understandings of the social-ecological system and legacies have to be questioned, in order to break open the understandings of possible futures (Esposito, 2008; Hall et al., 2017).

By strategy here we mean the function in governance of coordinating towards the long-term future. Community strategies are both a narrative and an institution, and at the same time they coordinate other institutions. In Chapter 10, we will delve into the nature and potential of community strategy. Strategies cannot be presented as technical tools of coordination, as a synthesis of existing policies, nor as a list of goals or principles, or as a compromise between several circulating lists. They will not work if they are not cohesive and if they are not persuasive. Strategy without a story will not be persuasive for the community and will find it difficult to create its own support in the community. In such cases, it can rely only on the tools and resources of governmental actors to work its way towards implementation. Which is not enough to truly function as desired, as a tool to harness resources and coordinate efforts towards a different future.

Strategy needs to be adaptive and evolving with the community, its changing circumstances and aspirations. Continuous adaptation of strategy is quite different from absence of strategy. Strategies can take the form of plans or policies and several strategic documents might co-exist. Strategies can also be informal, in the sense of unwritten. This does not necessarily hamper their coordinative function, but it does create risk in terms of transparency and legitimacy. Strategies can enable steering through governance and they can produce reality effects, i.e., they can change the material environment and they can change the stories people tell about their community and its futures (Gruezmacher & Van Assche, 2022; Lakoff & Johnson, 2008; Voß & Bornemann, 2011).

Our approach to strategy as building on a process of intense self-analysis has benefits for places where strategy is a tall order, where a new narrative about a desirable and achievable future is not immediately in sight and/or where the policy tools to move in a promising direction might not be available yet. Self-analysis can inspire several 'detours' spelled out in the last chapters of the book: community healing first, transitional governance and asset building before decision-making. The analytic and theoretically inspired earlier chapters of the book thus build up to a point where we can offer a path to a renewed self-analysis for resource communities, rather than pre-scribing one solution or one idealized form of governance. No specific form of governance would work for all situations, just as no strategy can be independent of context (Beunen et al., 2022; Grant, 2005).

Theory: Governance as central concept

The book thus works its way from theory to application, yet all chapters are inspired by empirical work which will be presented in numerous examples from across the world but also, indirectly, in theoretical work underpinned by empirical studies. The different chapters will lean on and borrow from different theories, yet the overall framing of governance, as the crucial inter-section of past, present and future, the site where legacies and memories compete and coalesce and affect decisions about the future, is inspired by Evolutionary Governance theory, or EGT (Beunen et al., 2015; Van Assche et al., 2013). Governance is thus a central concept, not only in our theoretical understanding of the ills of resource communities but also in our view on practical ways forward.

The accumulated effects of legacies on governance are understood as effects on the tools to get rid of or at least to modify such legacies. EGT is sensitive to this central insight, as it places great emphasis on processes of co-evolution which constrain the development path of a community and its governance system. A governance system, for EGT, is deeply structured by history, the history of the embedding community and the history of the governance system itself (Anderies et al., 2004; Luhmann, 1995). The modes of thinking and organizing available to actors in governance come out of these coupled histories of governance and community. We speak of cognitive and institutional path dependencies. How a community reacts to its environment and is able to restructure itself and its environment, depends on tools and ideas which stem from a history of interactions within governance and between governance and environment (North, 1990; Thelen, 2004).

Co-evolution is the key word here, as the mutual structuring of governance, community and environment, where the evolution and functioning of each cannot be understood without reference to the others. Co-evolution constrains the development path of a community, as it takes decisions binding the community to itself, codifying a past and a present as the basis for decision-making and as it tries to navigate its path towards a future it defined as desirable. Governance for EGT is never perfect, never comprehensive and always the result of steering attempts and other interventions that are not entirely predictable, as we are dealing with complex systems that are not fully transparent in their functioning and in their couplings with environments (Beunen et al., 2015).

EGT distinguishes first between *actors and institutions*, with actors defined as individuals, groups and organizations involved, formally or informally, in the taking of collectively binding decisions. The community is then what is bound by the decision and the actor is not only the person representing a governmental actor. A leader, as influential actor, is not necessarily a mayor, but leadership can be distributed, while conversely, a city council is not necessarily the main arena for local governance. Governance can therefore be understood as a configuration that has to be interpreted, carefully reconstructed in a process which requires deep familiarity with the community.

EGT recognizes policies, plans, laws and informal institutions as *institutions*, tools of coordination in governance, while governance also produces new institutions, to structure its further reproduction, but also to coordinate action in the community. Not all plans work, or have a coordinative function, so their labeling as formal institution does not imply that they are formal institutions. If they are not recalled, they might become what we call 'dead institutions', but just like in zombie movies, if they are not formally canceled, they could be revived. Similarly, not all formal actors fulfill the role they are formally ascribed. They could do something else, either in governance or for private benefit, or they could do nothing, for no one's benefit.

Actors co-evolve, institutions do as well. Actors and institutions, formal and informal institutions also co-evolve. This constitutes a web of co-evolutions, where relations with seemingly unrelated actors or informalities might enable or constrain the use or transformation of a particular institution. The web extends as EGT also concerns itself with patterns of inclusion and exclusion in governance, of actors and of forms of knowing. This is addressed through the concept of *power/knowledge configurations,* inspired by Michel Foucault (Foucault, 1980; Foucault et al., 2000). Power/knowledge configurations are less visible drivers of governance evolutions, yet, as actor/institution configurations, they are central to the reproduction of governance, both as infrastructures and as drivers. To achieve something actors need knowledge which will in turn have an effect in the restructuring of power. At the same time, to implement an idea they need power which will then shift patterns of inclusion of knowledge in governance. Once an actor identifies with a form of knowing and once an idea or form of expertise is built into an institution, such institutionalized knowledge will affect the paths of inclusion of new knowledges in governance, as well as the power relations in the system. Chapters 6 and 8 lean on this understanding of co-evolutions and apply it to the analysis of legacies in resource communities.

For EGT, governance systems develop, over time, their own patterns of flexibility and rigidity. They create tools that shape the future use of tools, establish patterns of inclusion and exclusion that are the basis for future inclusions and exclusions. Governance systems and create stories about the past, present and future which guide decision-making and are points of reference to new versions of past, present and future. EGT grasps the pattern of rigidities which develop by speaking of *dependencies.*

EGT distinguishes different types of dependencies, which will all assert themselves in later chapters, as they are all relevant to the analysis of the multiple presences of the past in the present of governance and community. *Path dependencies,* we already encountered, while *interdependencies* are easily understood as the relations in the present, constraining relations between actors, between institutions and between actors and institutions. *Material dependencies,* which will prove of special interest for our resource community story, are the effects, observed and unobserved, of material environments and structures, natural and human-made, on the reproduction of governance.

Finally, we speak of *goal dependencies* as the effects of visions for the future on the functioning of governance right now. The effects can be diverse as the effects of that vision, possibly codified in a policy or plan, on the community can be diverse. Implementation or rejection are not the only pathways available to get from idea to policy and there are other aspects beyond reality and effects that are relevant for the community. Indeed, if a newly articulated future or aspect thereof causes a shift in governance itself, this will affect the construction of new futures, the effect of new policies and plans.

We will expand the presentation and implementation of EGT ideas in the following chapters, but the preceding passages offer a sufficient base for understanding the rest of the story. In that story, we will engage, step by step with additional theoretical perspectives, which can provide insight in aspects of the predicament of resource communities, in aspects of their functioning, their evolution, in the ways they are haunted by their past.

Synopsis: Expanding analysis toward community strategy

We begin the next chapter by discussing the role of social memory and legacies in resource communities, distinguishing between cognitive, material and organizational legacies and between social memory and organizational memory. These are relevant because organizations are essential in governance. Social memory is presented as always plural, never entirely stable and as being crystalized and shaped by social identities. We draw here on anthropology of memory and social memory theory and indicate that legacies in governance and in the community are most likely coupled. Normatively, we argue that maintaining diversity in social memory and maintaining infrastructures of memory, can render governance less vulnerable to shocks and to processes of simplification, making it more resilient.

Chapter 3 stays mostly within the realm of anthropology when analyzing identity and reinvention processes, while integrating the notions of identity and reinvention in governance theory. Social identity emerges as a valued asset and cherished feature of many resource communities, but also an obstacle for change, especially when an alternative future must be imagined. The relations of social identity, place identity and social memory are considered and the difficulties facing a community when politics becomes identity politics are discussed both in cases of an overly homogenizing resource identity and in cases of polarization. Anticipating Chapter 10, we then analyze the options for community reinvention which emerge from the insights on identity and the notions on governance introduced earlier. We distinguish discursive and autopoietic identity, where the first is easier to access, to grasp and discuss from within the system than the second.

Chapter 4 then draws largely on ideas by sociologist Pierre Bourdieu to analyze symbolic violence in resource communities, as forms of violence that are not recognizably coercive or painful, but limit the autonomy of those subjected to it, by keeping them in their place in a social order designed by others, to benefit others. Symbolic violence in resource communities takes on special features, as these communities are often featuring prominently in the strategies of more important others and as a dependence on the resource and its powerful others, as well as an often relatively closed character of the community, conspire to incorporate the discourse of an oppressive other in discourses on self, environment and future.

Chapter 5 speaks of trauma and in doing so incorporates notions from classical psychoanalysis, later Lacanian analysis and recent literature on community healing. We engage critically and selectively with psychoanalysis but end up finding it truly helpful in understanding trauma at community level, the forms it can acquire in resource communities and the centrality of governance in the process of creating, maintaining and resolving trauma. It is argued that blind repetitions in governance, as well as difficulties in distinguishing vision from fantasy, can be symptoms of community trauma and that such trauma can be caused by a history of exploitation of people and resource alike and by the closure of a resource extraction operation which structured community life in more than one way.

Chapters 4 and 5 both develop the idea that weak integration of resource communities in the rest of society, remoteness and processes of simplification can combine to create violent and traumatizing environments where few tools remain for individuals to redefine themselves, but also that such reinvention becomes harder in the course of the history of the community. When the resource is gone and central actors around it as well, instability can occur or conversely a stifling stasis.

Chapter 6 takes a Foucaultian turn, dealing with power/knowledge in resource communities and investigates how a central place for natural resource governance in a community can shape power/ knowledge dynamics. We discuss the typical features of power relations in communities and the implications of the centrality of the resource for the evolution of governance, including its capacity to discern alternative futures. We dissect the discursive mechanisms which can connect actor identities, a communal resource identity and discursive configurations which can keep each other in place. Anticipating Chapters 7 and 10, we look at the relation between power and strategy, the limited power of the strategist over discourse and we diagnose the tendency of resource communities to get trapped in closed discourses which then tend to simplify themselves and their environment.

Chapters 4, 5 and 6 lead naturally into Chapter 7, where the *concentration problem* is fully introduced and analyzed, thus coming to a partial synthesis of the analysis. We start from a theoretically informed discussion on the value of diversity in a community and its governance. The concentration problem is presented as an unfortunate result of a series of unfortunate legacies or feedback loops, together amounting to a closure of the discursive worlds of the community and a simplification of governance. It also results in a slow atrophying of the governance tools and forms of expertise which could have been helpful to get out of the slump. The problem makes it hard to see the value in the policy tools which could address the problem. We connect a radical version of the concentration problem to the Lacanian idea of the Big Other, where a central player in the community, even after its own demise can structure the thinking, the patterns of identification and governance in the community, again making adaptation harder.

In Chapter 8, we synthesize what we learned into a perspective on legacies of resource centrality in resource communities. We develop the notions of legacy introduced in Chapter 3 and incorporate insights gained in the other chapters, especially Chapters 2, 6 and 7. We maintain the distinction between cognitive, material and institutional legacies and relate them to the dependencies as understood by EGT and slowly analyzed in the previous chapters. This allows us to shed a new light on the connections between memory, identity and the articulation of futures in resource communities. We revisit symbolic violence, trauma and the concentration problem in this light. The role of organizations is highlighted, in terms of legacies, but also as tools to break legacies proving to be constraining.

Chapter 9, ominously titled *Tripping over the Real* takes, only seemingly, a step away from the line of reasoning developed in the previous chapters yet makes it possible to introduce Chapter 10 with fewer false expectations. In this chapter, we offer an honest discussion of policy failure and especially of the difficulties to strategize in governance, difficulties to articulate and implement strategy. The EGT concepts of goal dependency and reality effects return here and we start from a distinction between tripping over reality and tripping over the Real. Tripping over reality refers to difficulties in implementation which stem from overlooked facts and perspectives which could, in principle, be introduced in governance, but which nevertheless create uncertainty and blind spots. New limits to observation will arise as soon as old limits are erased, new perspectives introduced, as the complexity of governance-community relations does not allow for complete observation and prediction. The Lacanian Real adds opacity and new series of obstacles for strategy, new reasons for tripping, in the resource communities. We demonstrate that this is the case largely because of unacknowledged inter-weaving of system and environment and unacknowledged yet active legacies from the past.

Chapter 10, considering the caveats offered by Chapter 9, then resolutely looks towards the future, a future which will have to break first, consciously, with many aspects of the past and overcome many obstacles, analyzed in earlier chapters, to break and first observe these legacies. In a community marked by trauma and symbolic violence, trapped in concentration problems, strategy must be preceded by careful and cautious self-analysis. Given the insights of earlier chapters, such analysis, in many cases, will take on features of a self-therapy. The self is important here, as outsiders, well-intentioned and highly skilled can offer input, yet an alternative interpretation of self and environment, a restructuring of social memory and identity, will have to emerge and be persuasive in the community itself. A working strategy must be derived from an analysis with such qualities, otherwise it will hit the obstacles encountered before.

Strategy, as said, is understood as necessarily located in governance, to be legitimate and impactful and as possessing a narrative and an institutional dimension, while on the institutional side, it will necessarily be an institution coordinating others, some existing, some possibly spawned by the strategy itself. This perspective on strategy is new and integrated into the perspective on governance offered by EGT. It owes to insights by Henry Mintzberg on emerging strategy and it finds inspiration in strategy as practice thinkers such as David Seidl, as well as thinkers on narrative and organization such as Barbara Czarniawska, Martin Kornberger and Mats Alvesson.

Chapter 11 will serve as a concluding chapter, summarizing insights gained, drawing out further implications, in order to answer the questions posed earlier, regarding the diverse ways resource communities are haunted by their past and possible routes to cut loose from the legacies that hold back thinking and organizing, the articulation and implementation of alternative futures. Whereas self-analysis preceding strategizing under difficult circumstances might have to take on unique qualities - possibly therapeutic ones - we also emphasize the importance of instilling new routines and new safeguards for *reflexivity* in governance in the longer run. Whatever the fate of the community strategy, such habits of governance can lower the chances that concentration problems reappear later.

Finally, in Chapter 12, we offer a more practical perspective on community strategy for resource communities. As before, we avoid formulaic and prescriptive answers. Rather, we present a concise guide to self-analysis and community strategy adapted to the conditions of resource towns in a situation where they discern a need and feel ready to embark on such process. The method offered envisions several sideways, where long-term perspectives might not be immediately clear and where the necessary policy tools might not be available yet.

References

Adalid, R., & Detken, C. (2007). Liquidity shocks and asset price boom/bust cycles. *ECB Working Paper No. 732*, 54–54.

Anderies, J. M., Janssen, M. A., & Ostrom, E. (2004). A framework to analyze the robustness of social-ecological systems from an institutional perspective. *Ecology and Society, 9*(1), 18–18.

Antze, P., & Lambek, M. (Eds.). (2016). *Tense Past* (2 ed.). Routledge.

Bainton, N., & Holcombe, S. (2018). A critical review of the social aspects of mine closure. *Sustainable management and exploitation of extractive waste: Towards a more efficient resource preservation and waste recycling, 59*, 468–478.

Berger, S. (2019). Industrial heritage and the ambiguities of nostalgia for an industrial past in the Ruhr Valley, Germany. *Labor, 16*(1), 37–64.

Beunen, R., Van Assche, K., & Duineveld, M. (2015). The search for evolutionary approaches to governance. In *Evolutionary governance theory* (pp. 3–17). Springer.

Beunen, R., Van Assche, K., & Gruezmacher, M. (2022). Evolutionary perspectives on environmental governance: Strategy and the co-construction of governance, community and environment. *Sustainability,* (14):9912.10.3390/su14169912.

Bradbury, J. H. (1979). Towards an alternative theory of resource-based town development in Canada. *Economic Geography, 55*(2), 147–166.

Collier, P. (AERC Senior Policy Seminar IX on Managing Commodity Booms in sub-Saharan Africa (March 2007: Yaoundé, Cameroon).

Conde, M., & Le Billon, P. (2017). Why do some communities resist mining projects while others do not? *The Extractive Industries and Society, 4*(3), 681–697. 10.1016/j.exis.2017.04.009.

D'Apice, V., & Ferri, G. (2016). *Financial instability: Toolkit for interpreting boom and bust cycles.* Springer.

Ellis, F. (2000). The determinants of rural livelihood diversification in developing countries. *Journal of Agricultural Economics, 51*(2), 289–302.

Esposito, E. (2008). Social forgetting: A systems-theory approach. In *Cultural memory studies: An international and interdisciplinary handbook* (pp. 181–190). Walter de Gruyter.

Foucault, M. (1980). *Power/knowledge: Selected interviews and other writings, 1972–1977.* Pantheon Books.

Foucault, M., Faubion, J. D., & Foucault, M. (2000). *Power.* New Press.

Fraser, A., & Larmer, M. (2010). *Zambia, mining, and neoliberalism: Boom and bust on the globalized Copperbelt.* Springer.

Freud, S., Ellman, M., & Whiteside, S. (2005). *On murder, mourning and melancholia.* Penguin UK.

Freudenburg, W. R. (1992). Addictive economies: Extractive industries and vulnerable localities in a changing world economy 1. *Rural Sociology, 57*(3), 305–332.

Freudenburg, W. R., Bacigalupi, L. M., & Landoll-Young, C. (1982). Mental health consequences of rapid community growth: A report from the longitudinal study of boomtown mental health impacts. *Journal of Health and Human Resources Administration, 4*(3), 334–352. JSTOR.

Freudenburg, W. R., & Gramling, R. (1994). Natural resources and rural poverty: A closer look. *Society & Natural Resources, 7*(1), 5–22.

Freudenburg, W. R., & Jones, R. E. (1991). Criminal behavior and rapid community growth: Examining the evidence. *Rural Sociology, 56*(4), 619–645.

Gourevitch, P. A., & Gourevitch, P. (1986). *Politics in hard times: Comparative responses to international economic crises.* Cornell University Press.

Grant, J. (2005). *Planning the good community: New urbanism in theory and practice.* Routledge.

Gruezmacher, M., & Van Assche, K. (2022). *Crafting strategies for sustainable local development.* In Planning. https://www.inplanning.eu/categories/1/articles/267?menu_id=publications§ion_title_for_article=New+Books

Hall, H. M., Vodden, K., & Greenwood, R. (2017). From dysfunctional to destitute: The governance of regional economic development in Newfoundland and Labrador. *International Planning Studies, 22*(2), 49–67.

Halseth, G., Markey, S., Ryser, L., Hanlon, N., & Skinner, M. (2017). Exploring new development pathways in a remote mining town: The case of Tumbler Ridge, BC Canada. *Journal of Rural and Community Development, 12*(2–3).

Halseth, G., & Ryser, L. (2016). Rapid change in small towns: When social capital collides with political/bureaucratic inertia. *Community Development, 47*(1), 106–121.

Halseth, G., & Sullivan, L. (2002). *Building community in an instant town; a social geography of Mackenzie and Tumbler Ridge, British Columbia.* University of Northern British Columbia Press.

Hessing, M., Howlett, M., & Summerville, T. (2014). *Canadian natural resource and environmental policy: Political economy and public policy, Second Edition.* UBC Press.

High, S. (2021). Constructing industrial pasts: Heritage, historical culture and identity in regions undergoing structural economic transformation, ed. S. Berger. *The English Historical Review, 136*(581), 1107–1109.

Keeling, A., & Sandlos, J. (2017). Ghost towns and zombie mines: The historical dimensions of mine abandonment, reclamation, and redevelopment in the Canadian North. In S. Bocking & B. Martin (Eds.), *Ice blink: Navigating northern environmental history* (1st ed., pp. 377–420). University of Calgary Press.

Lakoff, G., & Johnson, M. (2008). *Metaphors we live by.* University of Chicago Press.

Larsen, S. C. (2004). Place identity in a resource-dependent area of Northern British Columbia. *Annals of the Association of American Geographers, 94*(4), 944–960.

Lewis, H. M. (1983). Wales and Appalachia—Coal mining, culture, and conflict. *Appalachian Journal, 10*(4), 350–357. JSTOR.

Loayza, N., & Rigolini, J. (2016). The local impact of mining on poverty and inequality: Evidence from the commodity boom in Peru. *World Development, 84*, 219–234.

Luhmann, N. (1995). *Social systems* (Vol. 1). Stanford University Press Stanford.

Machiavelli, N., Skinner, Q., & Price, R. (1988). *The prince.* Cambridge University Press.

Maher, R., Valenzuela, F., & Böhm, S. (2019). The enduring state: An analysis of governance-making in three mining conflicts. *Organization Studies, 40*(8), 1169–1191.

Marais, L. (2022). *The social impacts of mine closure in South Africa: Housing policy and place attachment.* Taylor & Francis.

Marais, L., & Cloete, J. (2013). Labour migration, settlement and mine closure in South Africa. *Geography, 98*(2), 77–84. 10.1080/00167487.2013.12094371.

Marais, L., McKenzie, F. H., Deacon, L., Nel, E., Rooyen, D. van, & Cloete, J. (2018). The changing nature of mining towns: Reflections from Australia, Canada and South Africa. *Land Use Policy, 76*, 779–788.

Markey, S., Halseth, G., & Manson, D. (2012). *Investing in place: Economic renewal in northern British Columbia.* UBC Press.

Menkhaus, K. (2007). Governance without government in Somalia: Spoilers, state building, and the politics of coping. *International Security, 31*(3), 74–106.

North, D. (1990). *Institutions, institutional change and economic performance.* Cambridge University Press.

Ryser, L., Halseth, G., Markey, S., & Morris, M. (2016). The structural underpinnings impacting rapid growth in resource regions. *Extractive Industries and Society, 3*(3), 616–626.

Shandro, J. A., Veiga, M. M., Shoveller, J., Scoble, M., & Koehoorn, M. (2011). Perspectives on community health issues and the mining boom–bust cycle. *Resources Policy, 36*(2), 178–186.

Stedman, R. C., Parkins, J. R., & Beckley, T. M. (2004). Resource dependence and community well-being in rural Canada. *Rural Sociology, 69*(2), 213–234.

Storey, K. (2001). Fly-in/fly-out and fly-over: Mining and regional development in Western Australia. *Australian Geographer, 32*(2), 133–148.

Thelen, K. (2004). *How institutions evolve: The political economy of skills in Germany, Britain, the United States, and Japan. Cambridge University Press. Vancouver.* Cambridge University Press.

Tornell, A., & Westermann, F. (2002). Boom-bust cycles in middle income countries: Facts and explanation. *IMF Staff Papers, 49*(1), 111–155.

Umbeck, J. (1977). The California gold rush: A study of emerging property rights. *Explorations in Economic History, 14*(3), 197–226.

Van Assche, K., Beunen, R., & Duineveld, M. (2013). *Evolutionary governance theory: An introduction.* Springer.

Van Assche, K., Beunen, R., & Duineveld, M. (2016). Citizens, leaders and the common good in a world of necessity and scarcity: Machiavelli's lessons for community-based natural resource management. *Ethics, Policy & Environment, 19*(1), 19–36.

Van Assche, K., Deacon, L., Gruezmacher, M., Summers, R., Lavoie, S., Jones, K., Granzow, M., Hallstrom, L., & Parkins, J. (2017). *Boom & Bust. Local strategy for big events. A community survival guide to turbulent times.* Groningen/Edmonton, Alberta: InPlanning and University of Alberta, Faculty of Extension.

Voß, J.-P., & Bornemann, B. (2011). The politics of reflexive governance: Challenges for designing adaptive management and transition management. *Ecology and Society, 16*(2), 9. [online] URL: http://www.ecologyandsociety.org-9. [online] URL: http://www.ecologyandsociety.org.

2

HISTORY, MEMORY AND LEGACY IN RESOURCE COMMUNITIES

History

Things happen in the life of a community and the life of a country. Some of these things become 'facts,' the facts of history. What is selected as a fact and what is retained as a fact always depends on a perspective. Without a perspective there are no facts in history, only things happening and to give sense to them, those things require interpretation. Such interpretation requires a certain perspective and a perspective tends to be entangled with an interest, for example an interest in the community, in a position one tries to advance or a view of history which favors or enhances that position. Indeed, history is always written by the winners so this shapes the perspective of the losers and of the topics, resources and areas fought over (Ben-Amos & Weissberg, 1999; Certeau & Certeau, 1992; Esposito, 2008). Yet, also beyond a view of history as a series of wins and defeats, the fact remains that what counts as facts is determined by someone or something and that someone or something defines a perspective that becomes authoritative.

Making things authoritative by coercion is not a simple thing, even when a state has a frightful set of tools to coerce. Integrating an official history in curriculum is helpful, especially if the state controls the education system fully. Also helpful is crafting narratives and sets of narratives which reinforce each other. Narrative suggests structure, logic, morality and can make a set of facts more persuasive. For instance, the media's influence on the organization of cultural life or in a less positive perspective the media intentionally blocking off alternative histories and alternative interpretations of a certain situation thus preventing them from entering and emerging in the community. Having a tight control on education and the workplace can be an even

DOI: 10.4324/9781003332145-2

more effective way to reach similar results (Lefebvre, 1971; Luhmann, 1997; Zerubavel, 2003). A simpler strategy to control history is to move people around who do not adhere to a particular version of history, to an area where the dominance of the official perspective is more pronounced. Even simpler is to prevent self-organization, to neglect media and education.

Of course, in many times and places, the situation is not so dire and regimes are not so oppressive. Yet, sketching out the extreme situation helps in understanding how something becomes history and requires support by a regime able to legitimize it. Even where there is more freedom, history requires a stamp of academic and often official approval, to be taught, presented in museums, in cultural and political life. History can thus be defined as the official version of events, which means that, depending on the intricacy and capacity of state institutions, it is recorded and represented in a variety of ways, in various organizations, in such a way that it bestows not only legitimacy but also near unavoidability in a state. Various forms of recording, various sites of memory-making reinforce each other just like several narratives reinforce each other in discursive configurations that are difficult to change.

We speak of states here, not communities. This is no accident, as official history in most of the world and in recent centuries, is a history written by states. Those states are, in most cases, nation-states, so the perspective of the state is presented as the natural perspective of the group who built the state and is represented by it. At the same time there is nothing natural in such processes of state and identity building. Not only is the official memory a construct; the state itself and the nation it represents are constructs which co-evolved in a history of competition, coercion and homogenization (Anderson, 2006). French history is the history of something that was made in a contingent and often brutal manner; marginalizing, erasing, assimilating other groups, their languages, religions and regional cultures. 'The French' did not build the French state; the state, in many ways, built the French. Besides legislation, border-making and education, the creation of a shared memory codified in official history was an important tool. Centralization was a sub-process, an ancillary process, which made it easier to control the territory by sending signals to the peripheries in a unified manner but also by bringing people, goods, ideas from the peripheries and either erasing them or by being accommodating, by giving them a predefined position in a unified position of state, memory and identity building (Certeau & Certeau, 1992; Zerubavel, 2003).

Histories at community level are first shaped by the perspective and values of a larger polity, in most cases a nation-state. This means that often little attention is paid to local history and it means that what is written is discourse considered either as irrelevant or innocent, or framed by assumptions, narratives or identity categories as defined in national histories. Alternatively, local histories can be inscribed in national history in a more active way, as examples of state building at the local level, as morally exemplary cases of civilizing conquest, or peaceful coexistence, of a model melting pot, etc. We can consider as 'innocent' those local histories that focus mostly on families, small eccentric details of community life in the old days, or local histories considered as local nostalgia if there are no clear implications for the larger polity, its values and assumptions or its power relations. Disconnecting facts from narratives and larger interpretive frames is a common practice in local history writing, even in ambitious local book projects, supported by municipalities, local museums, etc. Such collecting effort of 'facts' is no threat to anyone, least of all to academia, where historians and others can stay in the role of offering more complex interpretive frames (Canagarajah, 2002). Of course, there are also practical reasons for these features of local historiography, as there are exceptions; locals miss the time, resources, education and organizational infrastructure to compete with the nuance and discursive proliferation of academic historians, geographers and sociologists, to name a few.

In addition, one has to mention that per definition, local history misses the authority of the nation-state, except where direct connections exist between the different scales of politics and administration and where the local history is merely a localized national effort (Schwartz & Cook, 2002). Another historical exceptions were city-states and networks (such as the Hanseatic league in medieval Europe) which were truly autonomous and self-defining and gave shape to larger political entities rather than being shaped by them - the budding nation-states, still *en route* to centralization (cf van der Steen, 2018). Machiavelli's history of Florence did not assume Italy as a naturally existing, God-given entity, on its way to unity and nationhood. He did use such discourse every now and then, but the self-organizing entity and the living identity he took for granted was the community of Florence, which started as a city and in his day was in a continuous struggle to expand into a region, a process which involved conquest of other proudly independent city-states (Machiavelli, 2023). Similarly, the history of current Belgium can be written off as the history of a weak state, but, maybe more convincingly, as a history of strong cities (Bruges, Ghent, Antwerp, Dinant, etc.) and sometimes, cohesive regions (Flanders, Brabant, etc.).

Nordegg, Alberta is a small community in the foothills of the Canadian Rocky Mountains. Established by German immigrant engineer-adventurer Martin Nordegg in 1911, it grew to a sizeable coal mining community, with a maximum population of over 2,000 and an ambitious comprehensive plan (1913) which demonstrated a long-term vision. It owed its viability to a rail line which arrived in 1912 – even now, the location is remote. Yet, changes in train technology also heralded the near-death of the town, as diesel trains made the Nordegg coal lose its value, and in 1955 the mine closed. A prison provided some employment afterwards but by the 1990s, the population had dropped to below

50, and many feared the death of the community. It was transferred to Clearwater County in 1996, and local activism which had started in the 1980s led to a recognition as national historic site in 2002. A few years earlier (2000) an ambitious revitalization plan appeared, a local initiative with regional support and by 2023, that plan began to bear fruit, with new residents moving in and new business and residential construction appearing.

History in Nordegg is not kept in Nordegg and was not written in Nordegg. Social memory was put to test by the skirting with ghost town status and institutional memory faded with the closure of the Brazeau Collieries since the mine with its archives moved as local government moved out. The person of Martin Nordegg moved out of Alberta, and he and his initial investors lost control over the mine to the owners of the railroad. Piecing the history of Nordegg together is not an easy feat therefore, but important for our discussion. There is no authoritative version of history present locally and hence there is a weak social memory since the interplay between social memory and history can hardly be established and one is not a reference for the other in the local community. Furthermore, governance is not the governance of Nordegg but of a much larger county, with a population over 10,000, concentrated in the city of Rocky Mountain House. History, memory and governance are thus dispersed and fragmented, and it took a volunteering group many years to draw the attention of county, provincial and federal actors and recognize a valuable past and a new future for Nordegg.

The pervasive influence of nation-states on the writing of history and the construction of identities, even where this history is short (as in the US and Canada) cannot be underestimated. Even the more critical currents, supporting often more critical political discourses, are structured by concepts borrowed from the official version of history. Local communities in many parts of the world are represented by local governments like municipalities which are often constructs of the higher-level polities (not usually the other way around, even if the smaller community was established earlier than the higher-level government and that was their historical pathway of development). Where local governance capacity is weak spaces for alternative narratives can be created; however, chances are small that such diversity of perspectives will coalesce in a stable alternative to the version of history emanating from above.

The importance of the nation-state for the understanding of history can be gleaned in many ways, but one glaring illustration is the way vanished polities are portrayed. The Habsburg and Ottoman empires are cases in point (Magris, 2016). As both were dismantled after the first World War, there are no clear representatives of these states. Neither were nation-states, neither still exist, few still identify with them and the official histories written in Austria and Turkey, the clearest successor states, had good reasons to differentiate from Habsburg and Ottoman historiography (Bartov & Weitz, 2013). In recent years, post-Kemalists found new reasons to look back in time and try to revive

Ottoman sympathies and identifications, yet this is not the revival of a truly Ottoman perspective. Rather, it is the selective reinterpretation of Ottoman history from the old core, from a vantage point which already incorporates a modern context and a history of trying to forget anything traditional in Turkey (the modernization project by Ataturk) (Kandemir, 2022). Internationally, Habsburg and Ottoman histories tend to be marked by a dismissive tone, an air of teleology, as if they were doomed by nature to succumb to a newer type of regime more worthy of existence, i.e., the nation-states resulting from their dismembering.

At a local level, one can find similar mechanisms at play where the historical perspective disappears when communities change radically over time. For example, when a city was self-organizing and marked by a strong local identity but was absorbed and assimilated into a state or when the place was central and typical for the ambitions and perspective of a regime or a state that does not exist anymore. Another example is a community that used to be cosmopolitan in nature but, due to economic and political shifts, became more marginal in international networks, less diverse, more closed in a cultural sense (Van Assche et al., 2009). The opposite is also possible, when a truly local identity and culture were gradually subsumed in a more complex society. A final example is the case where ethnic and cultural groups lived together, retaining a sense of identity but also together creating a unique urban fabric and urban cultural and political identity. When some of these groups disappeared, they left an impoverished and simplified community behind (Van Assche & Teampău, 2015). A state-centered historical perspective often gradually takes over local narratives, as local and regional differences slowly lose their significance, often after episodes of bitter contestation (Bartov & Weitz, 2013).

Coal mines from Asturias represented approximately 50% of the total national production in most of the 19th and 20th centuries, and many of the towns in this region are the best Spanish examples of mining communities, similar to those described in the classic book on Yorkshire mining, 'Coal is our life,' where almost everyone in the town has been dependent on the mine since time immemorial. Despite the decline of coal since the 1950s (the last mine closed in 2018), Asturias' identity is strongly linked to its mining past. The memory of workers' struggles, including dramatic episodes, such as the repression suffered by Franco troops during a revolutionary uprising in 1934, is today the main identity symbol of many of the municipalities that make up the autonomous community of Asturias.

Memory

All these local and national examples indicate the growing influence of the nation-state over the writing and imposition of official history but also on the functioning of social memory. They also bring up several points regarding the functioning of social memory and the relation between memory and history which are relevant for our discussion of resource towns and they ways they can be haunted by the past. Some of these points will be developed in later chapters (and summarized in Chapter 8) but the basic insights can be introduced here and do not need the context of resource towns to become comprehensible.

A first basic insight is that *time cannot be turned back.* Societies and communities evolve and no matter how cherished that past is and how strong the desire to go back to the past is, this is not possible. The international, national and local contexts have changed so much that any attempt at recreating something old is *de facto* the creation of something new. This applies to an identity, a history, a state, community, even a seemingly simple materiality such as a piece of infrastructure. In the following chapters, additional arguments, from additional empirical investigations and theoretical perspectives will emerge for this basic idea. Evolutionary governance, the overall perspective structuring this book, highlights the complex co-evolutions of elements in the governance system, of governance and community, community and environment and the complex evolutions shaping the community right now and molding the ways of thinking and organizing available to a community, including the way its history is written and the functioning of its identities.

A second point relates to this; *perspectives cannot be recaptured.* Once a form of polity, a form of organization, a cultural identity, a group with that identity is gone, it is gone and it cannot come back. If a century after a departure Armenian merchants return to their native Balkan town, neither people nor town will be the same; their role and perspective are bound to differ (Magris, 2016). They cannot play a similar cultural or political role in what is now a municipality, disconnected from their old networks. Their economic role is bound to differ in a radically altered economy, in a new nation-state with different expectations regarding identification and coexistence and different ideas of the material conditions of a good life (Van Assche & Teampău, 2015). Even for the well-studied Habsburg empire, the perspective of its governing elites as well as of its citizens in far-flung regions cannot be fully recaptured (Evans, 2020). The new elites, new centers and former possessions, now part of new nation-states, are not able to look back and regain the perspective of their predecessors. They cannot know to what extent they are shaped by new conditions, new powers, new networks and histories of identification.

Third, *memory is selective.* What is constructed as fact and as true and real narrative is contingent on the conditions of the moment, but those conditions also exert pressure on the process of retaining information. In other words, the present shapes both what is true in present and past and then what is remembered (Esposito, 2008). The narratives circulating about the present and past already introduce a selectivity, since what does not resonate with them will not be perceived as real or is not worth remembering. Those observations which introduce dissonance, by presenting facts, identities and narratives differently, will depend on how resilient the system is, how much diversity it is able to tolerate, how open it is for deliberation and for a possible codification of a new version of history (Baehre, 2015; Barth, 1998). Yet, there will always be a pressure from the existing system of memory and system of governance and always a double selectivity. By this we mean the fact that many things are not observed as relevant to begin with due to the organization of public discourse, and the narratives dominant in culture and governance. and Secondly, what does get through as an alternative interpretation will be judged by the criteria of the same system, with regard to the possibility of remembering, forgetting, or the options of opposing and erasing (Irwin-Zarecka, 2017; Moran, 2004; Ricoeur, 2004).

In the Free State Goldfields in South Africa people cherish the positive memories of mining that included the joy of raising children, and unthreatened and harmonious living. These memories contrast with the current economic hardship in a crime-ridden area (Marais et al., 2022; Sesele et al., 2021; Sesele & Marais, 2023).

Which brings us to our fourth point, *that forgetting is constitutive of memory.* This point, too will be developed in Chapter 8, but requires introduction now. Each act of remembering is an act of forgetting, by the mere acts of defining and selecting what 'is' and what is worth to remember, next what is worth to remember as a community. Forgetting can be primary and from there shaping what can be remembered and it can be secondary, as a result of the structuring of what is defined a real and important to remember (Esposito, 2008). More important, however, is to see them as co-constitutive, as part and parcel of one of the same process by which a system understands itself and its environment and guides itself when navigating that environment. This is, on purpose, a broad perspective, as this insight already follows from general systems theory. If we understand a community as a system and its governance configuration as a subsystem (see our introduction), then the remembering and forgetting of the governance system helps the community to make sense of itself and to adapt to, sometimes alter, its environment and the opportunities it offers (Bakken & Hernes, 2003; Luhmann, 1995).

Given the previous paragraphs, our fifth point might look obvious now: that *history and memory are made in the present.* They reflect identities, hopes and preoccupations of the present and cannot be extricated from this present. Both the construction and use of social memory and history as codified memory are informed by what is possible and expedient now, at this present moment. That present moment of course, is also shaped by history but this shaping happens in manners not always visible and thematized in the community and in governance. In later chapters, we will highlight this process as extending to the construction of futures, of narratives and images of possible and desirable futures, which are similarly marked by the conditions of the present. Indeed, the construction and use of both memories and futures has to take place in the present and their role in governance and the community at large can only be understood as a role in the present, resonating with the values and strategies of actors right now, with the sensibilities of the community as it exists right now. Certainly, this present is shaped by the past, yet the past that is consciously playing a role in culture and politics now, is a past constructed in the present (Canagarajah, 2002; Esposito, 2008).

In many African cases, mines have set up a welfare system: providing housing, large salaries, subsidized utility services and education. Knierzinger (2017, p. 87) refers to mine closure in Africa as 'mass depression' because the 'dream of modernity did not materialize.' An old future seemed close to an old present, it seemed realistic, and now the old, shattered dream left traces in the present and in the remembrance of the past.

The distinction introduced in the previous paragraph can be presented as our sixth point: *that memories differ from legacies.* What is remembered is partly selected as such as a product of legacies from the past, shaping the criteria of selection, the infrastructures of remembering and forgetting, but those legacies produce memories in interaction with the preoccupation and functionalities of the present. Memories, the result of the process of remembering and forgetting, are mostly conscious (we qualify this in our later chapters inspired by psychoanalysis) but legacies can take on many forms (see below) and often are not recognized as legacies from the past, nor as influencing the production of memories and futures. A legacy can be an environment scarred or positively formed by a history of resource extraction, but this is not always recognized as such; it is less likely even that it would be recognized as something constraining the production of memories or futures right now, or, more generally, the taking of collectively binding decisions in governance (D. Smith, 2009; L. Smith & Campbell, 2017). In the next section, we specify different types of legacies as they are essential to our overarching narrative.

Our seventh and final point is as similarly anticipated in the previous paragraphs: *that social memories and their infrastructures exist in the plural.* While history is, for the powers that be, ideally singular, social memory is always plural. This is the case even in the smallest and seemingly most homogenous resource community. One can be normative here and argue that such plurality is a good thing, a source of diverse interpretations of the past which can lead to a diverse pallet of possible adaptations and strategies for the future. Attempts to simplify and homogenize memory, beyond what takes place in the writing of history anyway, to actively suppress the emergence and functioning of social memory (partly through problematic writings and impositions of history), to dismantle infrastructures of remembering can be assessed as undesirable. This links to our overall analysis of resource communities as imbued with the problematic potential for simplification, in many cases becoming simplified communities marked by a host of problems, underpinned by a simplified functioning of social memory.

The infrastructures mentioned can be diverse. They can be sites of storytelling about the past, rituals of preserving memories, events, organizations outside the sphere of official remembering, organizations upholding diverse identities and their perspectives, but also media giving a voice to diverse groups, alternative understandings of the past and expectations for the future (Berliner, 2005; Smith, 2009). Infrastructure can include materialities such as archives, museums, buildings for civil society organizations, a printing press for the union, a basement where a certain cultural society can gather, even the store where ingredients for traditional ethnic dishes can be found, or the garden where herbs and ingredients for those dishes can be grown - otherwise not available in town. Preservation of sites with a special significance for a group, an organization, a culture, which is not in power now, can be part of efforts to maintain infrastructures of memory (the concentration problem analyzed in Chapter 7 associates with a simplification of memory and an erosion of memory infrastructure, both inside and outside the sphere of governance) (Hendon, 2010; Irwin-Zarecka, 2017; Nelson, 2008).

In Serón, in the Spanish province of Almeria, the lead and iron mining past has become an important part of local heritage through the numerous museums that have been created like the well-known Mieres Mining Museum, in Mieres, close to the city of Gijón. It was Spain's first mining museum when it opened in 1955. The museum is a site to learn about the area's mining history, and it showcases a variety of mining-related exhibits, including machinery, vintage mining equipment, and minerals. Another well-known mining location in Asturias is the Iron Age mines of Covadonga. They were the site of a conflict between ancient Greeks and Romans for independence. The mines were used to make iron and copper during the Roman era, and they were revived to make iron in the 1930s. They are now a UNESCO World Heritage Site.

Finally, we can mention here that *organizations* have their own memory mechanisms and infrastructures, but also that the existence of organizations themselves is important for the functioning of a diverse social memory in a community. Indeed, organizations can be tools for remembering, for reminding others about alternative interpretations of history, about alternative possible futures. Organizations need a memory to function, (see also Chapters 8 and 9), to adapt to their environment, give themselves direction, but they are also part of an environment where other organizations operate on different distinctions between remembering and forgetting and where a common good might only be remembered and observed in a subset of organizations (Rowlinson et al., 2010). We refer here both to administrative organizations and to civil society organizations and indeed, businesses (Bakken & Hernes, 2003).

Legacies differentiated

Besides history and memory, the past leaves traces, it has legacies, both at personal level and at the level of communities. Legacies are broader and more numerous than memories. Such legacies can take different forms in the present and they can shape the future of a community. We distinguish *cognitive, organizational* and *material* legacies. All three are important to understand how communities organize themselves, how they look at the future and how they can organize themselves for the future (Figure 2.1).

Cognitive legacies we see as narratives, images, concepts inherited or shaped by the past that affect the functioning of governance in a community. They can have the character of memories and histories of the community (as described above). Cognitive legacies can include omissions, blanks, difficulties in considering particular problems, images of other communities, of particular activities and attachments to particular problem definitions and types of solutions. Traumatic experiences, or, conversely, experiences and phases interpreted as the heyday of the community, can shape the interpretation of many things besides history; they can leave a multiplicity of legacies which have to be traced carefully. They cannot be anticipated generically, nor gleaned from a particular theory or by studying a seemingly similar community. Many cognitive legacies can come together in a social identity which

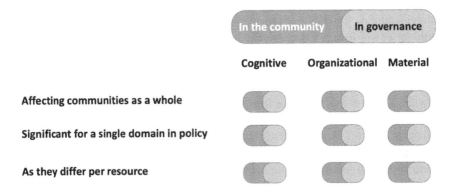

FIGURE 2.1 Typology of legacies. We distinguish between legacies in the community and in the governance system and those affecting the entire community, a single policy domain or a particular resource. They can be of a cognitive, organizational or material nature.

can guide the interpretation of past, place and future in a community. Communities can be traumatized, as individuals can be, they can be shocked and marked by histories of conflict, unfulfilled expectations, but just as much by hope, cherished success stories, resilience and social cohesion (Mah, 2012; Sesele & Marais, 2023).

Organizational legacies we see as tools and ways of organizing inherited from the past. These can be discerned in the collection of actors involved in local governance, in the types of institutions (policies, plans, laws) used and not used in governance, in the way these actors are organized and interact. Informal institutions and informal actors, sometimes illicit actors play a role. Just as narratives and ideas can be normalized, stop being scrutinized, forms of organization and decision-making can become a seemingly neutral background. That background is nevertheless a product of history and shapes how community futures can be envisioned and organized (Bakken & Hernes, 2003). Cognitive and organizational legacies shape each other over time, as stories and ideas can be entrenched or institutionalized in governance and as this process can make it difficult to take alternative ideas seriously.

Sulina, in the Romanian Danube Delta, was not a fishing village but a small trading town on the margin of the Ottoman empire until the 19th century when Russia invaded. After the Crimean War the CED or European Danube Committee, was established (1856). The CED was truly an experiment in international administration, as the great European powers collaborated to develop Sulina and the lower Danube ports into free ports, with international control over local governance, and local governance focused on the development of Danube trade (and keeping the Russians out). The CED regime encouraged multi-cultural coexistence, and attracted Greek, Armenian and Jewish traders. After World War II, CED was dismantled, and Romania took control over a rapidly shrinking and homogenizing community. Under communist industrialization people from other regions were moved in, mostly fishers from Delta villages migrated. Fewer and fewer people remembered the CED cosmopolitanism, yet a transition was possible, whereby the newcomers slowly enrolled into the Sulina narrative. Cognitive legacies proved stronger than organizational ones.

Material legacies are those features of a physical environment, which affect governance. Activities in the past might have had a strong influence on the natural environment creating or obstructing options for the future. Material legacies entangle with cognitive and organizational legacies. They can have the character of a particular form of spatial organization, a particular form and intensity of environmental pollution, a dominance of a certain type of infrastructure, an absence of certain land uses, a deterioration of buildings or a prevalence of a certain style. The material environment does not determine the way people think or organize themselves but it does constrain and positively shape what is seen as possible and desirable and how to move in that direction (Duineveld et al., 2017; Hendon, 2010; Marais, 2022).

We also know by now that we can also typify legacies in a different way distinguishing between legacies affecting communities as a whole, legacies more significant in one domain of policy and legacies as they differ per resource.

Legacies *affecting the entirety of the community* refer to legacies of the past in which several domains of policy are touched and involve a large part of the population. In resource communities, not all legacies of a resource-dependent past are important for all and for all topics of decision-making. Cognitive legacies might be restricted to a small group of people who were active in resource extraction or who are familiar with its history, while, in other cases, a whole population might not be able to see alternatives because nobody with influence entered the community with a different image of the place or with different intentions because of a dominant extraction history. If the image of the place for those in governance is entirely tied up with the resource history and identity, then more than one policy domain is likely affected (DeBoeck, 1999; Perchard, 2013). Everything that is not seen as compatible with the resource identity tends to be seen as a frivolity and maybe worse, as a threat to the identity to which most are clinging. Much depends, of course, on the nature of the resource and the nature of the dependence on the resource.

Many resource communities in South Africa have to deal with informal and illegal mining (also know as zama zamas*). The mafia-style takeover of underground gold mining in South Africa is common. Martin (2019, p. 2) says illegal artisanal mining in South Africa is 'among the most lucrative and violent on the African continent' and that it makes some mining areas in South Africa 'more chaotic and conflict-ridden than those elsewhere in Africa.' The loss to South Africa from illegal mining is about 14 b ZAR per annum, and the true costs include 'damage to public and private infrastructure' and 'the costs of security upgrades undertaken by mining companies' (Martin, 1992, p. 2). There is also a cost to society. Marais et al. (2022) found, for example, that gold mining areas in decline have some of South Africa's highest murder rates per 100,000 of the population. A similar trend can be seen in sexual offences, suggesting that there are gender implications. The high rates result from criminal elements associated* with zama zamas, *although not all these miners are linked to criminal activities. Madimu (2022, p. 438) argues for acknowledging the positive side of the story, as* the zama zamas *'do have proper governance structures, are generally orderly and are not always as violent as presented by the media.'*

Legacies can be *significant for a single domain of policy*. Long after extraction has ended, certain legacies might linger for ages, but might be restricted to certain domains of policy. One expert group might still be dominant in a part of administration that escaped reform for various reasons;

land ownership in a part of town destined to be important for economic development might still be in the hands of old industry players while a particular form of pollution might be a problem for one type of economic activity or for water management. It is also possible that a heightened sensitivity to a certain narrative or a kind of promise or an attitude from experts or outsiders, a certain method of investigation, has its roots in a period of resource dominance but is mainly observable in one policy domain or related to one topic of discussion.

Legacies can *differ per resource.* The nature of the resource and the relation of the community to the resource certainly make a big difference with regard to legacies which can later be spotted in governance. If the community was established because of a resource and stayed entirely tied to that resource, one can surmise that this creates a tight coupling between the community and the resource industry. In such cases especially, the kind of resource that created the community made a big difference, as different resources require different numbers of people employed, a different range of expertise or skills and as some resources are more or less mobile and more or less volatile in their dependence on commodity markets (Knierzinger, 2017). Maybe more interestingly, a tight dependence on one particular resource, especially a resource which requires many people with many specialized skills for extraction, can mean that many identities can form around the core extractive identity, that many places can see different specialized activities and that many specialized histories, memories and legacies can develop.

The American community of Hibbing, Minnesota, is first and foremost famous for being the birthplace of Bob Dylan, next for being located on top of one of the largest iron mines in the world. Similar to Nordegg, the town was founded by a German immigrant, Frank Hibbing, in 1893. He as Martin Nordegg felt proud of the new town and contributed greatly to its development. He organized and also provided finance from his personal fortune. Around 1920, the community of Hibbing moved a few kilometers south because of mining interests, as ore reserves proved enormous in the area where the settlement was located and fueled industrial development across the US in the early 20th century. Oliver Mining company and the village together developed a plan for the move that included the company building a new downtown and providing low interest loans. School, hospital and other public buildings were paid for by the company as well. Many existing homes were moved, however it took several decades before the last buildings were moved or demolished and mining activity really took over the old downtown.

Kiruna in Northern Sweden, also an iron mining town, is experiencing a similar fate. Established in the same period as Hibbing (Kiruna: 1890) for iron mining, the ore proved to extend under the townsite. A decision was taken, in 2013, to move the downtown a few kilometers east. Two differences between Kiruna and Hibbing are relevant: history and ownership. LKAB, the Kiruna mine, is state-owned and the move happened after the place developed truly into a community with a sense of identity and heritage. Many older buildings recognized as heritage assets will therefore be moved and a different sort of planning process and planning ambitions became possible. Hibbing did not have full powers of local government when the move happened, while Kiruna had. A strong planning tradition in Sweden, combined with the fact that mine and municipality are under the umbrella of the state made coordination and investment easier, made it possible to raise planning and design ambitions. At the same time, the Hibbing story is not one of wild west capitalism as village and mine did share ambitions to develop a high quality living environment for workers and managers alike and understood planning was necessary.

Material, cognitive and organizational legacies. are certainly entangled. And each can affect the larger community or a part of it, many topics of conversation and later governance or fewer, many places or fewer and they can be more or less tied to a particular resource. We cannot spell out all possible relations in this double typology but by simply envisioning the double typology (cognitive/organizational/material and resource/topic/space) can be helpful, as a tool, a heuristic device, to spot more resource legacies in a particular community and its governance system.

One additional and basic, distinction needed is that between legacies in the community and legacies in the governance system. What happens is governance ought to reflect what lives in the community but this is always an imperfect mirroring. Governance systems reproduce themselves and the balance between representation and participation differs per community. The narratives about past and future circulating in governance are not entirely the same as what people think in the community and the tools to steer the community in a particular direction are always shaped by the past.

Important to recognize here is the possibility of *decalage,* which means a systematic lagging behind between governance and community (Duxbury, 2015). This can work in two directions. Old ideas and identities might survive in the communities, while discourses in governance have moved on and tools in governance might reflect older realities, or older hopes for new realities. The economic realities of resource extraction, in an additional form of decalage, might be quite different from what is imagined in community and/ or governance system. The decalage between governance and community can also happen in the other direction, meaning that within the community, alternative ideas about the future and a concomitant reinterpretation of the past, might have emerged, while the actors dominant in governance do not reflect this (yet). Such lagging behind of governance can be the result of entrenched power positions, ideologies, narratives or simply passivity (Mah, 2012; Ricoeur, 2004). A contributing factor could be identity politics of a different sort, i.e., not associated with the resource but with an ideology or party which just happens to cling to old resource identities.

History and memory in resource towns

The following section, that is, the rest of this chapter is an exploration of history, memory and legacies in resource towns, an attempt to recognize typical relations, evolutions and problems. At this point we ask for patience since this exploration is not a final synthesis but rather a starting point for a gradual deepening of the analysis of legacies in resource communities and how they constrain the construction and implementation of community futures. In Chapter 8, we explicitly link the presence of various legacies with ways to imagine and organize the future. In Chapters 4, 5 and 6 we also develop the insight in various legacies, while Chapter 7 synthesizes a set of these legacies under the heading of 'the concentration problem.' Some of the ideas presented in the following paragraphs anticipate what will be fully articulated in those chapters.

One feature of resource communities, discussed in detail later, is that they often play a special role for larger polities. They can be important purely for economic reasons and they can be central to the survival of a political regime; in addition, a resource can be of strategic importance for national defense. Their establishment and growth receive therefore often special attention from central administrations (see later, Chapters 4 and 5) and this comes with consequences for the functioning of memory.

This entails often that history for resource communities is written more than for other communities, by the center of power and that social memory rarely is a product of multiplication of memories through differentiation and self-organization. Central administrations keep track of production, income, demographics, local governments are often weak (for reasons analyzed in the following chapters) and a slow formation of a local culture is an unlikely evolution. Both history and memory can be *somewhere else,* in other words, an illustration of the dependence of the community on other entities, either higher-level governments, or private companies (Baehre, 2015; Sebald & Schwartz, 2011). In the case of a dominance of a business, the memory of the community will be even more guarded, as subjected to the pressures of a more narrow, economic, interest. If a private governance regime, as in a company town, for example, is resisted by a union, history and memory are kept and evolve elsewhere perhaps closer to the center of union power.

A second problem relates to the transience of resource communities. A town itself might be short-lived, turning into a ghost town after a decade or so, a common occurrence in North America in the 19th and early 20th centuries. Such communities do not have the time to accumulate an archive, nor the time for local identities to evolve, or for existing groups to develop a social memory tied to the locale. Even if the town does remain, the circulation of workers can still bring about features of a transient community, with weak place attachment, little self-organization and governance capacity (see the introductory chapter). The existence of a physical town does not guarantee the existence of a community, a community which can create its own social memory and use that as a basis to have an input in governance. Of course, in those cases where the community is *de facto* a camp with a limited number of some services, as might be the case when for example a large camp is established near a small older village, the problems just mentioned will be amplified.

Where cycles of boom and bust are dramatic, the ups and downs will have profound effects on the functioning of social memory. These effects will hinge on the size and differentiation of the community, on the presence of infrastructures of memory and identities which can remain vital, despite the economic upheaval. If most residents are transient, even if this entails a residence of years, this often means that social memories lose diversity, can fragment and, where existent, can be disconnected from place. By which we mean that in older forms of organization, pre-existing identities might survive but the social memory reproduced there can be perceived as independent of place and be transferred to wherever the group moves or survives (Barth, 1998; Ben-Amos & Weissberg, 1999). For those remaining, throughout the cycles of boom and bust, those cycles can become normalized and the core of a social identity can be built around pride of surviving, sometimes pride of place, as those staying during a bust can do so because of a real attachment and a real interest.

In small communities experiencing a long period of decline, official history can be entirely erased, as its infrastructures can be lost and as a loss of hope for the future can lead to a loss of interest in the past. A weak local differentiation, a history of weak local governance, can contribute to a decline and narrowing of social memory. When the central industry is gone or almost gone, but people remain in place, nostalgia can take over, a form of social memory which is a simplification of more diverse and mutually balancing social memories (Berger, 2019; Savage, 2008). Economic decline in a context of weak governance will erode already fragile infrastructures of social memory. Where such infrastructures were strong, they tended to be associated with cultural, ethnic or national groups finding ways to organize themselves, in coexistence or competition with others (Certeau & Certeau, 1992; Zerubavel, 2003).

Simplification of social memory is an often-observed tendency in resource communities, therefore, a reflection of the simplification of governance and more broadly community life often observed (see Chapters 6 and 7). What happened in the past is first considered through the lens of the single industry (White, 2012). Many workers were not organized and even if so, many communities were not the places where families would take root and remain for many generations, a time frame which would allow for the evolution of more diverse perspectives, identities, activities, forms of organization and their memories (Perez-Sindin & Van Assche, 2020; L. Smith & Campbell, 2017). Where generations do stay, the main reason is the persistence of an industry which supports the community but keeps it in a state of non-diversification. In other words, whereas children and grandchildren staying in the place can be a condition for the formation of a differentiated community, where diverse social memories could compete and contribute in the orientation toward the future, it is not necessarily a sufficient condition (Assmann & Czaplicka, 1995).

One form of simplification of memory often encountered is an unhealthy focus on one period of extraction, a glory period, which is remembered in rosy hues and without much critical scrutiny. If a resource identity (see next chapter) is preserved, even when the industry is gone, this tends to reinforce such focus and vice versa. The glory period is often remembered in greater detail than other periods and a period of decline can be remembered in only the most general terms, sometimes glossing over decades of clear signals that the end was in sight (Berger, 2019). That glory period is then silently taken as the standard for an understanding of a good life, a good future, but also of the 'real' nature of the community. Everything else experienced as less real, since it is not living up to the 'true' potential of the community (Baehre, 2015; Van Assche et al., 2009).

In South Africa, the decline in the gold mining industry coincided with the transition from white minority rule to democracy (1992–1994). But despite the poor working conditions, wages and housing under apartheid, mining decline has left miners with memories of a booming economy, a feeling of loss, and regret for the disappearance of patriarchal protection by the companies. The main reason for the closure was that the mines were not profitable anymore (mainly because of the cost associated with deep mining). The link with the changing political regime is purely accidental. Yet, some people associate the good old times with apartheid. Sesele et al. (2021, p. 215) quote a respondent who contrasted comfort under apartheid with the current hardship:

We have witnessed apartheid. I want to make it clear: we regard the apartheid regime as good. We could live well, without the hardship we experience at the moment. We are experiencing terrible and the ugliest hardship today. Memories of the 'good old days' have become a framework to explain the current hardships. The inherent assumption is that there really was a better time, and that the solution to the current problems is to return to that point in history

Such simplification of memory and reality makes it difficult for new interpretations of the past to emerge, for diverse memories to find a place in community life. If the reality is the reality of one very selectively interpreted past and what is happening now is somehow less real and certainly less representative of the 'true' community, then there will be a pressure to exclude other memories, great difficulty to go against the grain (Assmann & Czaplicka, 1995; Berliner, 2005). Alternative memories are then seen as suspect, as associated with people who do not understand the community, its true nature, as reflected in its true past.

If community life is moreover built around the same industry, even when the industry is gone, memory functions of those organizations are not likely to be the beginning of an alternative form of remembering which could be the basis for new ways of looking at the future. Such narrowing infrastructure of memory will leave little space for the creation of new organizations, built around other identities, activities and aspirations. That is, except when younger people stay in town, but it is entirely clear to them that the industry offers no future, when e.g., alternative lifestyles and possible identifications do enter the community via schooling, jobs in government and via media.

What makes revival of diverse social memories difficult, is an often-occurring combination of de-differentiation and what we called elsewhere 'deep forgetting.' Deep forgetting is the forgetting of forgetting, the forgetting of the conditions of past successes and failures, the forgetting that infrastructures of remembering are necessary, but have locally eroded for a long time (Van Assche et al., 2009). Deep forgetting is typical for communities with a more prosperous past and a present that is not only less prosperous, but also less important, more marginalized in the larger polity. Certainly, many variants of deep forgetting exist, but resource communities in decline are prime candidates for such processes, especially if they are located in remote and sparsely populated areas, especially if the loss of economic importance was accompanied by a deep restructuring of economic and political networks that created the community in the first place. A town created by a state that does not exist anymore, a state which devoted extraordinary attention to a resource which is not valued anymore, is likely to be a town trapped in deep forgetting, with serious implications for its understanding of potential futures (see Chapter 8).

Social memory always operates on narratives which simplify. Yet, there are degrees of simplification, and depths of forgetting. Forgetting can be intentional, even if unconsciously so, and it can be the result of a focus on other things. In a Romanian community, a former quarry town, rife with conflict and possessing a rich multi-ethnic past, stonecutting was not forgotten but its identity was emphatically constructed as Romanian, harmonious, and agricultural. An American small town riddled by conflict brought about by oil extraction, where old prosperous families and new arrivals are adversaries and where stark distinctions between money 'useful to the town' and money 'flowing away like oil' are made with time simply becomes a 'family friendly place' in the minds of its inhabitants. In a Flemish town where in poorer periods people migrated to work in agriculture and mining in Northern France and Wallonia, and in more prosperous eras cottage industries mushroomed, as well as international trade, social memory sees the place as a 'always a farming village.'

De-differentiation will be discussed more in detail in Chapter 7, but this Luhmannian term can be invoked in a general sense here, as referring to a simplification of community life, a reduction in the diversity of perspectives present in the community and its governance (Luhmann, 1995). We can appreciate how this can be relevant for our discussion, as both deep forgetting and de-differentiation can be associated with a diminishing quality and diversity of infrastructures of memory. Moreover, they can both be associated with a growing dominance of a resource identity, a dominance which is not necessarily correlated with a thriving industry. For Luhmann, the relentlessness of forgetting is counterbalanced by new infrastructures of remembering and these are associated with new media becoming available (starting with the printing press), but also, importantly, the ongoing differentiation of society, where function systems such as law, politics and economy develop their own autonomy and memory functions (see later, Chapter 7) but also, where organizations can proliferate, each with their own memory, each potentially contributing to community life and governance in a unique way, representing a unique perspective on the place, its past and potential future.

Legacies in resource towns

The previous paragraphs already identified a series of cognitive and organizational legacies in resource towns. As said, later chapters will develop these insights. Here, we would like to mention the importance of material legacies, not mentioned above, yet quite important in the governance of resource towns and their possible futures.

Resource identities (see also the next chapter) could be considered the key cognitive legacy in resource communities, a meta-legacy which reinforces and produces other legacies, one that keeps a narrow social memory in place and connects to the future in narrow ways (Perez-Sindin & Van Assche, 2020). Even so, the awareness of material legacies can be limited. Of course, people understand their own environment and their own industry, but the effects of the industry on the environment are not always understood or observed (Van Horssen, 2016). Similarly, the mono-functional focus of the existing infrastructure is not always understood and grasped as a legacy of resource dominance.

A key organizational legacy is weak governance. We develop this idea further in the book (especially in Chapters 7 and 9) but we consider it can be introduced right now as we already discern that the singular focus of resource towns brings about a weak form of differentiation, a meager diversity in memory functions, a rigid resource identity and a dependency on other actors, beyond the community and its sphere of governance. One can understand therefore, that what often evolves is a community with a limited set of actors, topics of public discourse, tools for collective decision-making, a result of cognitive and organizational legacies which produce new organizational legacies. A history of limitation in the topics and tools of collective decision-making brings about a focus on a limited present and a limited time frame in governance, which further reduces the perceived need for governance capacity (Keough, 2015; Mah, 2012).

In Newfoundland, Canada, cod fishing was the main industry since the 17th century, coming to an abrupt halt in 1992 when a federal moratorium was enacted. In Newfoundland, local governments were not highly developed with capital St John's only incorporating in 1888. Even in the 21st century, after several waves of government-sponsored relocations and mergers many people continue living outside the jurisdiction of any local government. Those communities which are incorporated are usually small, with many responsibilities but few resources, little local expertise and low administrative capacity.

Identities can be strong and hyper-local, working often as obstacles against substantive collaboration. Ambitious development schemes initiated at provincial level struggle to gain traction partly because weak local governance means that local knowledge and organizational support for implementation as well constructive critique and debate are often missing. New initiatives towards re-scaling governance and finding new forms of regional collaboration, as a way to fill in the 'missing middle,' are slowly emerging yet sometimes struggle with the same set of dependencies that created the current situation.

Cognitive, material and organizational legacies thus entangle and reinforce each other, often in ways further simplifying the past, present and future of resource communities. Ways of understanding the world inherited in a history of resource dominance, ways of organizing community and environment, of taking collectively binding decisions formed in that same history and a material environment shaped by but also degraded by the same extraction focus, keep each other in place. A simplification of social memory, an absence of authors of official history and the interplay of legacies just mentioned conspire to create a set of problems for resource communities which are explored from Chapter 4 onward (cf. Berger, 2019; Perez-Sindin & Van Assche, 2020; Schwartz & Cook, 2002). In the next chapter, however, we stay closer to our current reflections and discuss more in detail the issues of identity construction and maintenance in resource communities, processes which we already know to be entwined with concepts of memory, history and legacy.

In South Africa there is ample evidence of how mining areas find dealing with mining growth and decline difficult (Marais et al., 2022). Weak governance also means that national government policies become applied uncritically at the local level, as in the case of blanket polices for home-ownership which create settlements in mining areas without considering the likelihood of mine closure or decline. Once settlements are there, this creates material legacies, landscapes, infrastructures and investments which cannot be ignored, as well as attachment to place, without really stabilizing this place or opening it up for alternative futures.

References

Anderson, B. (American C. of L. S. (2006). *Imagined communities: Reflections on the origin and spread of Nationalism* (3rd ed., p. 240). Verso.

Assmann, J., & Czaplicka, J. (1995). Collective memory and cultural identity. *New German Critique, 65*, 125. 10.2307/488538.

Baehre, R. (2015). Reconstructing heritage and cultural identity in marginalised and hinterland communities: Case studies from Western Newfoundland. *London Journal of Canadian Studies, 30*(1),17–38.

Bakken, T., & Hernes, T. (2003). *Autopoietic organization theory: Drawing on Niklas Luhmann's social systems perspective.* Copenhagen Business School Press. https://research.cbs.dk/en/publications/autopoietic-organization-theory-drawing-on-niklas-luhmanns-social.

Barth, F. (1998). *Ethnic groups and boundaries: The social organization of culture difference.* Waveland Press.

Bartov, O., & Weitz, E. D. (2013). *Shatterzone of empires: Coexistence and violence in the German, Habsburg, Russian, and Ottoman Borderlands.* Indiana University Press.

Ben-Amos, D., & Weissberg, L. (Eds.). (1999). *Cultural memory and the construction of identity.* Wayne State University Press.

Berger, S. (2019). Industrial heritage and the ambiguities of nostalgia for an industrial past in the Ruhr Valley, Germany. *Labor, 16*(1), 37–64. 10.1215/15476715-7269314.

Berliner, D. (2005). Social thought & commentary: The abuses of memory: Reflections on the memory boom in anthropology. *Anthropological Quarterly, 78*(1), 197–211.

Canagarajah, S. (2002). Reconstructing local knowledge. *Journal of Language, Identity, and Education, 1*(4), 243–259.

Certeau, M. de, & Certeau, M. de. (1992). *The writing of history* (T. Conley, Trans.). Columbia University Press.

DeBoeck, F. (1999). Domesticating diamonds and dollars: Identity, expenditure and sharing in southwestern Zaire (1984–1997). In B. Meyer & P. Geschiere (Eds.), *Globalization and identity: Dialectics of flow and closure* (pp. 777–810). Blackwell Publishers.

Duineveld, M., Van Assche, K., & Beunen, R. (2017). Re-conceptualising political landscapes after the material turn: A typology of material events. *Landscape Research, 42*(4), 375–384. 10.1080/01426397.2017.1290791.

Duxbury, N. (2015). Positioning cultural mapping in local planning and development contexts: An introduction. *Culture and Local Governance, 5*(1–2), 1–7.

Esposito, E. (2008). Social forgetting: A systems-theory approach. In *Cultural memory studies: An international and interdisciplinary Handbook* (pp. 181–190). Walter de Gruyter.

Evans, R. J. W. (2020). Remembering the fall of the Habsburg Monarchy one hundred years on: Three master interpretations. *Austrian History Yearbook, 51*, 269–291. 10.1017/S0067237820000181.

Hendon, J. A. (2010). *Houses in a landscape: Memory and everyday life in Mesoamerica.* Duke University Press.

Irwin-Zarecka, I. (2017). *Frames of remembrance: The dynamics of collective memory.* Routledge.

Kandemir, P. (2022). *The JDP and making the Post-Kemalist secularism in Turkey.* Springer Nature.

Keough, S. B. (2015). Planning for growth in a natural resource boomtown: Challenges for urban planners in Fort McMurray, Alberta. *Urban Geography, 36*(8), 1169–1196. 10.1080/02723638.2015.1049482.

Knierzinger, J. (2017). Mining towns as portals of globalization: The arrival of the global aluminium industry in West Africa. *Comparativ, 27*(3–4), Article 3–4. 10.26014/j.comp.2017.03/04.06.

Lefebvre, H. (1971). *Everyday life in the modern world.* Transaction Publishers.

Luhmann, N. (1995). *Social systems* (Vol. 1). Stanford University Press Stanford.

Luhmann, N. (1997). The control of intransparency. *Systems Research and Behavioral Science, 14*(6), 359–371. 10.1002/(SICI)1099-1743(199711/12)14:6<359::AID-SRES1 60>3.0.CO;2-R.

Machiavelli, N. (2023). *The history of Florence.* BoD – Books on Demand.

Madimu, T. (2022). 'Illegal' gold mining and the everyday in post-apartheid South Africa. *Review of African Political Economy, 49*(173), 436–451. 10.1080/03056244. 2022.2027750.

Magris, C. (2016). *Microcosms.* http://www.vlebooks.com/vleweb/product/openreader? id=none&isbn=9781446433768.

Mah, A. (2012). *Industrial ruination, community and place: Landscapes and legacies of urban decline* (p. 240). University of Toronto Press, Scholarly Publishing Division. https://books.google.ca/books?id=SKsAlP1kcC8C.

Marais, L. (2022). *The social impacts of mine closure in South Africa: Housing policy and place attachment.* Taylor & Francis.

Marais, L., Ndaguba, E., Mmbadi, E., Cloete, J., & Lenka, M. (2022). Mine closure, social disruption, and crime in South Africa. *The Geographical Journal,* geoj.12430. 10.1111/geoj.12430.

Martin, A. (2019). *Uncovered: The dark world of Zama-Zamas.* Pretoria: ISS (Institute for Security Studies).

Moran, J. (2004). History, memory and the everyday. *Rethinking History, 8*(1), 51–68. 10.1080/13642520410001649723.

Nelson, C. T. (2008). Dancing with the dead: Memory, performance, and everyday life in postwar Okinawa. In *Dancing with the Dead.* Duke University Press.

Perchard, A. (2013). "Broken men" and "Thatcher's children": Memory and legacy in Scotland's coalfields. *International Labor and Working-Class History, 84,* 78–98.

Perez-Sindin, X., & Van Assche, K. (2020). From coal not to ashes but to what? As Pontes, social memory and the concentration problem. *The Extractive Industries and Society.7*(3), 882–891.

Ricoeur, P. (2004). Personal memory, collective memory. In *Memory, History, Forgetting* (pp. 93–132). University of Chicago Press.

Rowlinson, M., Booth, C., Clark, P., Delahaye, A., & Procter, S. (2010). Social re-membering and organizational memory. *Organization Studies, 31*(1), 69–87.

Savage, M. (2008). Histories, belongings, communities. *International Journal of Social Research Methodology, 11*(2), 151–162.

Schwartz, J. M., & Cook, T. (2002). Archives, records, and power: The making of modern memory. *Archival Science, 2*(1), 1–19. 10.1007/BF02435628.

Sebald, W. G., & Schwartz, L. S. (2011). *The emergence of memory conversations with W.G. Sebald.* New York: Seven Stories Press.

Sesele, K., & Marais, L. (2023). Mine closure, women, and crime in Matjhabeng, South Africa. *Geographical Research, 61*(1), 18–31.

Sesele, K., Marais, L., van Rooyen, D., & Cloete, J. (2021). Mine decline and women: Reflections from the free state Goldfields. *The Extractive Industries and Society, 8*(1), 211–219.

Smith, D. (2009). Debating cultural topography: Sites of memory and non-places in the work of Pierre Nora and Marc Augé. *Irish Journal of French Studies, 9*(1), 31–48.

Smith, L., & Campbell, G. (2017). 'Nostalgia for the future': Memory, nostalgia and the politics of class. *International Journal of Heritage Studies, 23*(7), 612–627.

Van Assche, K., Devlieger, P., Teampau, P., & Verschraegen, G. (2009). Forgetting and remembering in the margins: Constructing past and future in the Romanian Danube Delta. *Memory Studies, 2*(2), 211–234.

Van Assche, K., & Teampău, P. (2015). *Local Cosmopolitanism: Imagining and (Re-) Making Privileged Places.* Springer.

van der Steen, J. (2018). Remembering the revolt of the low countries: Historical Canon formation in the Dutch Republic and Habsburg Netherlands, 1566–1621. *Sixteenth Century Journal, 49*(3). p713–741.

Van Horssen, J. (2016). *A town called Asbestos: Environmental contamination, health, and resilience in a resource community.* UBC Press.

White, N. (2012). *Company towns: Corporate order and community.* University of Toronto Press, Scholarly Publishing Division.

Zerubavel, E. (2003). *Time maps: Collective memory and the social shape of the past.* University of Chicago Press.

3

IDENTITY AND REINVENTION IN RESOURCE COMMUNITIES

Identity formation and memory

Identity is many things for many people. We understand it as a cultural construct, which means a discursive construct. People tell stories about themselves as a group, define symbols typical for that group and construct the group as such. Groups are also defined by contact and contrast with others. Appearance, language, rituals, symbols, art and many other features can provide distinctions which define two groups (Eriksen, 2010). People create boundaries, social boundaries, which support an identity, as much as internal and shared features define it. In some cases, the distinction with others comes first, in other places the focus on unity as defined from within comes first (Baehre, 2015; Yashar, 1998). Social identity is then, a set of images and narratives self-produced by the group, with the purpose of creating unity (Ben-Amos & Weissberg, 1999; Cohen, 2000; Liu & Hilton, 2005; Stets & Burke, 2000).

Identity cannot work without memory, social memory and identity can be considered legacies which shape the reproduction of the community and its governance system. In some cases, identities are tied to or produce formal histories, especially if the identity is one represented in and by a polity. Otherwise, the social memories can underpin, erode or contest the official memory that counts as history (Scott, 2010). Alternatively, they can exist in parallel, without much questioning and scrutiny, especially if the groups or the activities associated with the groups are not considered important in the polity. Social memory, or images of history, can help to define the boundaries of the group since identity can lean on a long-shared history or key events considered as defining for the group or a certain

DOI: 10.4324/9781003332145-3

shared experience which counts as defining (Mooney, 2011; Sullivan & Mitchell, 2012; Van Assche et al., 2008).

Identity, as shaping and shaped by memory, can be tied to a place, or not. Even if not, there tend to be references to places which anchor the narrative, as a group and its history do need a spatial context to appear real, to convey unity and existence (Koch et al., 2021; Scott, 2010). Possibly, the new world of the virtual changes some of these premises, but before the internet, the place reference was an intrinsic part of identity construction. Thus, one can consider spatial identity, social identity and social memory as mutually constitutive, with changes on one side likely triggering changes in the others (Cohen, 1975; de Vries & Aalvanger, 2015). If the narrative of the past changes, the identity changes and most likely one can expect a change in the construction of spatial identity

Identity and organization

Social identities can spawn organizations and they can spawn processes of community governance. In both cases, the process of organizing itself can contribute to the construction and maintenance of identity, as decision-making forces reflection on boundaries and key attributes. Organizations per definition have an identity, as in a narrative construct which guides decision-making, offering arguments why to do or not to do something and offering the opportunity to navigate various environments (Foucault, 2002; High & Lewis, David W., 2021). They are not necessarily linked to a social identity existing outside the organization but could do so. Sometimes, the organization comes first and intends to produce a social identity, or, in more activist terms, a movement.

The act of organization and at higher levels of complexity, meaning organization of governance, creates both problems and levers for social identities (Seidl, 2016). Identities can consolidate, tie themselves to their own decisions, as a collective, through governance and they can reshape their environment to fit their own self-image, image of place and history (de Vries & Aalvanger, 2015; Perchard, 2013). Conversely, the need for taking collectively binding decisions, the need to articulate boundaries and futures, in other words the requirements for governance, can expose weaknesses in the identity construction as well asrifts and incompatibilities andcompeting identities (Mate, 2002). A protest movement can turn into a union which could then alienate half of the movement and then split into three; an environmental movement can spawn a dozen organizations which then crystallize their own identities and start to compete on many topics (Luhmann, 1995); this illustrates the importance of forgetting in identity formation (Esposito, 2008; Ricoeur, 2004).

Identities evolve and there are no simple rules guiding that evolution. Shocks, conflicts, coalitions, persuasive ideologies, fashions, economic changes, nationalism and other things can reshuffle the landscape of social identities in a territory. Redefinitions of territory can engender such shifts. People might be used to a layered identification, where different identities coexist rather comfortably within an individual, where for instance being multilingual is not a betrayal (Ben-Amos & Weissberg, 1999; Lee, 2016). The rules of identification and the landscape of identities can change to such an extent that speaking a language becomes a symbol for an identity which is enforced or questioned, where friends should be similar, hobbies can be suspicious, etc. Forgetting former rules of identification, former identity constructions and rewriting history while forgetting that rewriting are all implied in such process (Eriksen, 2010; Magris, 2011). Again, selective remembering and selective forgetting are co-constitutive.

Identity transparent and opaque

Identity thus defined is a set of features of which a group can be aware of. Reflexivity can be cultivated such that this awareness is increased within the group. Civil society, academia, diversity in politics, media, can contribute to such reflexivity, to an increase in the transparency of social identity for the group itself and, by extension, in a community for the community itself (as a landscape of layered and partly competing identities). Questioning of social memory, of place identity, of the boundaries and key features of a social identity and of the linkages between place, group and history is critical work, which can help to break open discussions and lead to alternative understandings of self, of past, present and future.

A more complicated task is it to expose all legacies -more precisely to expose the way those legacies play a role in the reproduction of the community and its governance system. If we see a community as a social system and its governance as a subsystem (as the local and broadly defined version of the political system), then one can analyze those systems as *autopoietic,* or, operationally closed and self-reproducing. Each community then has a unique form of autopoiesis, as its reproduction mode is the result of a unique history, which gave it cognitive, organizational and material tools to shape itself (Luhmann, 1995). Governance systems structure this process of self-shaping, so the unique history of that system, or, the unique mode of self-reproduction and self-transformation, is key to the understanding of the unique path of a community and the unique set of options of transformation available to it (Bakken & Hernes, 2003).

This unique form of autopoiesis in communities, enabled through governance, is another form of identity, a unicity that deserves our attention. This autopoietic identity is less transparent for the community itself, even in

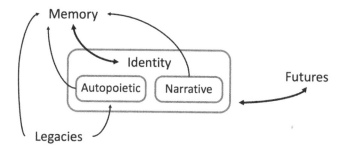

FIGURE 3.1 Role of identity in communities. Autopoietic and narrative identities are closely related to memory and futures in a community. Legacies in resource communities influence both memory and autopoietic identity, narrative identity shapes memory.

governance, where reflexivity can be structured, made part of decision-making routines (Van Assche et al., 2019). This is the case because no system can be entirely aware of itself, of all its features but especially of all legacies shaping its functioning and all aspects of its self-reproduction. Governance itself offers no perfect vantage point to understand everything in the community and steer the community perfectly through its decisions (see Chapter 9) and it certainly does not offer a perfect vantage point to look at itself. It is not able to question all its assumptions, all informal institutions enabling and limiting it; the images it has of itself are self-produced, hence structured by the same autopoiesis it is trying to reconstruct.

In the rest of this chapter and the rest of this book, we devote most attention to the discursive or narrative identity, but the less transparent autopoietic identity will rear its head every now and then, especially in Chapters 8 and 9, where it becomes relevant in understanding the diversity and diverse effects of legacies, the limitations in managing them and in grasping the limits of steering in and through governance. In Chapter 11, it appears in the examination on reflexivity and we will meet it here and there in the other chapters (Figure 3.1).

Memories and strong identities

In resource communities, the ambiguities of a strong social identity are brutally exposed. As discussed, explicit and implicit camp models make for weak social identities, where people working in an area do not become part of the community, do not identify with the place, do not stay, are not in-terested much in participation in governance and thinking about the future of the community (Markey et al., 2011). Weak social identities, that is, in relation to the place, weak integration in social memory, place identity and social identity, comes with a host of problems for the community; simply said, people do not care.

Weak social identities do not imply weak governance, but it is more common to observe a strong social identity associated with weak governance. It is not because people do identify with a place, a history, a certain group in a certain place that a history of governance reinforcing itself exists. Strong governance, as in the capacity to integrate and encourage diverse voices in the community and translate them into collectively binding decisions and the institutions to implement them and to continue future coordination, is not a direct correlate of strong social identities. Those identities can revolve around narratives critical of strong governance, of rules and regulations, of strategizing and thinking in the long run and they can circle around a key player which is expected to take decisions for them. They can, paradoxically, give central place to individuals who just happen to live together and only collaborate to protect that individuality, against perceived tyrants or external threats (Cohen, 1975; Marais et al., 2021; Ruiz Ballesteros & Hernández Ramírez, 2007).

We can observe here the relevance of the distinction between discursive and autopoietic identity, as a strong discursive identity does not entail awareness of the actual autopoietic identity of the community and therefore of the possibilities to move in a direction emerging as desirable out of the discursive identity. The discursive identity can naturalize the autopoietic identity without thinking much about it; it is quite common to take for granted that things happen because it's natural, logical or the most efficient way (Figure 3.1). However, this is not the only possible evolution: communities form where the dreams about the future are different from the present but entirely impossible to achieve in the actual autopoiesis of the community and its governance system (one could speak of The Real of autopoiesis here, see Chapter 9) (Bakken & Hernes, 2003; Eyers, 2012).

A resource identity, a social identity structured around the importance of the resource, around belonging to a community working in extraction, around a shared history of extraction and of working and living in the place and under the sign of the extraction, can develop easily when a community is established for the purpose of extraction, or when the resource sector becomes so overwhelmingly important for the town that anything else becomes marginalized. One can speak of a strong social identity, yet one that often associates with weak governance – an assertion argued for in detail in several of the coming chapters. A long history of extraction, of dependence, can reinforce a resource identity and entrench it deeply in governance. It can create myriad versions of the concentration problem, discussed in Chapter 7.

Identities, as the discursive products of memory further shape that memory. Memory, at the same time, shapes the understanding of a present and possible anddesirable future. Resource identities can tie past, present and future to the resource and in doing so impose severe limitations on governance. Resource identities can highlight certain aspects of the functioning of the community which are connected to the resource, certain qualities, certain episodes in its history, yet, unavoidably, they will elide and hide other aspects, qualities, episodes and connections. As many resource communities develop a resource identity in combination with weak governance, a weak capacity for self-determination and self-steering, the reflection on such selectivity tends to be weak and hence, its amenability to change limited. In other words, a combination of strong resource identity and weak governance reinforces the resource identity and the rigidities it introduces in the governance in the community (Hall et al., 2017; High & Lewis, 2010).

Changing policies in South Africa try to reinforce local identities. As is well-known, historical mining practices and migration patterns in South Africa were dominated by migrant labour. The apartheid government compelled mining companies to house their black workforce in single-sex hostels to prevent permanent urbanisation. The government prevented black mine workers from developing local place attachment and identity. By the mid-1980s, this policy had started changing and they could now live in urban areas and own their homes (Marais & Venter, 2006). Consequently, they were able to develop urban identities. One of the post-apartheid policy objectives was to bring stability to mining towns. To do this, the government had to stop migrant labour and enable homeownership (Cloete & Marais, 2021). However, the assumption that only homeownership provides stability and wealth is invalid. Marais, Owen et al. (2021) show that policies promoting homeownership did not necessarily create place attachment and local identity. They found that older miners in Rustenburg who were historically part of the migrant labour system were less likely to show place attachment, perhaps because for them the idea of moving on is ingrained. Marais (2023) argues that a substantial portion of miners will continue to migrate, as migration ensures a livelihood. The policy's over-emphasis on stability and place attachment ignores the value of migration. In aiming to minimize migration, create stability through homeownership and place attachment, and encourage miners to develop urban rather than rural identities, South Africa's policies and strategies ignore the reality of continued migration. In Tanzania, many mineworkers do not invest in housing in the mining area. Rather, migration is a livelihood strategy to avoid the effects of boom and bust.

Identities as rigidities

Those rigidities are very real, as weak governance and strong resource identity means that the sites and moments of self-reflection and steering in a community are increasingly rare and its adaptive capacity is likely to be limited. Moving in a different direction is difficult when the cognitive and organizational tools are not available and when the structures of memory and identity reinforce one way of thinking and organizing. A resource identity (see also Chapters 5 and 6) tends to include ideas regarding a limited set of relevant topics in governance and a limited need to think about governance (the simplification processes discussed in the chapters just mentioned). These ideas tend to generate meta-rules in governance, informal institutions keeping governance simple and even more likely to stay on the same track (Markey & Heisler, 2010; Van Assche et al., 2017).

Strong social identities can generate a focus on small differences, where other communities, especially in the same region, are considered totally different, impossible to work with, impossible to learn from (Blok, 1998). Even if there might be, from an outsider perspective, plenty of complementarities and similarities. Even when confronted with real problems, life-threatening problems for the community, such 'tyranny of small differences' can rear its head. This is not so strange, as moments of shock or conflict can create the need for unity, which can translate into a need to reinforce the resource identity and guard its boundaries. Historical differences can be brought back into public discourse, emphasized, magnified and connected to suspicious attitudes towards neighbors, towards higher-level governments, towards ideas coming from elsewhere, seemingly requiring a response emphasizing the unicity of the community, the incompatibility with the new ideas or propositions. The need for collaboration can be easily dismissed through such mechanisms as can be the need to adapt and certainly the need for larger municipal structures (Cohen, 2000; Hall et al., 2017).

In American mining communities in the 19th and early 20th centuries, various Southern and Eastern European ethnicities coexisted for generations. Even when their native languages had faded into the background, when they had become American in most respects, and even when their careers in the mine were not tied anymore to a cultural-economic hierarchy (with the Cornish on top), social and cultural life could be structured around the old nationalities (Emmons 1989). Meanwhile, in the mine, close collaboration was needed and they entrusted their lives to each other.

Sometimes, although the need for change might be understood and the idea of change might be widely shared, strong identities can stand in the way of actual change. They can create obstacles in a direct manner, leading to overly suspicious assessments of real options for change and it can happen indirectly, by ignoring real problems which could be addressed. These can include the creation of a welcoming environment for young people who might identify differently, even if they grew up in the area. Attracting young newcomers might be a taller order and if no attention is paid to adaptation, if the emphasis is on demanding conformity and loyalty, this is not likely to happen (Scott, 2010). One can refer to histories of struggle in the community, histories of marginalization, as well as pride in historical achievements and prosperity, as reasons for such difficulties and such reference makes sense, but the focus on boundaries of identity hinders adaptation, even where it is sorely needed.

When a community is aging and attachment to a declining industry is strong, this introduces yet another negative feedback loop. Deep social memory and place attachment can make it harder for outsiders and new ideas to be welcomed unless there is already a process of internal critique and interrogation of the past going on (Emmons, 1989). An aging population closing its ranks can scare off youngsters and newcomers, reinforcing the character of an outdated place and an aging population overly attached to an industry which offers little future, tends to close the door. One can therefore speak of cause and effects. The closing of ranks, the emphasis on boundaries, can be associated with positive and negative memories, with nostalgic reconstructions of a past deemed unique and wonderful and with attempts to open up, to change, which were experienced as disastrous and traumatic (Dennis et al., 1979; High & Lewis, 2010; Perchard, 2013).

Strong resource identities can attract and embrace newcomers when the industry is booming, when many are newcomers and clearly coming for the same reason, subscribing to and assimilating into the same identity. If, however, a community has existed for a long time and when cycles of boom and bust gave way to a steady decline, the situation tends to change. Especially when remoteness is a factor and reinforced by other layers of identity, such as religion, ethnicity or ideology, newcomers can be shunned simply because they are newcomers (Eriksen, 2010). If the newcomer then also questions the resource identity, things get worse. Newcomers might, over time, be tolerated, as they might be necessary to keep the community going, to allow for services, to bring in investment and tourists, but insider circles might still guard the arenas of decision-making (cf Koch et al., 2021).

Resource identities, especially when perceived to be under threat, can thus aggravate insider/outsider dynamics, which then hampers adaptation to changing conditions. We find another example of the paradoxical yet understandable influence of identities in communities under duress: just when adaptation is most needed, ranks close and adaptation becomes harder to imagine and organize. Loyalty to older circles and older ideas and identities takes precedence over a critical interrogation of the past and how it led to a critical juncture (Van Assche et al., 2021). Simply pointing this out does not help, as the insight in the problematic nature of the response must emerge from within. We discuss this in Chapters 9, 10 and 11.

Strong yet adaptive identities

Identities can be strong yet more amenable to adaptation (Hatum et al., 2012). If the dominant identity narrative is narrowly focused on one resource extracted in one way, for example if such identity is reinforced by common professional identities and social values in the community, imagining a different future will be difficult. If, in contrast, a process of reflection is taking place in the community which gradually takes a distance from a narrow set of professions and possibly one definition of family life, an internally supported broadening of the perspective might occur. An underground coal mining community might redefine itself as simply a mining community and from there a resource community, an identity which allows for a diversity of possible futures and activities to emerge, possibly enabling a more resilient and family-friendly future (Van Assche et al., 2022).

Insider/outsider, or newcomer/old-timer dynamics can develop into a polarization in the community and in governance. Politics can become identity politics and this inherently is a more rigid form of politics, as responses to opportunity and risk are informed by loyalty to a factional identity, not by a careful consideration of different responses, nor by learning processes in governance (Warner, 2019). Elsewhere in this book we emphasize the value of diversity, in terms of memories, discourses and perspectives, in governance (Chapter 2 and the following chapters), yet if diversity simplifies into polarization, the concomitant benefits disappear. The polarization can be newcomer versus old-timer, *pro* and *contra* resource, traditional versus new extraction technologies, in favor of or against the management of the resource company or in favor of or against diversification. The diversity of these polarities, all common in current and former resource communities, points at the risk of polarization in such places.

In a community in the Colombian Amazon, a palm species suddenly becomes valuable. Most locals are not aware of this, but a few people, with more connections and more travel experience, see the potential, the existing market, start to take over more land, and focus on that species. Which comes at the detriment of other species important to the local subsistence economy, but also to local institutions governing land use and governance more generally. Which triggers local conflict and creates a situation where neither traditional governance nor the formal system of Colombian multi-level governance works. This, in turn, means that conflict can proliferate, and governance capacity can weaken even further.

Indeed, going from a closed and unified resource identity to a form of governance which embraces and encourages a variety of identities and perspectives, is not an easy matter and a common step in this evolution is a split, a creation of two polarizing factions. Whereas a homogenous and strong identity has the benefit of simplifying coordination and policy integration (while possibly presenting those as less important), the next step towards a fruitful multiplication of perspectives in governance is often a polarized set of two identities, which is about the most difficult situation to coordinate decision-making and further public goods (Dunsire, 1996). Not only a closure of the minds and the community can ensue but also a history of conflict, instability and a chronic inability to define common goods. Polarization tends to reinforce itself, as conflict tends to reinforce itself (Luhmann, 1995), so what might appear as a logical step from one to many can easily maintain itself as unproductive polarity (de Vries & Aalvanger, 2015; Ruiz Ballesteros & Hernández Ramírez, 2007).

Identity politics

Both a strong unified identity and a split identity thus come with problems and engender a tendency to reduce politics to identity politics. Which means that constructing alternative futures and adapting to changing circumstances will be a real challenge. Old polarities can transform into new polarities with the same pernicious effects. A newcomer/old-timer distinction can evolve into a distinction between factions, underpinned by different ideologies, different understandings of what the qualities and assets of the place are and, over time, different social memories - when the newcomers are not so new anymore.

Where resource communities were always poor, marginalized or when a long period of decline makes for any livelihood difficult, a dense network of informal institutions is expected to evolve. In South Africa, for example, (Marais et al., 2022) emphasize the role of informality in negotiating the uncertainties associated with mining. Such informalities can help people and the community, to survive, to cope with scarcity, marginalization and weak governance. At the same time, such adaptations might make longer-term adaptation difficult as they do not tend to increase governance capacity, especially when the informality is less transparent and factional. This makes belonging to a faction most likely associated with one of the polarizing identities, a necessity of life. As such, conflict can perpetuate for generations and competing social memories can coexist without ever really coming into dialogue (Scott, 2010). Even the observation of threats then becomes tinged with identity politics and factional loyalty, hence the threshold for collaboration might be so high that the community might collapse before a shared interest is recognized.

Factionalism can easily evolve into patronage networks, which adds another aspect of path dependence. In patronage networks, the network does more than enabling survival. Networks and central figures within them, benefit and reinforce their position in the community. Patronage can keep people in a position of inferiority or superiority; it creates or maintains positions of power and affects the distribution of resources (Hardin, 2011). Patronage can connect to party politics, to higher-level politics, which can bring great rewards for the community and some of its factions but also long periods of marginalization, for example if the local clans are not in power at the centre, espouse the wrong ideology or live in a region deemed unimportant. Patronage networks thus reinforce faction-alism as what is at stake is control over resources and positions of power (Maconachie, 2017). Possibly, the patronage network itself becomes a source of identity, overlapping with a resource identity and creating yet another obstacle for deliberation of threats, opportunities and possible futures in the community (Cloete & Marais, 2021).

In the Romanian Danube Delta, fish was the key resource for centuries. The cultural landscape was multi-ethnic, yet this pattern was de facto a pattern of economic positions, a network of control over the main resource or lesser resources. People could speak Russian, be old believer Orthodox (Lipovan), and be fishermen, migrating back and forth across the Russian border; they could be Greek traders and fish merchants, Roma craftspeople, Romanian farmers. Yet all these categories were permeable, to a different degree, in the sense that, e.g., one could become 'Greek' by taking a position as a (fish) merchant and defending the Greeks would be defending the position of the merchants. In isolated villages in the marshes, merchants tended to become important anyway, not only for buying fish but also for providing locals with the necessities of life.

We haste to emphasize that not every step away from a unified resource identity leads to polarization and that not every form of polarization creates its own engine of self-reproduction through patronage networks (Auty, 1998). Moreover, not every form of multi-level governance extends patronage networks and comes with risks of long-term marginality for communities not benefiting the ruling centre. Polarization can tire and irritate people, conflict can cause a questioning of identities and histories rather than a reinforcing of old distinctions. And multi-level governance can be a mechanism of bal-ancing perspectives, of introducing difference into governance by enabling policies emanating from higher levels which would not be possible, or even debatable locally (Buchinger, 2007; Koch et al., 2021). People not fitting the local distinctions, at least in some of their opinions, can vote or argue for regional policies which simply ignore those local distinctions and, over time, might be able to weaken them (Liu & Hilton, 2005).

Reinvention

Some resource communities conclude that change -radical change- is needed. They are willing to question existing identities and existing activities. We can speak then of a desire for *reinvention*. Of course, there is a fair measure of ambiguity in any definition of reinvention or in any empirical occurrence of reinvention: how much change is needed? What is deemed essential enough to change before one can speak of reinvention? Rather than entering unpro-ductive debates on the delineation of reinvention, we focus on the idea of an intention to change and to question identities. We can point right away at one difficulty in practice, though not an objective for our theoretical perspective: to question an identity, that identity must have lost its grip already on the imagination of community members.

In the previous paragraphs, we already encountered an ambiguous obstacle for reinvention: a strong social identity. The stronger it is, the harder to bring in diverse identifications in public discourse and in governance. The more prevalent and the more dominant, meaning that it is more defining for the community and the individual than all other sources of identification, the more difficult it is to bring in new discursive identities or to construct a new one (Koch et al., 2021). Individuals are never merely miners or loggers, yet if the many existing layers of identity reinforce each other, keep each other in place, then the discursive identity of the resource community is also kept in place (Butters et al., 2018; High, 2018).

A remote fishing community might be predominantly Catholic and Irish. A fisher is religiously fervent, has a family, stays close to their extended family, all living in the same village, and raises theirkids to be fishers. There is no local school, and most training is practical, on the spot, in fishing boats owned by villagers. Those who do get a different education move out and rarely come back. Their experiences and stories do not change what happens in the village. One can speak here of discursive configurations reinforcing each other and creating little space for modification or evolution.

The ambiguity that interests us now is that a strong social identity can also enhance cohesion, coordination and policy integration If there is an agreement in the community that the identity ought to be stretched or revised, there is the possibility to maintain the unity of the tight-knit community and its advantages, while replacing part of the infrastructure of that unity, the resource identity. This will be easier in some places than in others because the diversity in opinions will differ and with it the seriousness of the problems and because some identity constructions (see above) are more inclusive and open to expansion than others.

The afore-mentioned idea that transformation will have to be self-transformation becomes visible here as well (Seidl, 2016). If a new narrative of self can be constructed within the community and understood as either a natural evolution of the cherished old identity, or, as a freely chosen new identification, then it stands a chance. People can shift identifications as they can embrace a different ideology, professional identity, religion and to a certain degree ethnicity (Mooney, 2011). A policy choice is not yet a change in identity, of course, so one needs to be careful with deducing shifting identities from policy shifts (Koch et al., 2021; Scott, 2010). Yet, through public discourse, strong persuasive leadership able to craft a new narrative which sounds new yet familiar, through participatory processes which do not feel alienating it is possible for a new narrative of place, a revised social memory and an evolved social identity to appear (Van Assche & Lo, 2011).

We argue here and throughout the book that this requires self-determination and self-transformation and one way to summarize this argument is to state that changes in discursive identity must respect autopoietic identity.

In Ely, Minnesota, a former mining town turned into a tourist community because of the quality of the surrounding landscape, a maze of lakes, streams, rivers, forest and granite outcrops, and because of a history of nature conservation efforts dating back a century, iron mining stopped in 1964. Mining does continue in the region, and this helps to keep the local memory alive. While the local economy is doing well, for decades, and while most locals are dependent on tourism, the acceptance of tourism as a mainstay, of the protected Boundary Waters Canoe and Conservation Area as an anchor of a new economy and identity, is reluctant. As the creation of the BWCCA and the decline of logging and mining are felt as imposed, as the result of outsider initiatives for generations, the relation with nature and its tourism is utterly ambiguous. A turn to mining nostalgia feels natural, even for people doing much better after mining, and for people who never experienced the mining history.

Governance and slow assessment of identity

In a practical sense, this also means that reinvention needs to go through governance. Governance decisions modify the autopoiesis of the community, the path it chooses, the tools to choose a path and move in a direction and the procedures to transform the rules. One can see the essence of democracy in the existence and control over rules to change rules, in other words over rules for self-transformation. This also explains why every democracy is different, a unicity which stems from the unique form of autopoiesis crafted for itself. Governance is also a matter of concentrating power to push the community in a direction, through collectively binding decisions. Here we need to broaden our perspective on reinvention and indicate that it is not merely a matter of questioning old identities but also strategically choosing a new direction, reflecting on the kind of activities, assets and values that might be central in the new version of the community (Van Assche et al., 2021).

The more practical discussions can help to soften the blow of the identity discussions and they might also bracket such discussions. A new identity might not be crafted, proposed, but rather emerge slowly in a process of questioning the suffocating effects of the old identity and/or from the collective deliberation of a new direction for the community. Such deliberation can come up through a process of self-analysis as proposed in Chapters 10, 11 and 12, a self-analysis which can take on, at times, the character of a therapy. This is not strange given the often-traumatic histories of resource extraction and the neurotic effects, as in a gradually building pressure to repeat and rehearse the same scenarios over and over again (Lee, 2016). Chapters 5, 6 and 7 dwell on this gradual simplification of governance and ossification of identity in many resource communities. At the moment it can suffice to say that methods might exist to open up constricting identities and that in many, if not most cases, an indirect approach towards identity building might be the most realistic one.

Most likely, to move in a different direction governance must be transformed to slowly deconstruct problematic aspects of the old identity. Governance change might come first or last here, as in one can start with changes in the governance configuration if doing so, will open up the space for rethinking memory, place, identity, or for strategizing towards different assets and futures. Choices regarding governance structures and processes can stem from a broader process of self-reflection (Van Assche et al., 2021).

Obstacles for reinvention

Identity thus can be an asset and a problem for reinvention. Weak governance, on the other hand, is an evident problem as we briefly discussed above and an idea which we will return to several times in the next chapters. Weak governance, as a limited capacity to organize anything through governance and as problematic inclusivity and diversity, will impinge on the faculty for reinvention (Van Assche et al., 2022). This is the case because of the simple fact that things need to be organized in self-analysis and in strategy for change, but also because weak governance (see Chapter 7) will come with limitations for an imaginative questioning of current versions of place identity, social identity and social memory.

Weak institutional capacity can be a label for the organizational side of weak governance, as the capacity to produce and use institutions, hence the capacity for coordination of collective action will be weak. We emphasize here that this is, for most intents and purposes, not a matter of financial capacity or even expertise. A poor community can have a strong institutional capacity and lack of administrative expertise might translate into a form of governance which is not immediately recognized elsewhere as strong, as it does not conform with national standards of administrative organizing, but it might work just as well as a community with more recognized experts and more standard procedures of administration.

What is more of a problem, in terms of institutional capacity, weak governance and its effects on reinvention potential is the situation, a common one in remote communities, where *internal expertise* vanishes as staff comes and goes. This can be an issue of limited career options for professionals in small towns, it can be an effect of problematic insider/outsider dynamics described earlier and there can be other reasons (Van Assche et al., 2022). Institutional memory and organizational memory get lost. In places where administration is not standardized, maybe less routinized, this is a problem. If the interplay between formal and informal institutions is complex such loss of memory is even worse because it makes the navigation of the governance system for newcomers almost impossible. This situation per definition, will undermine institutional capacity for the community (Dennis et al., 1979; High & Lewis, David W., 2021).

Reinvention has to take place from a discernable base. The initiative can come from outside, but if there is no linkage with local governance and its dominant narratives, the rebuilding will have to be a new construction from scratch, and this is more difficult and less predictable. In the Belgian Borinage, a former coal and steel area in the province of Hainaut, in decline for many decades, reinvention never fully succeeded, as even the most basic social services and opportunities, such as schooling and health care, were not connecting well with the poorest communities, slums often surviving for generations as islands in an otherwise reasonably functioning welfare state. Intergenerational poverty, undereducation and unemployment lingered in pockets, while those who did get schooling, usually moved to Brussels or more prosperous areas of Wallonia.

Rebranding attempts, regional plans and reuse of industrial heritage never succeeded in changing the image and structurally overcoming all negative legacies, yet, positively, one can say that infrastructure development, invest-ment in health care, schooling, environmental cleanup and higher education (e.g., Mons University) as well as strong local initiatives (e.g., in Mons under well-connected mayor and former prime minister Elio di Rupo) were able to diversify the economy, reduce social problems and pockets of poverty. One can note that the 'Borinage' identity is rarely recalled or reinforced in policy, that the region does not coincide with an administrative entity and that rather than reinventing a community, that community de facto dissolved once the industrial networks of coal and steel dissolved, and policy afterwards never attempted to bring it back. Older identities, such as the old urban identity of Mons, came to the foreground again, while the higher scales of policy integration were the Province and especially the more and more assertive region of Wallonia (in a more and more decentralized Belgium).

Obstacles for reinvention as seen by EGT

Finally, as we already mentioned in the introductory chapter, we can analyze obstacles for reinvention in terms of *dependencies,* understood from the per-spective of evolutionary governance theory (EGT). Interdependencies between actors, between institutions, between actors and institutions delimit what can be organized at a given point in time and how radical self-transformation can be. Diverse path dependencies, of cognitive and institutional sorts, mark the functioning and structure of the governance configuration, creating both enabling and disabling factors for change. Path dependencies might enable rapid change albeit in a direction resulting from the existing pattern of dependencies (Beunen et al., 2014; Van Assche et al., 2013). Whether this makes reinvention of any sort impossible is hard to say, as some types of self-transformation enabled by certain path dependencies might qualify as re-invention and in our view an aspiration for radical change and a local recognition of such change count as indicators of reinvention.

A fishing community might have governed itself in such a way that risks and opportunities are quickly grasped and acted upon in governance and self-transformation away from fishing might be less dramatic than initially thought because people might be convinced that such quick adaptation is more important for the community identity than the resource itself. Path dependency, re-interpreted through the lens of a revised identity, might then support reinvention.

Path dependence cannot be understood as an obstacle for change or as a force maintaining the *whole configuration* of governance. Certain traits inherited from previous iterations of the governance system might help its transformation and adaptation. One set of such features is associated with a simplified understanding of the situation (leading to quick action), another set is associated with the opposite; an increasing complexity in governance and of the environment - leading to deeper understanding of adaptation needs and options (Cheung & Oßenbrügge, 2020).

In the Free State Goldfields of South Africa, the tendency to think that new mining opportunities (Marais, 2013) will be discovered is an example of path dependency, suggesting that it is difficult to think outside of the existing context. At the same time, that particular path dependency leads to continuous search for opportunities, to learning and adaptation, although within the general direction of continued and expanding mining.

Goal dependencies in governance, as the effects of visions of the future on the reproduction of governance, can similarly function as obstacles and enablers for reinvention. Weak goal dependencies tend to be a problem, as it means that few visions of the future, few plans and strategies, will effect change in governance. They might change the community, have *reality effects* (see Chapter 10) and might be efficient in this way, yet if there are few pre-dictable ways to create effects in governance itself, then the reinvention strategies which require a restructuring of governance will find themselves in trouble. If goal dependencies are not weak and if they are more or less pre-dictable for those in governance, they can be managed and put to use in processes of reinvention. If they are highly unpredictable, if for example plans can, for seemingly minor reasons, trigger resistance and political shifts or a restructuring of administration, this will add sensitivity and complexity to any attempt at reinvention (Buchinger, 2007; Seidl, 2016).

Laws in South Africa require mining companies to invest in local communi-ties. In Koffiefontein, for example, De Beers provided salaries to employ teachers at secondary schools, thus ensuring that the schools could survive and provide education for the miners' children. When Petra Diamonds bought the mine from De Beers in 2007, it cancelled this support as the resource was declining and it had to downscale operations.

Material dependencies, as the effects of materiality on the governance of the community, also take on this double role of enabler and obstacle. They can represent a tight coupling with an environment which can generate other opportunities that can be capitalized upon easily. They can embody a tight coupling with a set of infrastructures which can, thanks to the keen understanding of their qualities, be used for other purposes and feature in other futures. However, material dependencies can also be unobserved and represent a dependence on a landscape, on a resource that is not entirely understood (Kluger et al., 2022). If this is the case, reinvention strategies might hit material limits that come as a surprise to the community and create disappointment or backlash.

In South Africa holding mining companies responsible for land rehabilitation became law only in 2002. Mining companies that opened mining operations before 2002 have no closure responsibilities and therefore these areas not only hold potential disaster risks but their possibilities for developing alternative economic opportunities are hindered. Nevertheless, many mining companies took on government responsibilities and functions which were difficult for small towns to take over.

The reinvention paradox

When reinvention succeeds another problem can occur. We refer to what we term the reinvention paradox, not meaning that a success story in reinvention turns into a failure. By reinvention paradox we intend to explain the idea that a reinvented community will have difficulties in assessing its own path and evaluating its own success (Van Assche et al., 2021). Successful reinvention strategies will change the community and most likely its governance system, to such an extent that the looking back and looking around in the present have changed too much to allow for an easy comparison with the older perspectives. In other words, the change is so structural that what it is looking back at its past is so different now that it does not recognize itself anymore and wonders how it got from A to B (Sanz-Hernández, 2020).

Recapturing old intentions, recapturing old problem definitions and feelings of urgency or opportunity is an almost impossible task, as is assessing success. Even the need for transformation might be hard to assess. In hindsight, some things might be clear but that is not the essence of the reinvention paradox. The issue rather is that the old situation is gone, the old states of the systems are gone, and that the perspectives which developed in the reinvented community is transformed in the process of reinvention. Transformation is self-transformation; the strategist changes asthe the strategy changes. The governance system observes itself during its own transformation, the structures of that observation are likely to change. Once a perspective on reality is gone, it cannot be recreated, as we know from our discussion of social memory and forgetting (Van Assche et al., 2008; Yashar, 1998).

A former logging and mining town in British Columbia, Canada, was able to reinvent itself through informal strategy, capitalizing on opportunities for winter resort development as well as summer tourism. Maintaining, restoring, up-grading the historic downtown, and keeping development and value capture away from the highway and from the high mountains (from the private resort established in 2007) was essential for this, as an attractive downtown could form the basis for year-round tourism while maintaining a footing in resource industries, which were strategically brought under local control. The increasing control over local resources enhanced the autonomy of the local community to strategize, to invest in the downtown, in small-scale tourism which could attract larger investors. After several decades, the strategy was successful, the com-munity reinvented, yet the rules started to feel as overly restrictive for new-comers unfamiliar with the past and with the strategic necessities of reinvention.

The reinvention paradox does not signify that strategic change is impossible, not at all. It does show that such change will have to be adaptive and it reveals that a community cannot entirely take a distance from itself, look at itself as a complete outsider and assess success and failure in re-invention from there. It also shows that governance is always imperfect, operating based on imperfect understandings of self and environment. Imperfect yet possible to adjust and possible to structure in such a way that strategizing for the long term and for radical change remains possible (as enough signals come from the environment regarding success or failure). Nevertheless, reinvention strategy introduces radical uncertainty which rep-resents a new risk, yet one can assume that embarking on a path of com-munity reinvention comes only after an awareness that other risks, such as the risk of doing nothing, are far greater.

References

Auty, R. M. (1998). Social sustainability in mineral-driven development. *Journal of International Development*, *10*(4), 487–500.

Baehre, R. (2015). Reconstructing heritage and cultural identity in marginalised and Hinterland communities: Case studies from Western Newfoundland. *London Journal of Canadian Studies*, *30*(1),17–38. 10.14324/111.444.ljcs.2015v30.003.

Bakken, T., & Hernes, T. (2003). *Autopoietic organization theory: Drawing on Niklas Luhmann's social systems perspective*. Copenhagen Business School Press.

Ben-Amos, D., & Weissberg, L. (Eds.). (1999). *Cultural memory and the construction of identity*. Wayne State University Press.

Beunen, R., Van Assche, K., & Duineveld, M. (2014). *Evolutionary governance theory*. Springer.

Blok, A. (1998). The narcissism of minor differences. *European Journal of Social Theory*, *1*(1), 33–56.

Buchinger, E. (2007). Applying Luhmann to conceptualize public governance of autopoietic organizations. *Cybernetics & Human Knowing*, *14*(2–3), 173–187.

Butters, L., Okusipe, O. M., Eledi, S. B., & Vodden, K. (2018). Engaging the past to create a new future: A comparative study of heritage-driven community development initiatives in the Great Northern Peninsula. *Journal of Rural and Community Development*, *12*(2), 186–209.

Cheung, T. T. T., & Oßenbrügge, J. (2020). Governing urban energy transitions and climate change: Actions, relations and local dependencies in Germany. *Energy Research & Social Science*, *69*, 101728.

Cloete, J., & Marais, L. (2021). Mine housing in the South African coalfields: The unforeseen consequences of post-apartheid policy. *Housing Studies*, *36*(9), 1388–1406.

Cohen, A. P. (1975). The definition of public identity: Managing marginality in outport Newfoundland following Confederation. *The Sociological Review*, *23*(1), 93–119.

Cohen, A. P. (2000). *Signifying identities: Anthropological perspectives on boundaries and contested values*. Psychology Press.

de Vries, J., & Aalvanger, A. (2015). Negotiating differences: The role of social identity in the emergence of institutions for local governance. In R. Beunen, K. Van Assche, & M. Duineveld (Eds.), *Evolutionary governance theory: Theory and applications* (pp. 291–304). Springer International Publishing.

Dennis, N., Henriques, F., & Slaughter, C. (1979). *Coal is our life* (1. publ. as a Social Science Paperback; reprint). Tavistock Publ.

Dunsire, A. (1996). Tipping the balance: Autopoiesis and governance. *Administration & Society*, *28*(3), 299–334.

Emmons, D. M. (1989). *The Butte Irish: Class and ethnicity in an American mining town, 1875–1925*. University of Illinois Press.

Eriksen, T. H. (2010). *Ethnicity and nationalism: Anthropological perspectives. Third Edition*. Pluto Press.

Esposito, E. (2008). Social forgetting: A systems-theory approach. In Erll Astrid – PhD Nünning Ansgar - PhD *Cultural memory studies: An international and interdisciplinary Handbook* (pp. 181–190). Walter de Gruyter.

Eyers, T. (2012). *Lacan and the concept of the "real."* Palgrave Macmillan.

Foucault, M. (2002). *The order of things: An Archaeology of the Human Sciences*. Psychology Press.

Hall, H. M., Vodden, K., & Greenwood, R. (2017). From dysfunctional to destitute: The governance of regional economic development in Newfoundland and Labrador. *International Planning Studies*, *22*(2), 49–67.

Hardin, R. (2011). Concessionary Politics: Property, Patronage, and Political Rivalry in Central African Forest Management: with CA comment by Serge Bahuchet. *Current Anthropology*, *52*(S3), S113–S125.

Hatum, A., Silvestri, L., Vassolo, R. S., & Pettigrew, A. (2012). Organizational identity as an anchor for adaptation: An emerging market perspective. *International Journal of Emerging Markets*, *7*(3), 305–334.

High, S. (2018). *One job town: Work, belonging, and betrayal in Northern Ontario*. University of Toronto Press, Scholarly Publishing Division.

High, S., & Lewis, D. K. (2010). *Corporate wasteland: The landscape and memory of Deindustrialization*. Between the Lines. Toronto

High, S. & Lewis, D. W. (2021). Constructing industrial pasts: Heritage, historical culture and identity in regions undergoing structural economic transformation, ed. S. Berger. *The English Historical Review, 136*(581), 1107–1109.

Kluger, L. C., Schlüter, A., Garteizgogeascoa, M., & Damonte, G. (2022). Materialities, discourses and governance: Scallop culture in Sechura, Peru. *Journal of Environmental Policy & Planning, 24*(3), 309–324. 10.1080/1523908X.2022. 2047620.

Koch, L., Gorris, P., & Pahl-Wostl, C. (2021). Narratives, narrations and social structure in environmental governance. *Global Environmental Change, 69*, 102317.

Lee, B. (2016). Causes and cures VII: Structural violence. *Aggression and Violent Behavior, 28*, 109–114.

Liu, J. H., & Hilton, D. J. (2005). How the past weighs on the present: Social representations of history and their role in identity politics. *British Journal of Social Psychology, 44*(4), 537–556.

Luhmann, N. (1995). *Social systems* (Vol. 1). Stanford University Press Stanford.

Maconachie, R. (2017). Navigating the intergenerational divide? Youth, artisanal diamond mining, and social transformation in Sierra Leone. *The Extractive Industries and Society, 4*(4), 744–750.

Magris, C. (2011). *Danube*. Random House.

Marais, L. (2013). Resources policy and mine closure in South Africa: The case of the Free State Goldfields. *Resources Policy, 38*(3), 363–372. 10.1016/j.resourpol. 2013.04.004.

Marais, L., Cloete, J., & Lenka, M. (2022). The plight of mining cities in South Africa: Planning for growth and closure. *Cities, 130*, 103965. 10.1016/j.cities.2022.103965.

Marais, L., Owen, J. R., Kotzè, T., Nel, P., Cloete, J., & Lenka, M. (2021). Determinants of place attachment among mineworkers: Evidence from South Africa. *The Extractive Industries and Society, 8*(3), 100943. 10.1016/j.exis.2021. 100943.

Marais, L., (2023). *The Social Impacts of Mine Closure in South Africa: Housing Policy and Place Attachment*. London: Routledge.

Marais, L., & Venter, A. (2006). Hating the compound, but… … Mineworker housing needs in post-apartheid South Africa. *Africa Insight, 36*(1), 53–62.

Markey, S., & Heisler, K. (2010). Getting a fair share: Regional development in a rapid boom-bust rural setting. *Canadian Journal of Regional Science, 33*(3), 49–52

Markey, S., Storey, K., & Heisler, K. (2011). Fly-in/fly-out resource developments: Implications for community and regional development. In *Demography at the Edge*. Routledge.

Mate, K. (2002). Communities, civil society organisations and the management of mineral wealth. *London: International Institute for Environment and Development (IIED) No, 16*.

Mooney, N. (2011). *Rural nostalgias and transnational dreams: Identity and modernity among Jat Sikhs*. University of Toronto Press.

Perchard, A. (2013). "Broken Men" and "Thatcher's Children": Memory and Legacy in Scotland's Coalfields. *International Labor and Working-Class History, 84*, 78–98. 10.1017/S0147547913000252.

Ricoeur, P. (2004). Personal memory, collective memory. In *Memory, History, Forgetting* (pp. 93–132). University of Chicago Press.

Ruiz Ballesteros, E., & Hernández Ramírez, M. (2007). Identity and community—Reflections on the development of mining heritage tourism in Southern Spain. *Tourism Management, 28*(3), 677–687. 10.1016/j.tourman.2006.03.001.

Sanz-Hernández, A. (2020). How to change the sources of meaning of resistance identities in historically coal-reliant mining communities. *Energy Policy, 139*, 111353. 10.1016/j.enpol.2020.111353.

Scott, R. R. (2010). *Removing mountains: Extracting nature and identity in the Appalachian Coalfields*. Univeristy of Minnesota Press.

Seidl, D. (2016). *Organisational identity and self-transformation: An autopoietic perspective*. Routledge.

Stets, J. E., & Burke, P. J. (2000). Identity theory and social identity theory. *Social Psychology Quarterly, 63*(3), 224–237. 10.2307/2695870.

Sullivan, C., & Mitchell, C. J. (2012). From fish to folk art: Creating a heritage-based place identity in Ferryland, Newfoundland and Labrador. *Journal of Rural and Community Development, 7*(2), 37–56

Van Assche, K., Beunen, R., & Duineveld, M. (2013). *Evolutionary governance theory: An introduction*. Springer.

Van Assche, K., Deacon, L., Gruezmacher, M., Summers, R., Lavoie, S., Jones, K., Granzow, M., Hallstrom, L., & Parkins, J. (2017). *Boom & Bust. Local strategy for big events. A community survival guide to turbulent times*. Groningen/Edmonton, Alberta: In Planning and University of Alberta, Faculty of Extension.

Van Assche, K., Gruezmacher, M., Summers, B., Culling, J., Gajjar, S., Granzow, M., Lowerre, A., Deacon, L., Candlish, J., & Jamwal, A. (2022). Land use policy and community strategy. Factors enabling and hampering integrated local strategy in Alberta, Canada. *Land Use Policy, 118*, 106101. 10.1016/j.landusepol.2022.106101.

Van Assche, K., Gruezmacher, M., Vodden, K., Gibson, R., & Deacon, L. (2021). Reinvention paths and reinvention paradox: Strategic change in Western Newfoundland communities. *Futures, 128*, 102713–102713. 10.1016/j.futures.2021.102713.

Van Assche, K., & Lo, M. C. (2011). Planning, preservation and place branding: A tale of sharing assets and narratives. *Place Branding and Public Diplomacy, 7*(2), 116–126. 10.1057/pb.2011.11.

Van Assche, K., Teampau, P., Devlieger, P., & Suciu, C. (2008). Liquid boundaries in marginal marshes: Reconstructions of identity in the Romanian Danube Delta. *Studia Sociologia, 53*(1), 115–133.

Van Assche, K., Verschraegen, G., Valentinov, V., & Gruezmacher, M. (2019). The social, the ecological, and the adaptive. Von Bertalanffy's general systems theory and the adaptive governance of social-ecological systems. *Systems Research and Behavioral Science, 36*(3), 308–321.

Warner, B. P. (2019). Explaining political polarization in environmental governance using narrative analysis. *Ecology and Society, 24*(3). https://www.jstor.org/stable/26796972.

Yashar, D. J. (1998). Contesting citizenship: Indigenous movements and democracy in Latin America. *Comparative Politics, 31*(1), 23–42. 10.2307/422104

4

SYMBOLIC VIOLENCE AND HEALING IN RESOURCE COMMUNITIES

Introducing Pierre Bourdieu

In this and the following chapter, the question of why resource communities tend to support a resource future even when the resource is gone and even when the community clearly suffered in the history of resource dominance is posed. In the next chapter, we will discuss violence and the resulting trauma from a mostly Lacanian perspective. In this chapter, we very selectively borrow from French sociologist Pierre Bourdieu to analyze more subtle forms of violence. His concept of symbolic violence will take central place and we define it as a form of violence exercised over people with a degree of complicity. It is moreover a non-physical violence, exercised through signs and symbols and mostly not perceived as coercion. The pressure can be subtle. It can be encoded in institutions, in space and in routine behaviors.

Symbolic violence can vary in its intensity over time, so an initially imposed code of behavior can become a part of identity later on, and can even be embraced and appropriated as a symbol of proud resistance against perceived elite behavior (Buchanan, 2000). Agency can grow over time, but so can assimilation, or enduring subjugation. The effects, in other words, can evolve along different paths. Even when an old elite is gone, when the aggressor is gone, traces of the old hierarchy might survive and different forms of symbolic violence exist. One can analyze this in negative terms as unconscious self-limitation (as in the next chapter) but, depending on the case and the angle chosen, one can also recognize paths to creative appropriation and new ways of identity formation. What started as symbols of oppression, can sometimes turn into tools of creative self-identification. Whatever the path that occurs, it is fair to say that lingering effects of a

DOI: 10.4324/9781003332145-4

former domination might structure current discourse and identity (Perez-Sindín & Van Assche, 2021; Perez-Sindin & Van Assche, 2020). People might not be aware of assumptions, traces of old power-relations inscribed in their own discourse, in the discourse structuring thinking and acting (Hillier, 2002; Van Assche et al., 2017).

Such combination of potential oppression and potential creativity is not only compatible with Bourdieu's ideas (and with Michel de Certeau's ideas; Buchanan, 2000) but also with our perspective on community identity and individual identity as continuously evolving narratives on self and environment, past and future, with place, history and social identity mutually shaping each other. These narratives do not come out of nowhere, their entanglement and structuring is constrained by power-relations, discursive configurations and a layering of institutions that define what is possible, allowed, governable (Pinçon-Charlot & Pinçon, 2018). This construction and embedding of narratives and their influence in shaping identity and environment can be explained through the concepts of habitus, fields and capitals discussed by Bourdieu.

Habitus

For Bourdieu, an individual is not merely marked by narrative structures, but also by a *habitus*. A habitus is personal yet structured by external webs of relations and power-relations. A habitus ends up becoming personal as a person moves through life, interacting with others, in arenas he describes as *fields* (politics, economy, religion ...) and over time acquires a unique identity which nevertheless cannot be understood without reference to the structure and internal hierarchies of the fields in a particular society at a particular point in time (Bourdieu, 1977). A habitus is neither material nor discursive, but a combination of both, as it becomes engraved in body and mind, forming grooves which become harder to skip with time.

Habitus is thus the result of mechanisms which both socialize and individualize. People who live in similar environments and interact according to similar traditions, routines and rules, are likely to share attitudes, beliefs and patterns of behavior. This is a result of interaction with others in the same fields and it helps to continue interaction. Belonging to a place, to a group, a religion, a class can all shape the habitus. The importance of class was emphasized by Bourdieu himself, but his theory stands even where class distinctions are becoming less important (and others take over). Habitus is built up over the years, in the family, at school, through recreational activities, clubs, work. The family can be clearly marked as working class and this can lead to a path of selecting certain schools, sports, musical tastes, a narrow range of potential jobs as well as favoring certain clothing choices and political preferences (Bourdieu, 1977). Yet in complex societies the web of couplings is not always tight and through welfare state investments schools and recreational options are available to more people. This makes it possible for more people to have an active role in forming their habitus and combining more features and activities which formerly would have looked as disparate and illogical (or, worse, as betrayal to a primary group).

Habitus is thus individual, but if certain groups are clearly defined in different dimensions (economic position, tastes, politics ...) one can also speak loosely of a group habitus. Both individuals and groups adapt to their environment and to changing environments. Habitus is eminently helpful in adaptation to the environment, yet potentially much more problematic when environments change dramatically (Bourdieu, 1985). Habitus takes time to develop and takes time to unravel, as it is both consciously and unconsciously tied to identity, both individual and at the level of groups. Habitus helps to navigate the group, but it also helps to keep the group together and for the group to maintain a position in society at large (Swedberg, 2011). Thus, habitus can reflect past realities and past adaptations. Aspects of habitus can become perceived as timeless, as natural, while, of course, they are not.

Capitals

Another useful Bourdieu concept for our analysis is that of capitals. Capitals are resources, of different kinds, useful for individuals, groups and organizations to move through life. Habitus determines access to certain capitals, but not entirely. Habitus enters the equation in several ways as it narrows down the ways to achieve certain goals in life but also shapes what those goals could be. It not only delineates certain options as attainable, but it also invests them with desirability. For Bourdieu, the fields of religion, politics, economy, are fields of circulation, production, accumulation of something; this can be goods, status but also knowledge and services (Trigg, 2004; L. Wacquant, 2018). Competition can be directly about those things, but also about positions in the field which can guarantee access.

Fields thus have resources, competition and rules. At the same time resources can be useful in the pursuit of more resources while in many cases, resources defined in other fields can help in the competition in one field. Each society is thus marked by a set of conversion rules, between capitals and even knowledge about those (often informal) conversion rules, must be considered a valuable resource: knowing how to dress, how to speak, what to speak about on certain occasions, can make or break a career, a slip of the tongue can reveal a background that is not an asset but rather a liability (Bourdieu, 1977, 1985). As rules change, as the structures of fields change, so do conversion rules. Certain habits of conversion, as part of an acquired habitus, might slowly lose their adaptive value; perhaps the appreciation of opera is less helpful for career advancement than it used to be (Eichholz et al., 2013).

Thus, habitus contributes to the formation of goals and motivation but capitals are very helpful in moving through the fields and trying to achieve those goals. Bourdieu distinguishes economic, social, cultural and political capital, with economic capital referring not only to money but also to natural resources that can function as capital (Bourdieu, 1977, 1985). Cultural capital and social capital are connected but distinct, with social capital being embodied mostly in networks which can help to pursue other goals and cultural capital being more diverse and diffuse, ranging from education, skills, language skills, rhetoric and style, to taste in music, clothing and architecture (Swedberg, 2011). While these features can all be assets and can be wide-ranging, they do need to cohere in a manner that makes sense for those that need to be persuaded. That is, in many cases they need to amount to a recognizable habitus, which could also allow for a degree of tolerance for rule-breaking and eccentricity in elite circles (Bourdieu, 1989).

Political capital is capital that can affect a whole community, which can benefit the community itself (if public goods are pursued) or the individuals or organizations deploying the capital itself. Rules can be made, policies formulated which can bind a whole community. Power here is the power to bind a collective to a decision where the benefits go in the direction the strategist intends and, more elementarily, it can be the power to access resources (Hillier, 2002). Political and social capital come close, but the presence of political capital comes with a promise of access to the collective, to rule-making and possibly a threat of state coercion (Bourdieu et al., 1994; Eichholz et al., 2013; Trevisani, 2010). In capitalist societies, economic capital has the widest variety of possible uses and can most easily be converted into the other forms, although each form of capitalism and each polity has its own conversion rules (Bourdieu & Wacquant, 1992).

In a community, individuals and organizations compete, interact, move through the different fields, develop a habitus they believe to help them in their pursuits, while simultaneously taking over many aspects of that habitus from the social structures they are embedded in. In a community, hierarchies, capital accumulations and identities evolve, so what counts as an actor in governance will evolve as well. The specter of political power is always present, as the promise of political capital is the promise of redefining the community and one's position in it.

Natural resources

Access to natural resources is interesting for political and economic actors, for the political and economic field. Natural resources represent economic capital in an immediate sense, yet, they are also inputs for other processes of capital creation; they are resources in the end and in capitalism, a never-ending stream of products can be derived from resources. This creative side of capitalism, besides the law of demand and supply, makes its valuation of resources different from Marxism, where an intrinsic value is attributed to a resource (Van Assche et al., 2017). Natural resources, however, also lure political power, as political actors can extract rent more easily from natural resource extraction than from most other economic activities and, in more ambitious regimes driven by images of collective goods, natural resources become the symbol of and input for development projects (de Vries, 2007; Jaramillo & Carmona, 2022). Chances are exceedingly high that natural resources will have a monetary value, useful for economic development in other sectors, or that they can directly serve as input for development projects and in both cases extraction will be encouraged and regulated (Molle et al., 2009; Wilson, 2014). The principle can be observed in a wide variety of different polities, capitalist, Marxist and beyond. Ambitious regimes will aspire for control over natural resources, for private or public gains (Lesutis, 2023; Scudder, 1981).

Access to resources drove political expansion since ancient times and it still does (Van Assche et al., 2016). Larger extraction projects also need state support, in the form of subsidies or guarantees, infrastructure development, town planning and in many other forms (Gunder & Mouat, 2002; Molle et al., 2009). Hence, the traditional entangling of state and resource extraction, even where wild capitalism at first sight seems to rule. Political and economic capital tend to overlap in the resource sector and discovery of resources quickly draws the attention of politics (Trevisani, 2010). That politics is in many cases not without its forms of inclusion and exclusion, its hierarchies, its elites and forms of oppression, its forms of abuse of cultural and social capital for economic gain and to maintain elite status (Eichholz et al., 2013; Ojha et al., 2009).

Once resources are discovered, these hierarchies are not forgotten; often, elites will benefit most and will secure positions of preferential access to maintain their elite position (Ballet et al., 2007). In many western and developed countries, colonial hierarchies, class structures and religious divides were maintained through resource extraction. Only rarely did resource economies offer chances for social mobility, for colonial emancipation or for personal or territorial reinvention. On the contrary, for colonial territories, the presence of valuable resource tended to be a curse in more than one sense as it made it less likely that the colonizer would lose interest. Even after independence, neocolonial connections were often maintained because of resources. Resources tend to keep power relations in place and if investments are large, infrastructures complicated, this tendency is even more outspoken (Molle et al., 2009; Scudder, 1981).

Even if resources are central for a regime, that does not mean that the place of extraction is important (cf Scott, 1998). Even when the place is important, it does not mean that the residents have much say over their own organization. Company towns (with state backing) had notoriously little participation and democracy but also in supposedly self-organizing communities (the most common form being municipalities), the degree of self-determination, of autonomy, tends to be low (Ojha et al., 2009). This tends to be the case precisely because a national interest or elite interest is perceived and decisions ought to be taken elsewhere, closer to centers of power, where that interest is understood.

Caring for the place of extraction might be real, but that care is often focused on maintaining production and ensuring a degree of comfort for residents – so they don't run away or start a revolution (Tsuji & Otsuki, 2023; van der Watt & Marais, 2021). Yet, both under capitalist and Marxist systems, production infrastructure tends to take priority over infrastructures fostering a vibrant community life and possibly a more diversified future later. Often higher-level actors are not interested in such diversification nor in the long-term existence of the community, or only insofar as it supports resource extraction. As we noticed in other chapters, resources featuring in higher level interests and plans often generate resource towns as simplified environments with little say over their own future (Bradbury, 1979). This can be intentional, as in the reasoning above, as self-determination can undermine strategic interests and it can be the result of the set of factors analyzed in other chapters, the result of unintentional evolutions leading to a closing of minds, to tight identifications and simplified futures.

Symbolic violence

It is against this background that the concept of *symbolic violence* needs to be understood. Hierarchies and relations of domination in social fields are bound to be at play in resource communities, in the identification of people working in the industry, in their habitus, in their attitudes towards governance and control over their own future. There is real violence involved in many places (see next chapter), in others there is coercion and symbolic violence. Symbolic violence becomes a force in shaping the habitus of workers and other residents. It can take many forms, yet always rests on the subtle imposition of categories of thinking by the powerful on the powerless. If those lower on the ladder incorporate the thinking of the powerful in their own navigation of the social fields, it is likely to reproduce the structure of the field and to mask forms of oppression.

The ideas which come from somewhere else but are considered as their own, can be ideas of class structures, of environmental quality, masculine virtues, decent behavior, appropriate clothing, work ethic, potentially anything that can support those benefiting from the existing order. Symbolic violence does not necessarily stem from ideologically biased schools, media propaganda, subjugate or corrupted unions, elite-oriented government policies, in a rather closed community. All this is possible, but for Bourdieu, the structures of class and other hierarchies created by a particular structuring of the field and accumulations capital, have in turn a structuring effect, creating a habitus which is not easy to undo, a habitus which reflects adaptations benefiting those adapting but also naturalized impositions (Jaramillo & Carmona, 2022; Lesutis, 2023). Class structures and other hierarchies (which can include simple insider/outsider distinctions) thus exert symbolic violence themselves and habitus can be a medium for this (Atkinson, 2013; Van Assche et al., 2017).

When people leave town, when they make money or change jobs, this does not unmake the habitus and undo symbolic violence. Indeed, it is not entirely a conscious process and for what is conscious, many beliefs look like either freely chosen, or reflecting a natural order of things, while they are neither (Weininger, 2002; Wilson, 2014). In addition, at community level, relations of power may persist even if the initiator, a set of actors initially benefiting from the structure of the field, has gone. The structures which evolved from the initial power relations might be intact and habitus might survive, as well as symbolic violence, long after the elite left and long after the resource economy collapsed. In Chapter 7, we will speak of the Big Other, as an authority which can easily survive itself and haunt a community for generations.

Symbolic violence can be directly institutionalized more easily when resource communities figure prominently in national level ambitions, especially in regimes not too fond of participatory democracy. National governments, in authoritarian and other regimes, can concentrate power and decide on literally everything in the community. Resource communities are often built from scratch and can be highly planned, so the planning government can have a strong influence on what appears as reality, as natural and fair for the residents. This is not only because everything was built by the government, all initial decisions were taken by them, but also because the entwining of political and economic power imbues existing social relations with an air of legitimacy (Harrits, 2011).

As we mentioned, a direct interest by higher level governments (or large companies backed by governments) does not always bode well for the resource communities themselves, either through visible limits on self-governance but also through the myriad ways in which, invisibly, symbolic violence can be exerted (Borges & Torres, 2012; Görmar et al., 2022). The often limited ways resource communities are truly self-organizing, the often oversized impact of small groups of private or public actors in their establishment and the role they can play for larger polities make for myriad entries of symbolic violence.

As Pontes is a town located in Galicia, Spain. The surrounding area experienced dramatic rural transformation, driven by the largest coal power plant in Spain, where both the plant and the supporting mines served as a source of income and identification for decades. Recently, 5,000 residents, together with public authorities and a dozen of mayors from neighboring municipalities demonstrated against the State Company's intention to close the power plant – the mines had closed before. Despite environmental degradation occurring for decades, and even though the power plant no longer provides as many jobs as in the past, it is still perceived as an anchor of the local and regional economy, and everything that is not keeping the plant afloat is seen as the 'death of the town.' The place is largely a creation of the 1970s, when the oil crisis forced European countries to rethink their energy policies, a creation of the national Spanish government, yet the origins of As Pontes' coal dependency must be traced to the Spanish Civil War (1936–1939). Hardly can a passer-by imagine the importance the agrarian cooperative movement of the 19th and early 20th centuries had in the town. The movement was crushed violently by Franco's dictatorship and union leaders were persecuted, exiled or executed, the town's economic driver shifted from agriculture to coal.

Space and symbolic violence

Symbolic violence exerted through space starts with the planning, design, the spatial structure of the community (cf Gottdiener, 1993; Gunder & Mouat, 2002). This can fundamentally express the centrality of the resource, marginalizing other activities and meanings. It can express the power of the regime or company establishing the town, directly or indirectly. And it can express hierarchies in the company, in town and beyond. Once an environment exists, it tends to become the natural background for the lives of people, structuring their behavior, instilling quietly the hierarchies and value systems of those in power (Borges & Torres, 2012). A new town might be established over an old town, with structural disinvestment and marginalization of the old town; new quarters might be arranged in hierarchical order, with areas for management, engineers, permanent workers and temporary workers. Such hierarchies can be overlaid and reinforced by ethnic and cultural distinctions, where immigrants from less prestigious areas crowd less attractive neighborhoods and work in lower-level jobs (Bradbury, 1978; Marom, 2014). Such jobs can also be outside the main company or industry, if the resource itself is seen as prestigious and everything else, all services and governmental jobs, are seen as inferior. Unions, initially protecting workers and unifying them as a group can, also after a while, divide and create new hierarchies which can be expressed in spatial organization and in other ways (Chau, 2008; Friedmann, 2005).

The spatial organization can thus exert symbolic violence, reinforcing distinctions and hierarchies, shaping habitus. Some neighborhoods start to feel like a bad place to be for a person like you, some routes become natural, creating an image of the town that starts to look like the only real one and your place in the town slowly starts to feel like a reflection of a natural order which is hard to escape (Atkinson, 2013; Pinçon-Charlot & Pinçon, 2018). One can add here that symbolic violence is not restricted to oppression of what is constructed as lower ranks in society, as what is reinforced through symbolic violence is a whole order, a system where different groups are expected to occupy a place, a role (Eichholz et al., 2013). Hence, in premodern Europe, the violent reaction against elite members who 'betrayed rank' and became too close or too similar to lower classes.

Symbolic violence makes people think that certain ideas, narratives, behaviors, are theirs, self-chosen, that their individual agency is not affected by histories of hierarchy (Atkinson, 2013). At the same time, it makes their environment look like a reflection of a natural or rational order, not of power relations that could have been different and maybe should have been different (Görmar et al., 2022). Identity and environment thus reinforce each other and the latent structuring of neither is easily revealed. The measure of isolation of the community, in physical and social sense, makes a difference (see also next chapter) as a closed world allows for forms of symbolic (and other) violence which are harder to imagine in communities more integrated in the rest of society (Chioneso et al., 2020). The interplay between identity and environment just mentioned, amplifying symbolic violence, can be stronger in remote, closed and controlled environments (Ballet et al., 2007).

The availability of goods and services in resource towns and in certain parts of the town, at certain prices, is another source of distinction, an input for the formation of habitus, establishing a web of relations and interactions that will look natural after a while and can keep people in their place (Bradbury, 1978; Laermans, 1993). If at some point it starts to feel as coercive or overly limiting, it will not be symbolic violence anymore but now close enough to the consciousness to rouse people and trigger calls for change. If the lifestyles people were used to become inaccessible because goods disappear or because the control of the company over social space and social time increased, what might have been symbolic violence enters the realm of experienced oppression which, in the longer run most likely will not benefit the powers that be (Gottdiener, 1993; Trevisani, 2010).

The root of symbolic violence in As Pontes (Galicia, Spain) is found in the fact that the dominated think of themselves with the categories of the dominant. The Franco-era development projects from the 1930s, which created its identity, are not highlighted, nor the social, economic and spatial divisions of post-Franco Spain and instilled by the Company, divisions which reinforced each other and left strong legacies on the town and the people. Rather, what is foregrounded is the presence of a magnificent resource (coal) just waiting to be exploited. The current shared identity (as coal and energy town) is thus presented as natural and necessary, and the coal and energy developments as inevitable. The inevitability of resource development entwines here with the 'natural' process of modernization. 'Finally, progress' came to 'retarded' rural Galicia (Pérez-Sindín López, 2015). *Alternative development paths are disregarded, dismissed as 'not real,' and unreliable. People who seemingly do not benefit much from the current socio-economic organization, including recently arrived peasants speaking Galician, embrace the 'industrial' identity, as it makes them part of a new community, and marks their progress away from 'the village.' What to outside observers looks like assimilation of the categories of the dominant looks for them like progress.*

Media, discourse, organization

Symbolic violence can be exerted by local media, who, without any real intention can reproduce categories and narratives which keep the social and economic order in place (Chioneso et al., 2020). Once symbolic violence works, once they believe that the way things work is natural and acceptable, once they believe that their identity is self-chosen, people will want to read stories confirming this positionality and this context. Critical journalism might occur but without questioning the basic assumptions structuring the field (Burawoy, 2019). Critical investigations too remote from the sensibilities of locals, assuming people of a habitus that does not really exist locally, will not trigger much reaction, rarely an uprising and, on the contrary, the journalists or letter writers in the local newspaper can face backlash, being perceived as outsiders or, worse, traitors.

Similarly, public discourse, already weak when self-organization is weak, will probably spark not much change if not rooted in the categories perceived as real, as natural, as unavoidable in the community. If the key distinction locally is between union and management, calls for change which operate outside the discursive worlds of these two groups will find little resonance. A clothing store not addressing local tastes, which reflect a habitus formed under symbolic violence and perpetuating it, will not thrive. That is unless tastes do change under external influence (Laermans, 1993).

Social and cultural organizations can function as mediators of symbolic violence. If miners go to the miners café, are members of a theatrical group organized by the union, a Catholic fanfare or scouting club and the fanfare plays on Sunday, after a mass where the priest preached a conservative message supporting the regime that established the town, the implications are clear (Wacquant, 1987, 2018). None of the organizations have a clear incentive to alter the social order, none of them might strategize to keep the social ladder as it is, but nevertheless contributes to its reproduction (Bourdieu, 1989). If members, through socialization in many sites, come to see their reality as hard and hardly avoidable, then the organizations do contribute to the symbolic violence exerted by the social field (Burawoy, 2019).

All these forms of symbolic violence can coalesce into and be perpetuated by a system of formal and informal institutions. The systems of rules of interaction and transaction, written and unwritten, exert continuous pressure not only on what is allowed and promoted, but also on how to identify and what to take as facts and reality, as a starting point of discussions on public goods and desired futures (Trigg, 2004). Institutions keep each other in place, and new institutions come out of old ones, while some institutions are not questioned after a while. In resource communities, the idea of the town itself, its function, its role in grand national development plans, can be a naturalized starting point, a decision out of view for the locals, yet a decision at the source of myriad local institutions which exert symbolic violence. This does not mean that the initial plan envisioned or condoned all forms of symbolic violence which developed over time; rather that the framework of institutions enabled the evolution of forms of symbolic violence, as long as the resulting community remained compatible with the aims of higher-level politics (Chau, 2008; Harrits, 2011). In resource towns where such a supra-local interest and an initial plan did not exist, the evolving institutional configuration still exerts symbolic violence, yet at the behest and the benefit of less strategic and more localized hierarchies.

*In South Africa, mines are required by the government to develop social and labour plans to ensure that local communities benefit. Despite the good intentions, the outcomes are limited (*van der Watt & Marais, 2021*). We highlight four types of symbolic violence in South Africa's mining policy and social and labour plans.*

*To begin with, there is little evidence of collaborative planning and local participation. The accountability lies with a national government department (*Van der Watt & Marais, 2021*), which does not need to liaise with the local government, communities or the mines to ensure local participation. Consequently, mines are not transparent about their plans and budgets because their social and labour plans are part of the formal licencing agreement. Mining companies are unlikely to share their contracts publicly. Progress reports become overly technical and untransparent.* Van der Watt and Marais (2021, p. 1) *note that the regulatory framework 'does not facilitate positive relationships or suggest procedures to ensure joint planning, mutual accountability and transparency.'*

Second, collaboration is implemented haphazardly. There is little evidence of alignment between mines' and municipalities' plans. Van der Watt and Marais (2021) *point to examples where the mines provided the infrastructure (for example, a clinic), but the government was unable to provide the operational costs (such as staff salaries). The lack of collaboration and alignment deprives poor people of basic health services. Third, gender concerns are underrepresented in these plans (*Sesele et al., 2021*). Men dominate mining employment and mining communities experience adverse effects of overly dominant* *masculinity. Although mining companies have been able to address the HIV&AIDS concerns of their workforce, they have been less successful in addressing the social concerns related to masculinity that mining creates. The inability to counter masculinity and the absence of gender issues in social and labour plans, despite the guidelines making provision for them, are examples of symbolic violence against women.*

Finally, the social and labour plans and integrated development plans seldom consider mine closure. They assume that mining is unlikely to end or that economic diversification will counter mine closure. Both these assumptions can be classed as symbolic violence, as they disguise the likely outcomes of mine closure. Consequently, for many people, mine closure comes as a shock, with substantial risk to their livelihoods. Despite the government's good intentions in aligning mining plans with local government plans, the failure of the government and mining companies to implement the plans or the haphazard implementation represents symbolic violence depriving people of basic rights, perpetuating discrimination, undermining local governance and causing overall instability in the community.

Limitations and ambiguities

We do encounter limitations of the concept of social violence or at least limitations to the centrality of symbolic violence in practice. From the preceding pages we can extract two such limitations. First, a community, especially in recent times, is never entirely closed, nor disconnected from the rest of world. Remoteness does not have the same meaning anymore and in most political regimes, coercion is not such that resource towns can be entirely controlled or totally sealed off. If kids go to school, parents watch television, if there is internet, new sorts of organization, new connectivity, new styles and lifestyles are hard to keep out.

A *second* observation is that some of the conduits of symbolic violence can also help to emancipate individuals or groups (Swartz, 2012). A Catholic and nationalist scouting club can also, through its tight organization and formative effect on the coming-of-age in a community become a powerful agent of change, when for example new ideas start to appear in such environment and gain traction among young people easily influencing each other (Friedmann, 2005; Görmar et al., 2022).

A *third* ambiguity, which we encountered early in this chapter, is that people can appropriate, creatively interpret and modify what is given to them as a natural order (Laermans, 1993). This does not necessarily entail a conscious resistance or rebellion against perceived symbolic violence. It can also be resistance against tradition as such, against the tradition embodied by their parents, the political discourse they hear, a discourse that starts to sound hollow to them, without grasping the underlying hierarchies which are perpetuated (Van Assche et al., 2016). It is also possible that there is no resistance at all, only creativity, reinterpretation. What can be craved is change, without knowing this change is also altering symbolized positions of power (cf Buchanan, 2000 on Certeau).

Finally, one can point at the possibility that people are both subjected to and distanced from symbolic violence. We tend to agree with the position of psychoanalysis that the 'true' person is not an essence, that internal contradictions occur, that what seems a deep identity structure can turn out to be a shallow adaptation and vice versa. For our discussion, this is relevant because it means that people and whole groups can identify and behave in a manner which is structured by symbolic violence, without much reflection, irony or critique, but this position can shift in an instant, or can shift situationally. If circumstances change, people can adapt unexpectedly well, they can simply move and blend into an entirely new social setting, which by itself hints at the difficulty in discerning whether symbolic violence truly 'works,' or whether people willingly adapt, knowingly accept and order and stop thinking about every detail and how it might reflect a hierarchy they might not agree with (Bowden, 2014). Conversely, an urbane and ironic distance might still be accompanied by a pliant and compliant attitude, referred to by Zizek as 'I know very well that ... , but ....'

Mining was prominent in the Spanish region of Andalucia during the 19th and 20th centuries. By the end of the 20th century, many of the mines were abandoned, while the 'sun and sand' tourism industry experienced a significant development. Despite the potential of transforming the materialities of the mining past into heritage, in some of the most representative mining towns, people feel detached from that past (Ruiz Ballesteros & Hernández Ramírez, 2007). *In Seron, where iron was extracted until 1968, few people are interested in the mining legacy. The mining identity is limited to a minority locally and to people who emigrated to Catalonia later. There is no local symbolic expression with any mention of mining, indicating a separation between current local society, mining identities and the old mining population. The local community strove to forget the mines when they closed and many workers left and instead built its identity around other symbolic reference points, most notably ham and pork products. Local identity is created in opposition to symbolic mining references that are even utilized to support the 'us' against 'them' conflict between the townspeople and the miners (largely independent of the more complex relations and overlaps in the past).*

Healing and extrication

What can healing mean in the case of symbolic violence? We believe the previous paragraphs contain some intimations of ways out of symbolic violence. One can try to reconnect, as individual or as community to a wider world, where other perspectives on life and social order exist and where the possibilities for reinvention are greater (Bourdieu & Wacquant, 1992). One can, as individual, try to move. There are the ambiguities inherent in symbolic violence, where the creative side can start to prevail over the oppressive aspects, or, where the positive aspect is less creativity than the creation of a comfortable material and discursive home (Friedmann, 2005). One cannot dismiss the possibility that a niche created in a system marked by symbolic violence forms the basis for the construction of an identity, a way of life and an environment that are not felt as oppressive and that, even if perspectives broaden and alternatives are visible, becomes truly chosen (Burawoy, 2019).

As outsiders, one has to take great care, therefore, not to deconstruct what might feel real, functional and homey in a resource community. At the same time, symbolic violence is part of the reality of many resource communities, one of its most classic features, we would argue. We would say that symbolic violence might be part of any social fabric and part of any process of identity construction; it is just that in the simplified and polarized realities of resource towns, it can be rampant (Bradbury, 1978). Which means that its damaging, limiting and unjust aspects can become very clear to outsiders, while remaining largely invisible, naturalized, for insiders (Swartz, 2012).

Lacan would remind us that all identity construction takes place using borrowed material and subjecting us to an order we do not choose (Gunder & Hillier, 2009). At the same time, some orders are more oppressive than others. In some cases, there is not simply the violence that comes with subjection to the world of signifiers and its rules, fashions and narratives, but also a subjugation to an order which knowingly benefits some groups more than others – and where elite strategies can either be at the origin of such order, or at least at its cultivation (Bowden, 2014; de Vries, 2007; Hillier, 2002). Hence the limiting, unfair and damaging aspects.

In later chapters, we will develop a set of arguments and methods for cultivating reflexivity as way out of the limited and limiting world of resource communities and a way forward *for* resource communities. At this point, we can highlight that encouraging reflexivity in the community and in governance can help to scrutinize assumptions, traditions and naturalized realities, and help to reveal inherited symbolic hierarchies which might not be desirable anymore (cf Ojha et al., 2016). Reflexivity can also disclose the community to the outside world, can make it examine alternative forms of organization and of identity construction. A reassessment of self naturally leads into a re-examination of the outside world, of one's position there.

If we phrase this in terms of healing as taking a distance from a damaging past, a limiting past, one can say that the order which was imbued with symbolic violence does not necessarily have to retain these damaging and limiting effects but, on the other hand, it could. Which means that what needs to be exposed is not only the existence of naturalized hierarchies and symbolic violence, but also whether that violence has the same effects and, finally, whether a critical distance can be introduced so the effects can be more objectively assessed and so alternatives become imaginable and observable (de Vries, 2007). At that point, agency can emerge more clearly and a distance from oppressive aspects of the past does not have to lead to a total rejection, of the past, of the structure of the field and of one's own habitus.

A growing awareness of past oppression does not have to produce identities which either reject or maintain that past. It is not necessary to maintain any reference to that past (positive or negative), yet it remains possible to positively select and embrace aspects of that past, including spatial structures, rituals, social organization and discourse. Healing here is thus becoming more conscious of the hierarchies shaping social and individual identity, of the functioning of the community and the limiting effects of its rules and roles (Chioneso et al., 2020). Healing of this sort is not always moving from an unhealthy to a healthy state of being, nor the simple release of a toxic past and its harmful hidden hierarchies; it is the gradual opening of perspectives so what is changed and what is not takes on the character of a conscious decision.

In Belgium, the Limburg mining region is not an old one. Although exploration goes back to the 1870s, the seven mines which came to dominate the regional economy until the 1980s, opened only in the 1920s and 30s, together producing about one third of the overall Belgian coal, which served heavy industries in Wallonia and France. While the media presentations of the mining decline, since the 1970s, were dominated by uproar in Brussels, strikes and images of social devastation and marginalized immigrant communities, and while the popular image of the 'solution' to the decline of the region centered around state subsidies for unprofitable companies, then state takeover and overly generous compensation packages and early retirements, a more quiet revolution had been taking place in the formerly rural and poor region, as part of the strong overall economic recovery in Belgium. Both local entrepreneurship and foreign investment (Ford, Phillips), as well as investments in education and infrastructure made for increased opportunities and labor mobility, so by the time the miners' struggles drew national attention, the mines and the miners were a minority in the regional economy. Old forms of symbolic violence had been gradually loosened, old hierarchies erased, and the narrative and physical traces of mining (with a well-considered planning process starting in the 1980s towards adaptive reuse, rewilding and redesign) could be simply regarded as 'interesting,' as an asset, rather than as either a source of problematic identification, or a source of social forgetting. The former foreign and Walloon control over these Flemish mines could easily have led to the forgetting and rejection option.

References

Atkinson, W. (2013). Economic crisis and classed everyday life: Hysteresis, positional suffering and symbolic violence. In W. Atkinson, S. Roberts, & M. Savage (Eds.), *Class inequality in austerity Britain: Power, difference and suffering* (pp. 13–32). Palgrave Macmillan UK. 10.1057/9781137016386_2.

Ballet, J., Sirven, N., & Requiers-Desjardins, M. (2007). Social capital and natural resource management: A critical perspective. *The Journal of Environment & Development, 16*(4), 355–374. 10.1177/1070496507310740.

Borges, M., & Torres, S. (2012). *Company towns: Labor, space, and power relations across time and continents.* Springer.

Bourdieu, P. (1977). *Outline of a theory of practice* (R. Nice, Trans.). Cambridge University Press. 10.1017/CBO9780511812507.

Bourdieu, P. (1985). The social space and the genesis of groups. *Social Science Information, 24*(2), 195–220. 10.1177/053901885024002001.

Bourdieu, P. (1989). Social space and symbolic power. *Sociological Theory, 7*(1), 14–25. 10.2307/202060.

Bourdieu, P., & Wacquant, L. J. (1992). The purpose of reflexive sociology (The Chicago Seminar). In An invitation to reflexive sociology, 61-215. Chicago: The University of Chicago Press.

Bourdieu, P., Wacquant, L. J. D., & Farage, S. (1994). Rethinking the state: Genesis and structure of the bureaucratic field. *Sociological Theory, 12*(1), 1–18. 10.2307/202032.

Bowden, M. (2014). *Crime, disorder and symbolic violence: Governing the urban periphery.* Springer.

Bradbury, J. H. (1978). Class structures and class conflicts in 'instant' resource towns in British Columbia – 1965 to 1972. *BC Studies: The British Columbian Quarterly, 37*, 3–18.

Bradbury, J. H. (1979). Towards an alternative theory of resource-based town development in Canada. *Economic Geography, 55*(2), 147–166. 10.2307/142657.

Buchanan, I. (2000). *Michel de Certeau: Cultural Theorist.* Sage.

Burawoy, M. (2019). *Symbolic violence: Conversations with Bourdieu.* Duke University Press.

Chau, A. Y. (2008). An awful mark: Symbolic violence and urban renewal in reform-era China. *Visual Studies, 23*(3), 195–210. 10.1080/14725860802489882.

Chioneso, N. A., Hunter, C. D., Gobin, R. L., McNeil Smith, S., Mendenhall, R., & Neville, H. A. (2020). Community healing and resistance through storytelling: A framework to address racial trauma in Africana communities. *Journal of Black Psychology, 46*(2–3), 95–121. 10.1177/0095798420929468.

de Vries, P. (2007). Don't compromise your desire for development! A Lacanian/Deleuzian rethinking of the anti-politics machine. *Third World Quarterly, 28*(1), 25–43. 10.1080/01436590601081765.

Eichholz, M., Van Assche, K., Oberkircher, L., & Hornidge, A.-K. (2013). Trading capitals? Bourdieu, land and water in rural Uzbekistan. *Journal of Environmental Planning and Management, 56*(6), 868–892. 10.1080/09640568.2012.708650.

Friedmann, J. (2005). Place-making as project? Habitus and migration in trans-national cities. In *Habitus: A sense of place* (2nd ed.). Routledge.

Görmar, F., Grillitsch, M., Hruška, V., Mihály, M., Nagy, E., Píša, J., & Stihl, L. (2022). Power relations and local agency: A comparative study of European mining towns. *Urban Research & Practice, 0*(0), 1–24. 10.1080/17535069.2022.2051066.

Gottdiener, M. (1993). A Marx for our time: Henri Lefebvre and the production of space. *Sociological Theory*, *11*(1), 129–134. 10.2307/201984.

Gunder, M., & Hillier, J. (2009). *Planning in ten words or less: A Lacanian entanglement with spatial planning*. Ashgate Publishing, Ltd.

Gunder, M., & Mouat, C. (2002). Symbolic violence and victimization in planning processes: A reconnoitre of the New Zealand resource management act. *Planning Theory*, *1*(2), 124–145. 10.1177/147309520200100203.

Harrits, G. S. (2011). Political power as symbolic capital and symbolic violence. *Journal of Political Power*, *4*(2), 237–258. 10.1080/2158379X.2011.589178.

Hillier, J. (2002). *Shadows of power: An allegory of prudence in land-use planning*. Routledge.

Jaramillo, P., & Carmona, S. (2022). Temporal enclosures and the social production of inescapable futures for coal mining in Colombia. *Geoforum*, *130*, 11–22. 10.1016/j.geoforum.2022.01.010.

Laermans, R. (1993). Learning to consume: Early department stores and the shaping of the modern consumer culture (1860–1914). *Theory, Culture & Society*, *10*(4), 79–102. 10.1177/026327693010004005.

Lesutis, G. (2023). Scenes of subjection: Extractive frontiers, symbolic violence, dispossession. *Geoforum*, 103681. 10.1016/j.geoforum.2023.103681.

Marom, N. (2014). Relating a city's history and geography with Bourdieu: One hundred years of spatial distinction in Tel Aviv. *International Journal of Urban and Regional Research*, *38*(4), 1344–1362. 10.1111/1468-2427.12027.

Molle, F., Mollinga, P. P., & Wester, P. (2009). Hydraulic bureaucracies and the hydraulic mission: Flows of water, flows of power. *Water Alternatives*, *2*(3), 328–349.

Ojha, H. R., Cameron, J., & Kumar, C. (2009). Deliberation or symbolic violence? The governance of community forestry in Nepal. *Forest Policy and Economics*, *11*(5), 365–374. 10.1016/j.forpol.2008.11.003.

Ojha, H. R., Ford, R., Keenan, R. J., Race, D., Carias Vega, D., Baral, H., & Sapkota, P. (2016). Delocalizing communities: Changing forms of community engagement in natural resources governance. *World Development*, *87*, 274–290. 10.1016/j.worlddev.2016.06.017.

Pérez-Sindín López, X. (2015). *De mina a lago. Actores sociales y discurso. El caso de As Pontes (España) y comparación con el caso de Carmaux (Francia)*. https://ruc.udc.es/dspace/handle/2183/13987.

Perez-Sindín, X. S., & Van Assche, K. (2021). "Coal [from Colombia] is our life". Bourdieu, the miners (after they are miners) and resistance in As Pontes. *Resources Policy*, *71*, 102006. 10.1016/j.resourpol.2021.102006.

Perez-Sindin, X., & Van Assche, K. (2020). From coal not to ashes but to what? As Pontes, social memory and the concentration problem. *The Extractive Industries and Society*. 10.1016/j.exis.2020.07.016.

Pinçon-Charlot, M., & Pinçon, M. (2018). Social power and power over space: How the Bourgeoisie reproduces itself in the city. *International Journal of Urban and Regional Research*, *42*(1), 115–125. 10.1111/1468-2427.12533.

Ruiz Ballesteros, E., & Hernández Ramírez, M. (2007). Identity and community— Reflections on the development of mining heritage tourism in Southern Spain. *Tourism Management*, *28*(3), 677–687. 10.1016/j.tourman.2006.03.001.

Scott, J. C. (1998). *Seeing like a state: How certain schemes to improve the human condition have failed*. Yale University Press.

Scudder, T. (1981). What it means to be dammed: The anthropology of large-scale development projects in the tropics and subtropics. *Engineering and Science*, *44*(4), 9–15.

Sesele, K., Marais, L., van Rooyen, D., & Cloete, J. (2021). Mine decline and women: Reflections from the Free State Goldfields. *The Extractive Industries and Society*, *8*(1), 211–219. 10.1016/j.exis.2020.11.006.

Swartz, D. (2012). *Culture and power: The sociology of Pierre Bourdieu*. University of Chicago Press.

Swedberg, R. (2011). The economic sociologies of Pierre Bourdieu. *Cultural Sociology*, *5*(1), 67–82. 10.1177/1749975510389712.

Trevisani, T. (2010). *Land and power in Khorezm: Farmers, communities, and the state in Uzbekistan's decollectivisation*. LIT Verlag Münster.

Trigg, A. B. (2004). Deriving the Engel curve: Pierre Bourdieu and the social critique of Maslow's hierarchy of needs. *Review of Social Economy*, *62*(3), 393–406. 10.1080/0034676042000253987.

Tsuji, H., & Otsuki, K. (2023). The trajectory of extractive urbanism: Examining the implications of Vale's presence and withdrawal for the coal frontier and its urban spaces in Tete. *The Extractive Industries and Society*, *13*, 101170. 10.1016/j.exis.2022.101170.

Van Assche, K., Beunen, R., & Duineveld, M. (2016). Citizens, leaders and the common good in a world of necessity and scarcity: Machiavelli's lessons for community-based natural resource management. *Ethics, Policy & Environment*, *19*(1), 19–36.

Van Assche, K., Beunen, R., Duineveld, M., & Gruezmacher, M. (2017). Power/knowledge and natural resource management: Foucaultian foundations in the analysis of adaptive governance. *Journal of Environmental Policy & Planning*, 19(3), 308–322. 10.1080/1523908X.2017.1338560

van der Watt, P., & Marais, L. (2021). Implementing social and labour plans in South Africa: Reflections on collaborative planning in the mining industry. *Resources Policy*, *71*, 101984. 10.1016/j.resourpol.2021.101984.

Wacquant, L. (1987). Symbolic violence and the making of the French agriculturalist: An enquiry into Pierre Bourdieu's sociology. *The Australian and New Zealand Journal of Sociology*, *23*(1), 65–88. 10.1177/144078338702300105.

Wacquant, L. (2018). Bourdieu comes to town: Pertinence, principles, applications: Forum. *International Journal of Urban and Regional Research*, *42*(1), 90–105. 10.1111/1468-2427.12535.

Weininger, E. B. (2002). Pierre Bourdieu on social class and symbolic violence. *Alternative Foundations of Class Analysis*, *4*, 83.

Wilson, J. (2014). The violence of abstract space: Contested regional developments in Southern Mexico: Contested regional developments in southern Mexico. *International Journal of Urban and Regional Research*, *38*(2), 516–538. 10.1111/1468-2427.12023.

5

TRAUMA AND HEALING IN RESOURCE COMMUNITIES

Invisible legacies and sources for optimism

Problems in resource communities

Communities can be shocked, shaken up, take abuse and their environments can suffer in a history of resource extraction. Just as people can suffer, resource communities, certainly in less prosperous countries, do show a lot of human suffering. Suffering can leave scars, with people and with communities and it can cause trauma. Not all suffering and not every shock creates scars, and not every scar is a trauma. Certain communities and certain people, moreover, seem to endure suffering and shocks more than others. Without moralizing, one can observe such differences and the reasons can be complex. In this chapter, we investigate what community trauma could be and how it could possibly be alleviated. In the chapter on strategy, we will devote our attention to the kinds of self-analysis which can precede community strategizing and which could help in working through trauma. This chapter will give the first few pointers.

In the introductory chapter of this book, we already encountered some of the problems of resource communities and we will not repeat everything said there. Now, we would like to draw the attention to the problems of power and marginality in resource communities and their effects on the safety and wellbeing of inhabitants. Resource communities are often in remote places that are not entirely integrated in the systems of governance existing at larger scales. They can be located in the margins of the nation, in inhospitable landscapes and climates, where not all social safety nets function, where not all mechanisms of participation and representation work, where not all services are offered and where public discourse (which could expose problems) is impoverished (Miller & Sinclair, 2012; Wenar, 2008).

DOI: 10.4324/9781003332145-5

Companies can exert too much power over the lives of workers, enabled by weak local governance and by a national government more interested in resources than in resource communities. Companies might offer some form of medical services, retirement and schooling, where governmental presence is weak, but that also means that access, quality and permanence are not guaranteed and are subjected to the whims of management (Dinius & Vergara, 2011; Hayter, 2017). As resource towns are often male dominated for a long time, until a community has developed which is safe and attractive enough to persuade people to raise families there, that period can be one of danger for women and children (Fitzpatrick, 2005; Nyamunda & Mukwambo, 2012). Negative spirals can develop where the transition to a family-friendly community never happens because the transitional environment itself is seen as too risky.

Where barracks and company-owned sleeping quarters are the normal arrangement, a safe and nurturing family life is not likely to find a place (Hayter, 2017). Where possible, people will fly in and out and this situation reinforces the lack of attachment to the place but also lack of care for the place, which cannot truly be called a 'community.' Women in such environment tend to be vulnerable and children are not often seen. The rule of the company, moreover, is not really a rule of law, as management is not impartial and complaining is not often followed by fair procedures. Escalation to actual courts is rare as the company prefers to avoid such trouble and reputation damage (Moonesirust & Brown, 2021).

Resource extraction in many parts of the global south is not conducive to a strengthening of local and regional governance and a reinforcing of the rule of law (Sesele et al., 2021; Wenar, 2008). In many cases, it does not contribute to local and regional development, as in the creation of communities where people want to live with attractive and safe environments, with a rich social and cultural life and a variety of services. National governments, tend to be interested in the economic development potential, especially as resource extraction is a relatively simple way to boost national level macroeconomic indicators, but less so in the places where extraction takes place, especially as they are often in social, spatial and economic margins. Local governance thus tends to be weak and new private actors are not necessarily interested in improving this situation, as long as their operations can thrive. If it is necessary to have many workers living there the pressure to build some sort of livable community can exist, but the general tendency is in the other direction, i.e., to rely more on fly-in fly-out arrangements.

The result, in many cases, is either instability or totalitarian control. Old style company towns and modern work camps can be considered totalitarian, as workers officially do not live there, have no voting rights and their input in the governance of the place is virtually zero (Marais et al., 2018). Many other places such as 19th century resource towns in western countries and 20th and

21st century settlements in many parts of the global south were distinctly unstable and often dangerous. For many African former colonies, colonial-era work camps were followed by new camps, under the influence of glob-alization and de-regulation (Rubbers, 2021). Work conditions might be unsafe, but also the streets. Inequality further contributes to tensions, as do the meagre options in social and cultural life. Drugs and addictions are a part of the equation in the 'social' life of resource communities across the world and contribute to the volatility of many encounters and situations that would elsewhere be safe and predictable. When something happens, the rule of law turns out to be weak (Roche et al., 2021; Saunders & Nyamunda, 2016; Woodhead et al., 2018).

In between two large mines lies Jagua de Ibirico, the main town of the Corredor Minero. Locals reminisce about the town's agricultural past "when we were a quiet and prosperous town". There's even a nostalgia for the 80s and 90s, when coal mining was more artisanal, and more people were employed. With the arrival of multinationals, mechanization came, and many well-paid young males –Drumeros –who did not take root. Often, they commute or live in camps. Disruptions in normal patterns of interaction, damage to the social fabric, and social ills (crime, substance abuse, prostitution) followed.

Vallenato is a popular folk music genre in the region. The lyrics of an award-winning song at a local festival are illustrative: 'mi negra (my wife) has already broken up with me because what I earn is not enough. She said she wants a better man, one who works in the Drummond (the Company) and who gives her all the pleasures of life' and continues 'I don't know what happened to the women from La Jagua, that if you're not a drumero, they don't want to see you anymore.'

Instability and volatility

Of course, places differ and they evolve over time. Nevertheless, it is not too difficult to recognize resource towns are often troubled and instability is one of those issues (Marais et al., 2022; Perez-Sindín & Van Assche, 2021; Perez-Sindin & Van Assche, 2020). Vulnerability is a consequence, a vul-nerability aggravated by the male-dominated world of many resource oper-ations and the lack of employment options for women – see also Chapter 7 on the concentration problem. The difficulty to attract and keep families makes it less likely that social networks develop that could contribute to a safer environment, to raising children collectively, to mutual help and support. The 'eyes on the street' in the more unstable resource towns, are not necessarily the eyes a family wants to be there.

The cycles of boom and bust discussed in the introduction, do not help either. If towns shrink and grow dramatically but without much guidance, if workers are fired and hired in large numbers and if local governance did not take or never believed in counter-cyclical measures, this can have profound implications for the safety and well-being of residents.

Africa has seen its fair share of resource busts. Bryceson and Mackinnon (2013) *note that the effects of mining booms and busts on urbanization vary across Africa. Zambia is notable as mining companies established large mining towns in the Copperbelt (Fraser & Larmer, 2010). Neighboring Angola and the DRC show a different pattern, yet also significant and rather chaotic urbanization. Busts affected the future of these towns. Some towns retained their growth despite mine closure (Gough & Yanksen, 2012). The factors contributing to the effects boom and bust have on urbanization are varied, but instability, violence and lack of opportunities in the rural areas, as well as ethnic or regional marginalization, can make the boomtown look attractive, even when the boom is gone. Regime shifts can engender institutional transformation and new economic priorities, but also forced displacement. Even under conditions of bust, individual and local agency might be higher than in the rural areas (Udelsmann Rodrigues et al., 2021), while the young boom towns remain dependent on rural relations. Urban-rural lifestyles can stabilize for a long time, and contribute to the resilience of the community, while lack of infrastructural investment and proper urban governance structure (and capacity) prevent the formation of recognizable urban centers. The economy, however, can already move forward in terms of diversification, partly because rural opportunities were missing and because the new settlement was de facto more than a mining town, even if its existence was triggered by the mine.*

If the community is large enough to offer diverse jobs, one partner can be unemployed for a while, waiting it out until the next boom. Often, waiting is not an option and if boom and bust succeed in perpetuating the short term, it becomes difficult to maintain a long-term perspective as a family and as a community and in governance. Being fired can leave scars, moving and moving again, losing the house, losing networks of friends and colleagues. If it is possible to remain in the same region and to rely on family networks, coping strategies can be found and relative stability can ensue (e.g., with one partner traveling), but in many regions this is not possible. Instability breeds instability, and the riskier an area is perceived to be, the harder it becomes to attract enough people and activity to then ensure a strong enough presence of government to stabilize things (Marais et al., 2018; Van Assche et al., 2022) – except for very special circumstances, where economic and urban development are state priorities, as in some resource areas in the former USSR.

Boom and bust cycles do not always remain cycles of course and many resource towns stop to be resource towns when one bust is simply too dramatic. Sometimes, there is no town left, only a cluster of buildings slowly falling apart, a ghost town. If there still is a town, legacies of weak governance, marginality, incomplete rule of law and a loose social fabric will not make it a more attractive place. A history of instability in a community always already close to unraveling, will leave more than traces when the main industry disappears. Those who cannot leave and cannot find jobs, can lose hope and the services that were provided by industry vanish, without being replaced by government initiatives, as the presence of government was weak, as infrastructures are missing and as incentives for higher-level governments to introduce them later are low. Exceptions always exists, as when a particular place features high on the agenda for government, if it has a perceived strategic importance, or if government sees a potential that locals do not see.

Marginality, integration and resilience

One can also look at this set of problems as an issue of poor integration with the rest of society, where remoteness, transience and underdeveloped education and social services make it harder to cope with shocks. If a resource town was better integrated to begin with, if people could move between towns in the same region, staying in the same industry, or if a diversity of services could be accessed, a social safety net, without moving out of the region, this could enhance the resilience of both town and region (a variety of accessible adaptation options). An individual might be better able to deal with economic shock, a community, a region. If resource towns are spaces of exception, if many of the normal rules and expectations are not valid, if the rule of law is not expected to fully function, the lack of connection with the rest of society, its opportunities, its safety nets, will reduce the resilience of all (see Luhmann, 1990 for the contrasting situation of the welfare state). In such an environment, shocks can cause more scars, scars can turn into trauma more easily and trauma can be more complicated to heal.

Community resilience in this perspective is a matter of community completeness and community integration (Luhmann, 1990; Shields, 2013): if many features common in other communities, forms of support, basic safety, infrastructures, are missing and if weak integration with other areas creates obstacles for compensation somewhere else and for correction of local problems through incoming flows, of ideas, rules, resources, people and goods, then it is difficult to bounce back from shocks (Barnes et al., 2001; Hayter, 2017; Van Assche et al., 2022). If community resilience in this sense is weak, then dealing with environmental shock, another prominent feature of many resource community histories, is severely hampered. In later chapters, we will analyze the capacity to bounce back in terms of the functioning of governance, where collective answers and collectively binding decisions have to be formulated.

Community resilience can reduce the chance of community trauma and help with the healing of scars and working through trauma. Yet, the idea of trauma at community level itself requires our attention. If we say trauma, we refer to shocks that leave legacies communities are only partly aware of.

A second feature is that the legacy creates problems for the community. The limited nature of the resource community, a set of limitations which we consider from different angles throughout this book, makes it more vulnerable to shock and makes it harder to overcome the scarring effects of shock. We can distinguish between environmental shocks, in difficult environments (or caused directly by extraction histories), the shock of the extraction history itself and the shock of closure.

The trauma of mine closure for women in the Free State Goldfields in South Africa has been well documented. Historically, women in the Free State Goldfields were not employed in the mines. But the patriarchal mining system meant that they did not need to work, because the mining benefits were extensive. When mines close, and their spouses or partners lose their jobs, they are obliged to become the bread-winners but they have very few skills to fall back on. A further cause of distress is that they are expected to not only bring in household income but also retain their functional role as carers: a situation that Sesele et al. (2021) describe as a double-edged sword. The double responsibility of providing income and care is compounded by the fact that the men migrate, looking for alternative employment. In such a situation, women risk becoming victims of crime. Gangs and organised crime target women. Crime figures show increased household and sexual violence (Marais et al., 2022).

The sexual and violent nature of these crimes adds to the trauma associated with mine decline. The suffering is worsened for women when they see their children becoming involved in crime. This creates internal conflict. Women who were interviewed said they knew their children were doing wrong but also felt personally at fault because they could not provide for them (Sesele & Marais, 2022). Women themselves can become involved in crime. This includes prostitution and knowingly allowing their children to be involved in it. Most respondents interviewed by Sesele (2019) also described the associated trauma. Most of them found it difficult to justify this behaviour but accepted it because it provided resources for household survival.

Scars and belonging

The extraction period itself, the dangers of work in mines, drilling rigs, can leave scars and can be traumatizing for both individuals and community (Buckley, 2004). If the community itself is unstable and unsafe, this aggravates the situation, as it means that a stable home base is not really there (Sesele et al., 2021). A safe community can be a nurturing one, one where it is possible to heal from otherwise damaging work environments. If the whole community is a work environment and de facto an unsafe one, if transience and weak attachment are the order of the day, this does not make for a restorative community. A community is indeed more than a place; the network of ties which support safety and collaboration can also support restoration and healing (Edkins, 2006). Especially when government and rule of law are weak, this sense of community and the associated forms of self-organization, are even more important (Meadowcroft et al., 2012). Thus, safety, belonging and healing can be supported through different routes, but if few of those routes are available, tensions, conflicts, volatility at work can translate into trauma for the individual. One can also speak of layered support mechanisms, where each of the layers can be weakened in resource towns: family, network and community, governmental safety nets and safety mechanisms.

Feelings of belonging, however, are not positive *per se*, just as a strong community identity is not positive in itself. If home ownership is encouraged and permanent settlement is pushed hard by governments when the resource futures are bleak and alternatives are unlikely to appear easily, this puts a heavy burden of responsibility on the shoulders of government. Especially if mobilities are limited, if there are few other opportunities easily accessible for the new residents of a declining place, ownership and deep place attachment might add obstacles to mobility, to a possible strategy of 'smart shrink.' Healing can be healing in place, but circumstances might also make moving more rational and might make healing by moving more realistic. This, however, requires a capacity to observe that moving might be better, that the situation is untenable and such capacity can be hampered by deep feelings of place attachment, which can in turn be reinforced when place identity and individual identity are entangled – 'I am a fisherwoman, I belong in this fishing community.'

Extraction can be painful for the workers, the work can be traumatic, yet the attitudes towards the work can be complex. One can be scarred deeply without knowing it, one can be in denial for years about the damage the work did to body and soul. This is not so strange, as identity and work can be closely connected, as social support and social networks can be organized in and around the work. If the community is weakly integrated in the rest of society, if few other lifestyles are known, if education levels are low, the work and the resource company are the devils people know, the devils essential in their identity construction. The relation between company and workers can be abusive, for generations, but people still identify with the work, the place, even the community.

Such deep ambiguity can explain the feelings after closure of the resource operation. People might visibly be scarred by the work, mentally and physically, but long nostalgically for the good times of resource booms. Of course, reference will be made to the money and the perceived stability of intergenerational employment in the mine, fishery, forestry. This stability will be exaggerated in memory, as periods of closure, reduced work hours, lowered salaries and labor struggles, are systematically forgotten or minimized. Tensions within the company and within the community, e.g., between ethnic and religious groups, are typically glossed over. Salaries were high in certain periods, but those periods do not have to be typical to be remembered as typical.

Simplification and forgetting

The narrowing down of ideas of self, of community, of the world and of possibilities to navigate that world can be seen as coping strategies with life in remote communities, doing dangerous work, ways to simplify life and self, in order to function, in order to ignore risk and emphasize reward (Buckley, 2004; Patterson, 2007; Richards, 2007). Hence, in our view, also the emphasis on self-reward when money is flowing, the buying of 'toys' like smart TVs, trucks, cars, boats, snowmobiles and other forms of extravagant spending. The longer time horizons coming with investing, could be there, but an enabling condition which is less commonly present is the idea that things can be different and that individual agency can make for a different path through the world (cf Barnes et al., 2001). The simplification of self and world can be a coping strategy but also a product of the extraction history itself: an environment is created which offers its own ways of dealing with the problems of that environment (Kojola, 2020).

In our view, such simplification can by itself be a symptom of trauma. It is not necessarily so, as, indeed, people can freely choose the work, the lifestyle, the identity, even the risk (Buckley, 2004; Cottle, 2013). Work and life in an isolated resource town can be felt as more 'real,' manly, closer to essential values, closer to the earth, closer to a natural division of labor and gender roles (Barnes et al., 2001; Van Assche et al., 2021). All of this is possible and all those positive images have been elaborated in popular culture, in films, songs, novels and TV series (Hayden, 2020; Richards, 2007). Remoteness itself can be romantically portrayed as bringing people closer to themselves, to their true feelings and identity and closer to each other, making for a tight-knit and warm community, an extension of the family and the home. All of this might occur, might function as such, but we argue the reality of remote resource towns is such that many of the reactions are not freely chosen, but rather symptomatic of trauma (cf Loney, 1995). The distinction can be subtle and cannot be summarily made by outsiders. Our point is rather that people are often not aware of the effects of scarring encounters and even more so when those encounters take years, a life of work and when one feels entirely dependent on the scarring other (Freud, 2015).

Other symptoms occur and we cannot map them all here. We would like to highlight the tendency to repeat behaviors, to repeat ideas, to stay trapped within certain ways of understanding self, environment and others (Gunder & Hillier, 2009; Zizek, 2013). One can also point at the creation of fantasies, which can be escape fantasies, or reward fantasies – away from it all or it was all worth it (Fink, 1995). A reduced awareness that fantasies are fantasies can be mentioned, a more limited testing of ideas about the future and, possibly easy dropping of such ideas (Van Assche et al., 2021). A wavering between overly optimistic and pessimistic assessments of the future can keep people trapped, especially after the collapse of the resource industry (Bullock, 2013).

A restructuring of memory, following psychoanalysis here, is typical of trauma, a non-remembering of what caused the trauma, or, a warped inter-pretation omitting crucial details, omitting agency, intention and negative aspects of the experience (Kojola, 2020; Miller & Sinclair, 2012). Beyond detail and emphasis, a narrative of the past can be constructed which keeps identity intact but circles around what was traumatizing (Walkerdine, 2009). Such kernel is hard to symbolize, hard to integrate into narrative identity (Zizek, 2013). One reason for this can be a relation of dependence which can lead to a partial identification with that what is damaging.

The memory of an agricultural past and a town 'perhaps not richer but calmer,' as well as the fight against the excesses of mining companies, has been one of the main sources of local identity in the Colombian municipality of Victoria de San Isidro, a place riddled by violence and challenging socio-economic conditions. Nostalgia is a feeling that constantly appears in dis-courses about the community, its past, and its future. Many remember the 2007 protests against the mining companies and deteriorating social and environmental conditions as a historic day, as the day the community finally spoke up and stood up for its interests. Yet, the increasing centrality of mining companies in the daily life of the community, as well as the evident transformation of the landscape, makes farming identities cohabitate with mining identities in an asymmetric relationship that favor the latter. This is clearly reflected in the local cultural production. The day called 'Agrarian Festival' is today 'Agrarian and Mining Festival.' Posters combine orugas *(Caterpillar) and other heavy machinery with more traditional elements. Mining becomes also aspirational. The composer of a vallenato song –also a local social science teacher –wrote 'I will do a course on heavy machinery or if not, I will name my fish cart "oruga", to see if it gets me another woman.'*

Trauma and nostalgia

Trauma can thus be caused both by extraction and its cessation and nostalgia for what was problematic yet also foundational can dominate once an industry left. Nostalgia is a good entry point to discuss community trauma, as what makes it difficult for many resource communities and former resource communities to take a different path, to see a different path, is not merely a sum of individual experiences.

In previous chapters, we analyzed communities as narrative constructs, with identity narratives as key connections between individual and community governance, between thinking and organizing, as identity narratives give direction to collective action. Both individual and community identities can be understood as narrative constructs and as both rely on memory to construct understandings of present and future, nostalgia for a perceived better past, a past that is better aligned with a preferred identity can occur at both levels (Moonesirust & Brown, 2021). Nostalgia can be created and maintained in a community and can circulate and dominate governance, even if competing narratives exist and even if not all residents recognize themselves in the narrative of a golden past (Roche et al., 2021; Weeks, 2019). People and communities can also have deeply contradictory feelings about a past, with nostalgic narratives functioning in one situation and more critical ones appearing elsewhere (Gunder & Hillier, 2009; Waddington, 2001).

For us it is important to see which narratives have an impact on governance, on the way the community organizes itself, takes decisions and constructs futures (cf Meadowcroft et al., 2012). Social memory in many resource communities and former resource communities often is tinged with nostalgia and indeed, with trauma as the circling around a kernel of collective experience which is hard to symbolize. Negative experiences might be hard to integrate in community identity, but also the dependent relation itself, on the resource, on a company (Dinius & Vergara, 2011; Edkins, 2006). Identification with the resource only goes so far as a response, more so when the resource is gone or extraction stopped (Waddington, 2001; Woodhead et al., 2018).

The hole in the memory of many resource communities can have a variety of effects, just as individual trauma can produce a wide variety of neuroses, where listing of the symptoms themselves is not all too revealing. One can say that the need to not-incorporate the traumatic kernel, can quickly diminish the collective capacity to look at other things, other aspects of the past and the present (Turner, 2022; Žižek, 2000). This then has implications for constructions of the future, where reality testing will be affected making it difficult to distinguish between innocent fantasy and fantasy as a product of trauma (Walkerdine, 2009). Innocent is hard to define here, except in contrast with the other, traumatic category, where collective fantasy will more easily lead to a confrontation with reality and to repetitive behaviors and neurotic repetitions of futures (Glynos & Stavrakakis, 2008). In this case the trauma expressed through collective fantasy refers to a desire to either return to a past seen through a nostalgic lens again and again or to a breaking away in the direction of a fantasy which is largely untested and disconnected from diverse and sharp observations of changing environments, of what might be possible and desirable (Barnes et al., 2001; Roche et al., 2021; Weeks, 2019).

Both the desire for complete self-identity, where the ideal identity is placed in the past and the desire to break free, to do something entirely different, can be symptoms of collective trauma (Bullock, 2013). In both cases, the autonomy of the community in deciding its future is not as free as it could be, because it remains tied to a past it could not fully incorporate in its identity. The connections with that past can therefore be observed only with great difficulty and assessing those connections is similarly difficult. In both cases, the unobserved past of trauma, shapes determinations of the future in ways that undermine adaptive capacity and the capacity for reinvention.

The Africa Mining Vision (African Union, 2009) was an ambitious document, a vision produced by the African Union, which intended to maximize the development potential of African resource endowments and minimize the risk of ending up in a resource trap, or resource curse, where local benefits dampen, profits go to local consumption or flee the country. It also intended to dispel the ghosts of colonialism, by finding new forms of cooperation across colonial-era borders and using the anticipated profits to speed up infrastructure and more general development. New relations with China and India were expected to break open old hierarchies. The vision is not predicated only on large scale mining as part of national strategies and does not consider small and artisanal mining simply as a problem; it is seen as a complementary driver of development which however needs some regulation. Constraints for the vision are acknowledged.

Yet in the final pages, spurring to action, the perspective suddenly changes, and looks much less realistic, a diminished realism also borne out by the results (Van Assche et al., 2022; Waddington, 2001)(Beland et al., 2021). In those last pages the initial steps to be undertaken, in order to use mining positively as a continent-wide development driver, look like more than overcoming a few constraints. Rather, it starts to look as if all problems of development have to be resolved first, before mining could be the core of a responsible and fair development strategy. Infrastructure, schooling, rule of law, institutional capacity and investment capacity all have to be addressed first. While the history of ups and downs in resource economies are not considered in all their implications for modernization (e.g., large job losses in Zambia in the 90s; Ferguson, 1997) asneither is the trauma caused by mining, mining in conflict areas and conflicts caused by mining in areas marked by weak governance.

Governance and identity construction

In governance, discursive and organizational features have to be brought together in an always imperfect and imperfectly stable way. Community identities are reflected in the structure and functioning of governance, in the kinds of institutions used and decisions taken. Competing narratives can find a place, new narratives can be created. Governance itself can be a site of reflection on the past, of working through the past, reinterpreting it and from there, gaining more degrees of freedom when thinking about and organizing for the future (Van Assche et al., 2021; Waddington, 2001).

In Chapter 7, we will speak of the previously introduced concentration problem in detail. The concentration problem can be an indication of and partly a result of community trauma, of difficulties in facing the future because past issues need working through (Samson, 2017). The concentration problem we located in governance, so governance is a problem, yet at the same time, governance has to be part of the solution. Reflection on the past, a careful dislodging of false certainties about the past can take place outside governance, in schools, media, public discussion, museums, cultural and environmental organizations and such settings might provide more freedom, flexibility, time, to approach the past and community identity gently and from different angles (Gunder, 2005). Yet, at some point, the discussion will have to be continued in the governance system and a decision will have to be taken. This might go as far as considering reinvention, or it might lead to a strategy for reduced dependence and wise use of the resource, but some collectively binding decision will have to be taken.

A collective rethinking of the past will be necessary to expose trauma, relieve its symptoms, give more space for thinking and organizing in other directions, less steered by the past but steering consciously in a self-chosen direction (Meadowcroft et al., 2012; Samson, 2017). The confrontation with the past is not only a matter of facts, of reconstructing what actually happened, but also of narratives: how are facts constructed and given place in narratives which define place and community, which explain what is good and what a good future could be (cf Roche et al., 2021). Thus, a new scrutiny of the past is also a matter of confronting desire: what did we want and why? What do we really want now and why? Is what we see as the best option really inspired by a thorough understanding of resource economies, of quality of life in the past, in other places? People are desiring beings and without desire it is virtually impossible to create and maintain images of a desirable future (Gunder & Hillier, 2009). In communities, attractive images of the future will not be persuasive, will not spread, will not forge coalitions, if they are not invested with desire and if they do not resonate with existing community desires.

In the Goldfields of South Africa, nostalgia is rampant, as mining declined over three decades. 'The gold is growing' is a typical expression, indicating a belief that, despite downturns, it is worth waiting for a return of the gold. It cannot be stopped, it is a force of nature, it will always grow (Sesele et al., 2021). Good times will come back, as it is nature itself which is resilient. Sesele (2019) (2018) distinguishes between nostalgia for the good old mining days, and nostalgia for the pre-industrial societies, which can still be associated with mining, in the form of 'artisanal' mining. The artisanal is mostly a leftover of the industrial production, and one marked by the double trauma of industry closure and often intolerable and largely unregulated working conditions. Thus, legacies are erased in an ambiguous manner, with two golden pasts, a present deemed either a partial return to a past or a waiting area (while the gold grows) for a future return to the other past.

For psychanalyst Jacques Lacan, desire is what makes subjects cohere, more than the images it collects to construct its ego (Fink, 1995; Gunder & Hillier, 2009). Slavoj Zizek, more than Lacan himself, explored what this means for politics, ideology and communities (Zizek, 2013; 2006). What we called community identity and place identity, is for Lacan and Zizek an always unstable construct because it does *not* start from desire, but functions rather as an ego at individual level, an assemblage of stories and images, coming from the past, from somewhere else, from culture, ideology (Žižek, 2000). The ego, for Lacan, cannot be taken as the measure of all things, as a core of reality. Identity stories will transform, will suggest a coherence that is not there and the ego for him as to be distinguished carefully from the subject, which is the subject of desire (Turner, 2022). What an individual feels at a certain moment, what he says about his feelings, what a community expresses as its identity, as overriding concerns, all these things must be taken seriously by external observers trying to assist and by the community itself (Fink, 1995; Gunder, 2005). They cannot be taken for granted, as that what reflects the deepest core of being, that what has to be taken literally (no questioning is allowed). Rather, in a patient process of analysis, or self-analysis (in communities), other stories, other desires, other possible versions of the self can slowly emerge, either learning to live with certain symptoms, or trying to dislodge them.

The symptoms themselves then require not so much discussion, as the past and the difficulty lies in the slow extraction of the subject from the ties of a traumatic past. This does not always mean fully bringing the trauma to the consciousness (central in classic psychoanalysis). It can also entail a non-understanding of the past, rather a loosening of the grip of that past by changing the associations around that past (Fink, 2010). A slow restructuring of social memory, sometimes with elements of shock therapy, that is, con-frontation with difficult questions, can be necessary, unavoidable. More likely, the shock element will be a gentler yet confrontational pushing away from narrative comfort zones, by stopping a narrative, changing angle, asking unexpected questions. The free association of psychoanalysis, at community level, can then be the creation of many spaces where reflection on the past can be free, without immediate implications, codification, ties to politics and decisions (Gunder & Hillier, 2007). A process of reflexivity (see Chapter 11) therefore, a process beneficial in opening up the past, is not only a process of creating new understandings, but also a process of shifting signifiers, creating new association, of letting things come up, of expressing without immediate reflection (Fink, 2010). This is only possible when there are spaces where morality and judgment are suspended for the moment.

Self-analysis in governance as therapy

For Lacan, the order of ego and of narrative identity is the order of imaginary. What we experience as reality is an entangling of the imaginary, the symbolic and the Real. We will discuss the Real in Chapter 9 and here we can suffice by contrasting the imaginary to the symbolic order. For Lacan, the symbolic order is also the Big Other (see Chapter 7), the order of signs which gives meaning in a manner perceived as more neutral, as a set of rules of signification coming from the outside (Hook, 2017). Hence the functioning of our system of meaning-making as a system of authority. Both the symbolic and the imaginary orders create freedoms and constraints for subjects to develop. True identity for Lacan is identity of desire, of a unique interweaving of symbolic, imaginary and Real, as that which resists symbolization and imaginary capture.

The true desire of a community trapped in the past thus must be distinguished from what can be immediately gleaned from fantasy, from public and expert discourse. It has to be slowly understood in a process of self-reflection and self-expression where what was unacknowledged can come to the surface (the traumatic kernel can be revealed, as a piece of the Real). Such desire is not likely to be something specific and more likely, a desire to be free from constraints from the past. We emphasize self-in self-reflection and expression as we believe, in line with psycho-analysis, that suggestion by experts and outsiders aspiring to be community therapists, might be helpful later on, when deciding on strategy, when offering pieces of information, helping to think in scenarios and comparing with other places, but not in the properly therapeutic part of self-analysis in a community. Only the subject itself can dislodge problematic entanglements of signifiers, can come to alternative interpretations which can affect thinking and acting in such a way that change occurs. Otherwise, the suggestions will be incorporated into the imaginary, will be modified by the rules of the symbolic, but then will lose their potency to effectuate change (Beach, 2017; Fink, 2010).

Only the community can decide if it wants to be free, whether it has a problem or not, whether it needs a form of self-analysis or not and whether some of its problems come out of a traumatic presence of the past, or not (Gunder, 2005). Scholars studying community woundedness come to similar insights. A distance from oppressive aspects of the past does not entail a total rejection of the past and a growing awareness of past oppression, of current trauma, does not need to entail maintaining an identity in reference to the past or to a traumatizing other or oppressor (Freire, 2018;

Van Assche et al., 2021). Recognizing symptoms, working through fantasy can help communities to choose the kind of reference to others and the past more freely, just like the oppressed often struggle to stop identifying the oppressor as a norm (Freire, 2018; van der Watt, 2018).

Self-analysis of this sort, working through trauma in this manner, can help to open the little, closed, and not so cozy worlds that can be created in resource communities. It will become clear that more futures are possible but that not every fantasy about the future can be treated as a community vision, a possible basis for strategy. It is also possible that self-analysis will hit its own limits and those can be limits of a Real of dependence on higher-level governments, which are necessary to reconnect, reintegrate and support a community, before it is able to draw the full conclusions out of its own self-analysis, or even before any self-analysis can be productive. Discerning and deciding when this is the best way forward, is a process fraught with moral and political questions, which we cannot answer here. The process is akin to the decision whether a community deserves another lease on life and that decision must be taken according to the rules of the multi-governance configuration in which the community is embedded. What is seen as legitimate and acceptable in these matters, will depend on the context and will most likely be hotly debated.

In a Canadian former mining town, regular planning processes get stranded, are opposed, the resulting plans not implemented. Planning itself, trying to move in a desired direction as a community, becomes suspicious, either as government overreach or as a waste of resources. Diversification, capitalizing on tourism potential, is seen as marginally beneficial. A return to the past is deemed as the only path forward for the community itself, and the planners – representatives of a regional organization –presented as outsiders who do not understand the place. Each outside perspective on the place, each analysis, is either rejected or ignored, while self-reflection, as in a local assessment of possible futures, does not take place. The desired future, as a return to the past, becomes visible in public and private discourse, and in voting. As confrontation with other perspectives, other facts and other pasts can be avoided. The future can stay frozen as a return to an idealized past.

References

African Union. (2009). Africa mining vision. *Addis Ababa: African Union.*

Barnes, T. J., Hayter, R., & Hay, E. (2001). Stormy weather: Cyclones, Harold Innis, and Port Alberni, BC. *Environment and planning A: Economy and space, 33*(12), 2127–2147.

Beach, A. I. (2017). *The trauma of monastic reform: Community and conflict in twelfth-century Germany.* Cambridge University Press. 10.1017/9781108277341.

Béland, D., Campbell, B., Coderre, M., & Haang'andu, P. (2021). Policy change and paradigm shifts in Sub-Saharan Africa: Implementing the Africa Mining Vision.

Canadian Journal of African Studies / Revue canadienne des études africaines, 56(1), 79–97. 10.1080/00083968.2021.1886955.

Bryceson, D. F., & MacKinnon, D. F. (Eds.). (2013). *Mining and African Urbanisation: Population, Settlement and Welfare Trajectories* (1st edition). Routledge.

Buckley, K. L. (2004). *Danger, death and disaster in the Crowsnest Pass mines, 1902–1928.* University of Calgary Press.

Bullock, R. (2013). Mill town identity crisis: Reframing the culture of forest resource dependence in single industry towns. *Social Transformation in Rural Canada: New Insights into Community, Cultures and Collective Action,* 269–290.

Cottle, D. (2013). Land, life and labour in the sacrifice zone: The socio-economic dynamics of open-cut coal mining in the Upper Hunter Valley, New South Wales. *Rural Society, 22*(3), 208–216. 10.5172/rsj.2013.22.3.208.

Dinius, O. J., & Vergara, A. (2011). *Company towns in the Americas: Landscape, power, and working-class communities.* University of Georgia Press.

Edkins, J. (2006). Remembering relationality. In D. Bell (Ed.), *Memory, trauma and world politics: Reflections on the relationship between past and present* (pp. 99–115). Palgrave Macmillan UK. 10.1057/9780230627482_5.

Ferguson, J., (1997). *Expectations of Modernity: Myths and Meanings of Urban Life on the Zambian Copperbelt.* Berkeley: University of California Press.

Fink, B. (1995). *The Lacanian subject: Between language and jouissance.* Princeton University Press.

Fink, B. (2010). Against understanding: Why understanding should not be viewed as an essential aim of psychoanalytic treatment. *Journal of the American Psychoanalytic Association, 58*(2), 259–285. 10.1177/0003065110369349.

Fitzpatrick, D. (2005). Evolution and chaos in property right systems: The third world tragedy of contested access essay. *Yale Law Journal, 115*(5), 996–1049.

Fraser, A., & Larmer, M. (2010). *Zambia, mining, and neoliberalism: Boom and bust on the globalized Copperbelt.* Springer.

Freire, P. (2018). *Pedagogy of the oppressed.* Bloomsbury Publishing USA.

Freud, S. (2015). *Beyond the pleasure principle.* In J. Miller & M. C. Waldrep (Eds.) (p. 64). Dover Publications.

Glynos, J., & Stavrakakis, Y. (2008). Lacan and political subjectivity: Fantasy and enjoyment in psychoanalysis and political theory. *Subjectivity, 24*(1), 256–274.

Gough, K. V., & Yankson, P. W.K. (2012). Exploring the connections: mining and urbanisation in Ghana. *Journal of Contemporary African Studies,* 30(4):651–668. 10.1080/02589001.2012.724867.

Gunder, M. (2005). Obscuring difference through shaping debate: A Lacanian view of planning for diversity. *International Planning Studies, 10*(2), 83–103.

Gunder, M., & Hillier, J. (2007). Planning as urban therapeutic. *Environment and Planning A: Economy and Space, 39*(2), 467–486. 10.1068/a38236.

Gunder, M., & Hillier, J. (2009). *Planning in ten words or less: A Lacanian entanglement with spatial planning.* Ashgate Publishing, Ltd.

Hayden, K. E. (2020). *The rural primitive in American popular culture: All too familiar.* Rowman & Littlefield.

Hayter, R. (2017). Single industry resource towns. In *A Companion to Economic Geography* (pp. 290–307). John Wiley & Sons, Ltd. 10.1002/9781405166430.ch18.

Hook, D. (2017). *Six moments in Lacan: Communication and identification in psychology and psychoanalysis.* Routledge.

Kojola, E. (2020). Divergent memories and visions of the future in conflicts over mining development. *Journal of Political Ecology, 27*(1), Article 1. 10.2458/v27i1.23210.

Loney, M. (1995). Social problems, community trauma and hydro project impacts. *Canadian Journal of Native Studies, 15*(2), 231–254.

Luhmann, N. (1990). *Political theory in the welfare state.* De Gruyter.

Marais, L., McKenzie, F. H., Deacon, L., Nel, E., Rooyen, D. van, & Cloete, J. (2018). The changing nature of mining towns: Reflections from Australia, Canada and South Africa. *Land Use Policy, 76*, 779–788. 10.1016/J.LANDUSEPOL.2018.03.006.

Marais, L., Ndaguba, E., Mmbadi, E., Cloete, J., & Lenka, M. (2022). Mine closure, social disruption, and crime in South Africa. *The Geographical Journal*, geoj.12430.

Meadowcroft, J., Langhelle, O., & Ruud, A. (2012). Governance, democracy and sustainable development: Moving beyond the impasse. In *Governance, Democracy and Sustainable Development* (pp. 1–13). Edward Elgar Publishing. https://www.elgaronline.com/display/edcoll/9781849807562/9781849807562.00009.xml.

Miller, B., & Sinclair, J. (2012). Risk perceptions in a resource community and communication implications: Emotion, stigma, and identity. *Risk Analysis, 32*(3), 483–495.

Moonesirust, E., & Brown, A. D. (2021). Company towns and the governmentality of desired identities. *Human Relations, 74*(4), 502–526. 10.1177/0018726719887220.

Nyamunda, T., & Mukwambo, P. (2012). The state and the bloody diamond rush in Chiadzwa: Unpacking the contesting interests in the development of illicit mining and trading, c.2006–2009. *Journal of Southern African Studies, 38*(1), 145–166.

Patterson, P. B. (2007). Attributions of danger and responses to risk among logging contractors in British Columbia's Southern interior: Implications for accident prevention in the forest industry. In D. C. Wood (Ed.), *The economics of health and wellness: Anthropological perspectives* (Vol. 26, pp. 103–125). Emerald Group Publishing Limited. 10.1016/S0190-1281(07)26005-6.

Perez-Sindín, X. S., & Van Assche, K. (2021). "Coal [from Colombia] is our life". Bourdieu, the miners (after they are miners) and resistance in As Pontes. *Resources Policy, 71*, 102006.

Perez-Sindin, X., & Van Assche, K. (2020). From coal not to ashes but to what? As Pontes, social memory and the concentration problem. *The Extractive Industries and Society*.7(3), 882–891.10.1016/j.exis.2020.07.016

Richards, J. S. (2007). *Death in the mines: Disasters and rescues in the anthracite coal fields of Pennsylvania.* Arcadia Publishing.

Roche, C., Sinclair, L., Spencer, R., Luke, H., Brueckner, M., Knowles, S., & Paull, M. (2021). A mining legacies lens: From externalities to wellbeing in extractive industries. *The Extractive Industries and Society, 8*(3), 100961.

Rubbers, B. (2021). Inside mining capitalism; the micropolitics of work on the Congolese and Zambian copper belt. Woodbridge: James Currey.

Samson, C. (2017). The idea of progress, industrialization, and the replacement of Indigenous peoples: The Muskrat Falls Megadam Boondoggle. *Social Justice, 44* (150), 1–26.

Sesele, K., & Marais, L. (2022). Mine closure, women, and crime in Matjhabeng, South Africa. *Geographical Research*, 61(1), 18–31 10.1111/1745-5871.12563.

Saunders, R., & Nyamunda, T. (2016). *Facets of power: Politics, profits and people in the making of Zimbabwes blood diamonds*. African Books Collective.

Sesele, K. (2019). Women and mine decline in the Free State Goldfields. Unpublished PhD thesis in Development Studies, UFS.

Sesele, K., Marais, L., van Rooyen, D., & Cloete, J. (2021). Mine decline and women: Reflections from the free state Goldfields. *The Extractive Industries and Society*, 8(1), 211–219. 10.1016/j.exis.2020.11.006.

Shields, R. (2013). *Spatial questions: Cultural topologies and social spatialisation*. Sage.

Turner, K. (2022). *Lacanian fantasy: The image, language and uncertainty*. Taylor & Francis.

Udelsmann Rodrigues, C., Mususa, P., Büscher, K., & Cuvelier, J. (2021). Boomtown urbanization and rural-urban transformation in mining and conflict regions in Angola, the DRC and Zambia. *Sustainability*, 13(4),2285. 10.3390/su13042285

Van Assche, K., Gruezmacher, M., & Beunen, R. (2022). Shock and conflict in social-ecological systems: Implications for environmental governance. *Sustainability*, 14(2), 610. 10.3390/su14020610.

Van Assche, K., Gruezmacher, M., & Granzow, M. (2021). From trauma to fantasy and policy. The past in the futures of mining communities; the case of Crowsnest Pass, Alberta. *Resources Policy*, 72, 102050–102050. 10.1016/j.resourpol.2021.102050.

van der Watt, P. (2018). Community development in wounded communities: Seductive schemes or un-veiling and healing? *Community Development Journal*, 53(4), 714–731.

Waddington, D. (2001). *Out of the ashes?: The social impact of industrial contraction and regeneration on Britain's mining communities*. Psychology Press.

Walkerdine, V. (2009). Steel, identity, community: Regenerating identities in a South Wales Town. In M. Wetherell (Ed.), *Identity in the 21st century: New trends in changing times* (pp. 59–75). Palgrave Macmillan UK. 10.1057/9780230245662_4.

Weeks, E. C. (2019). Mill closures in the Pacific Northwest: The consequences of economic decline in rural industrial communities. In *Community and Forestry* (pp. 125–139). Routledge.

Wenar, L. (2008). Property rights and the resource curse. *Philosophy & Public Affairs*, 36(1), 2–32.

Woodhead, A. J., Abernethy, K. E., Szaboova, L., & Turner, R. A. (2018). Health in fishing communities: A global perspective. *Fish and Fisheries*, 19(5), 839–852.

Žižek, S. (2000). Melancholy and the act. *Critical Inquiry*, 26(4), 657–681.

Zizek, S. (2013). *Enjoy your symptom!: Jacques Lacan in Hollywood and out*. Routledge.

6

POWER KNOWLEDGE AND THE GOVERNANCE OF RESOURCE COMMUNITIES

Introduction: Michel Foucault

Michel Foucault and his notion of power/knowledge, a notion later incorporated into EGT, have wielded great influence in policy studies, planning and environmental studies. In modernist theories of planning, policy and administration, power was notoriously undertheorized. Meanwhile, work on natural resource governance was notoriously limited to natural resource management studies, focusing on the optimization of the extraction in economic terms. More neo-liberal studies emphasized the role of private companies and privatization as only the means to regulate resources in common enabling conditions to trigger a private-led resource boom. Others, assuming a larger role for government were focusing on the utility of resources and resource towns for regional and national development. In the USSR and more generally, in neo-Marxist analysis, natural resources are understood to have an intrinsic value and an intrinsic importance for economic development. We will come back to the importance of ideology later in this chapter and now turn to Michel Foucault and his ideas on power, knowledge and power/knowledge.

Foucault did not develop a unified doctrine or definition of power, as his work evolved continuously, in dialog with colleagues, opponents and with the archives he so scrupulously scrutinized. He sometimes changed his mind, for example in the slowly refining analysis of oppression and being oppressed, where he found reasons to question the possibility of total power and complete powerlessness (Elden, 2007; Richardson, 1996). Another example is the evolving analysis of inclusion and exclusion, where in his later work, the matter was not to expose exclusion and condemn it but to show how

DOI: 10.4324/9781003332145-6

governance systems and knowledge systems always produce patterns of inclusion and exclusion, where some are more problematic than others, on political, ethical or cultural reasons (Van Assche et al., 2014, 2017).

Power can be ascribed to many things and understood in many ways. We will not attempt to summarize the literature here, but we can point at basic understandings which can be found in academia and general culture. Power can be the power to do things or stop things, to boss people around, make people, organizations and communities do things. Political power is then power at community level, power to make a whole community move in a particular direction, or, more elementarily, to follow certain rules (Cleaver & Whaley, 2018; Fischer, 2000; Svarstad et al., 2018). Those rules and directions can benefit the community itself, or the people in power. In democratic theory, power that is used towards public goods and public goals, is acceptable. In more deliberative and participatory versions of theory, that power is expected to be distributed, not vested in one person without opposition and not held by people for a long time (Flyvbjerg, 1998, 2011). When private interests start to override public interests, one can speak of corruption.

Affordances and materiality

As natural resources are usually (animals being an exception) tied to a place, whoever is in charge in that place, has control over natural resources. Where political control is weak, where governance is weak or corrupt, private actors can hold more power over them. When governance is very weak, criminal actors tend to come in, in complex patterns of overlap with governmental roles and roles in private companies (Madimu, 2022; Moreno & Wilton, 2014). Boundaries tend to become blurred, while such boundaries play a pivotal role in maintaining the rule of law and the potential for redistribution of resource income for public goods. Where power is centralized and strong, benefits can be centralized and redistribution can be used for many places and public goods can be incorporated more easily into collective strategy; this also comes with drawbacks. In this case, local support might be weak, local knowledge might be missing and this can undermine the legitimacy and efficiency of the resource operations. In extreme cases, it can lead to an undermining of extraction, to local corruption or to destabilizing of a national regime. In the case of indigenous communities, local governance can be strong but decoupled from the overarching governance system. A similar situation can occur in places that have been far removed from centers of power, that have evolved governance structures independent from the dominant structures and are therefore dislodged from the governance system.

The nature of the regime, the type of multi-level governance structures in place and the balance between participation and representation in place, thus play a role in the functioning of power in resource management and the benefits for community and environment (Escobar, 1996, p. 199; Rinfret, 2009). The resource itself, its physical characteristics, the technologies and economies of extraction also exert an influence, one can say power, over the forms of political organization and power that can enable it and can benefit from it (Michael & Still, 1992; Richardson & Weszkalnys, 2014). Highly expensive large-scale projects, such as oil sands, need a lot of support from governments, as private actors alone are not willing or able to carry all risk involved and build all necessary infrastructure, provide training, housing, etc. (Richardson, 2016).

Or, when a large private actor does embark on such enormous projects, the political risk is very high, that is, the risk of undermining democracy, weakening governance and introducing elite corruption (where these things do not already occur). This is the case because an entirely private enterprise of such scale indicates either a weak form of governance already there, easily corruptible or a reigning ideology of very small government and maximal private benefit, which in turn is likely to further shrink government and put barriers for the pursuit of public goods (Bevir, 1999; Newig et al., 2007).

One can speak here of *affordances,* inspired by anthropology (Ingold, 2018). Resources comes with affordances, certain effects on human organization of the materiality of the resource. The pattern of affordances can be complex and cannot be interpreted as determinism: there is no resource that *imposes* a particular use or form of organization, there is always cultural mediation, technological and economic mediation. The affordances can be considered as multi-origin, as they can stem from the resource itself, its material characteristics, but also from its location on a vertical plane, deep or shallow, between hard or soft layers, liquid or solid. Or, from the landscape or climate where they are found; oil in the seas of the high arctics has different affordances than oil in a shallow well. Affordances can stem not from the resource itself but from particular technologies of extraction and processing. When technologies change, affordances change.

Small nuclear reactors make for different possible forms of organization, for different connections with political regimes. One does not need billions of (foreign) support and expertise available only in a few (possibly unfriendly) countries, nor years of development, droves of foreign workers, and complex logistics. Private companies might supply them, install them quickly, and help with an affordable maintenance package where local experts can be involved quickly. Similarly, bigger boats and newer nets change the affordances of the sea floor and its resources. New fishing technologies alter what people can do, what ecosystems can yield, how they limit and shape fishing. Damage done by those technologies (say, bottom trawling) can alter the ecosystem, which again changes its affordances, and its resilience.

And affordances can stem from infrastructures and logistics.

Roads open remote landscapes for cheaper exploration and bring resources within reach. They can bring remote areas under political control, stabilizing a situation, imposing a form of rule of law, of institutional predictability, which might make it attractive for business and residents to come in and invest with a longer time horizon. At the same time, roads can open up areas for criminal activities, for plundering of resources, for rapid unregulated expansion of agriculture. The Brazilian initiative to build ports and roads through the Amazon revealed all such side-effects, as well as the difficulty in guiding development strategically once connectivity is established, once a road has been built.

In other chapters in this book, we speak of material dependencies, when materiality, e.g., the materiality of the resource, affects the functioning of governance. Of course, the opposite direction, the way governance structures the extraction and use of resources, is much easier to observe. We will say therefore that the partial opacity of material dependencies makes them hard to manage, not only the obdurate nature of materiality itself. In terms of actor network theory (ANT) one can speak of not just the resource itself, in its material aspects, but also machinery, plants, roads, other infrastructures, as *actants,* in the networks enabling resource extraction. Not all actants are recognized by the decision-makers in the network of extraction, let alone by those in governance or by the rest of the community (Agrawal & Gibson, 1999; Latour, 2004).

Social-ecological systems

These considerations point back to our reflections in previous chapters, on the nature of natural resources. Something is never a resource by nature and some attribution of value and form of organization is needed. In line with Erich Zimmerman's (Zimmermann, 1951) functional definition of resource, something becomes a resource in a community and its use and circulation require cultural supports (Descola, 2013; Escobar, 1996; Van Assche et al., 2017). Gold only has value because some cultures attributed value to it and started to use it as a means of exchange, so it could become a symbol of many other things which could be purchased by means of it. In contrast, oil only became valuable because technologies of extraction developed and because possible uses in an industrializing society were recognized. The materiality of gold itself thus is less important than with oil, to understand its recognition as natural resource. Yet, rather than a 'more or less' or one-dimensional approach to the problem, it is better to think in terms of patterns of interaction and interweaving of natural and cultural elements (Descola, 2013; Descola & Palsson, 2003; Whatmore, 2008).

Gold does have material features which trigger certain interpretations and uses, even if this triggering is not universal and not mechanical It is relatively easy to melt, it shines, its radiant appearance can invoke comparisons with the rays of the sun. It is also rare, yet it could be found in many places. It is remarkably heavy, contributing to its mystery. The transformation of little speckles into a shiny metal clump, which could be shaped relatively easily, sparked comparisons with mythological and religious transformations, meanings of the sun and its light and found resonances in the role of priests and shamans, which could transform themselves and contact celestial beings. Later, when market economies emerged, other material affordances came to the foreground and preferences for gold over other metals as payment became institutionalized and backed by the power of governments, empires and their mints.

In terms of social-ecological systems, one can say that not all elements of ecological systems become resources. Only those who find a use and/or meaning in social systems will be ascribed value, which will then drive exploration, extraction and circulation. Political power comes in through various channels in this process (Bevir, 1999; Biermann & Anderson, 2017). Governments can encourage extraction, build infrastructures, attribute and stabilize value, create property arrangements. They can promote narratives of value or disinterest, of religious meaning, of identity. They can sponsor research on particular environments which lead to the discovery of resources, which can then be promoted, or they can sponsor the mapping, exploration, or conquest of territories, because of resources, or, a posteriori, they might need to justify the conquest by looking hard for existing resources (Latour, 2004).

The use of natural resources in a community and, on a larger scale, a state can be coordinated or not. For many forms of extraction, even illegal ones, some form of coordination is needed, even when government does not interfere (Bevir, 1999; Madimu, 2022; Van Assche et al., 2017). If this coordination is dominated by private actors for private benefit, we speak of private governance. If there is no governance at all, we speak of uncoordinated extraction and here we can think of hit-and-run tactics, illegal small-scale mining (in absence of informal coordination), logging, fishing, etc. Uncoordinated can mean unobserved, as most likely it means illegal, in areas where some form of rule of law and formal governance exists. This is not always the case, as many regimes have degrees of tolerance, double standards and resource-related corruption is common in many parts of the world. In addition, uncoordinated and illegal use might be observed within the community and those observations might reach officials or others involved in collective decision-making, but that does not mean that there will be action taken based on those observations (Agrawal & Gibson, 1999).

Illegal small scale gold mining is prevalent in the Amazon basin. The people involved can be locals, but also people from other regions in the Amazon, even from neighboring countries. They can be reliant on low tech solutions, or bring in newer technologies, which indicates a higher level of coordination, and connections with criminal gangs, corrupt officials and/or resource companies turning a blind eye to the practices of some of their suppliers. As we're in the sphere of illegality, one cannot speak of formal governance considering public goods, but this does not mean there's no (informal, private) governance, and the connections between formal and informal actors also entail that some formal rules cannot be evaded, that some are selectively applied.

Rules might exist, laws, policies, plans, maybe even overarching development strategies based on using or not using these resources, but this does not mean that they are enforced and implemented. Non-enforcement can reflect an inability of governmental actors, or the whole governance system, to enforce. It can also express an unwillingness of key actors to enforce, which can in turn have a multitude of reasons. One reason for a lack of willingness to enforce can be an ambiguity towards ideas or ideology associated with the rule, policy or strategy, another reason can be outright competition between governmental actors, where certain institutions are associated with one actor might be thwarted by others. It is possible that an institution was adopted for reasons quite different from their stated intention, so when the question of implementation comes up, that stated intention plays no role.

A local sustainability plan can be adopted to get subsidies from the regional government, a biodiversity policy can be articulated in participatory fashion, simply because the process of participation was pleasant or lucrative, or to show the organizers that there was participation. Participation in policy formation or approval can be performance, and the reasons to do so can be far removed from the policy objectives at play.

Governance of natural resources

In multi-level governance systems, these issues of ambiguity and competition in resource governance can become complex. That is, competition between actors at one level can be accompanied by competition and ideological difference between levels of governance. Or, certain actors at one level might be interested in undermining certain actors at a different level and non-implementation of resource policy can be one way of achieving this. A federal administration dominated by one ideology might support a different approach to resource governance than a provincial government which then only imperfectly imposes its perspective on local governments, where ideological diversity might be greater, as well as resource dependence.

The power of the institution, of the policy, plan, law, strategy regulating the use of resources, their extraction or processing, will thus hinge on the distribution of political power, while in polities with strong governance and functional checks and balances, the opposite will also be true. That is, existing institutions can in most cases be applied and enforced and this can change the position of power of certain actors in governance (Van Assche et al., 2016).

Governance of natural resources is therefore the coordination in a community of the use, valuation, extraction and processing of natural resources, the coordination of collectively binding decisions on all this (Svarstad et al., 2018; Van Assche et al., 2017). Which requires the articulation and implementation of institutions, which can be simple rules, but also more complex institutions such as policies, laws and plans. Complex societies, marked by multi-level governance, are most likely to have institutions to regulate resources at each level and for different resources, as well as area-based policies and strategies which might affect a diversity of institutions. Governance is never perfect in the sense that it can never cover all resources in all uses, all possible situations and in the sense that perfect implementation and enforcement rarely occur (Armitage, 2005). Furthermore, there is always a variety of unanticipated effects, where implementation, even with the best intentions and good information, leads to a degradation of the resource, the environment, or to undesirable effects on other aspects of life – we discuss this in Chapter 9.

The existence of governance and its institutions is thus a deliberate concentration of power, as collectively binding decisions are produced and enforced. Political power can only reach as far as the power of its institutions (Bryant & Bailey, 1997). In the Middle Ages, the picture is often one of boundless domination by ruthless rulers, but in practice, many freedoms existed, as governance was not effective, not consistent, not fine-grained and observation and regulation of everyday life existed only in rudimentary fashion. Natural resources, if they are valuable and especially if few other activities exist, attract attention by regulators, as their governance can stop some uses and users, benefit others, as the structuring of property arrangements and collectively binding decisions on their use have great consequences for the distribution of wealth in the community – and flows out of the community (Agrawal & Gibson, 1999; Brosius, 2004).

Decisions over natural resources, production and enforcement of institutions regulating resources thus naturally attracts competition, discussion and strategizing. Resource governance notoriously attracts shadow governance and corruption and remaining neutral when few other sources of wealth exist, can be utterly difficult for economic and political elites (Madimu, 2022; Svarstad et al., 2018). Political elites regulating resources therefore often blend with economic elites; that is, political elites can enrich themselves and economic elites find access to the regulation of natural resources, entrench themselves in the political elite (Bryant & Bailey, 1997).

Power and strategy

This brings us to a different face of power which is often discussed in policy studies in planning: power as strategy. In much of the literature on deliberative policy making, inspired by Jurgen Habermas and other modernists, power has a bad name and is equated with strategy (Flyvbjerg, 1998; Hillier, 2002). Power is seen to distort reality, undermine equality and fairness, make real participation difficult, as well as twisting rationality and negating the power of rational persuasion, that is, the natural and acceptable power of the best argument. In such perspective, fair and rational deliberation does not allow for strategizing actors, as strategizing means twisting stories and arguments, for private gain. It means creating opacity and false transparency, posturing, performing, forming sneaky coalitions and in the long run undermining the rule of law. Strategy, therefore, in this perspective, breeds opacity and opacity breeds corruption. Strategy also comes to oppose rationality which from other theoretical perspectives, seems rather odd.

We prefer to take the side of Niccolo Machiavelli, who would be one of those people finding it odd. To be rational, for Machiavelli, means to strategize and that entails the use of rhetoric, of performance, the deployment of knowledge and narrative where necessary and of transparency and opacity where useful (Flyvbjerg, 1998; Van Assche et al., 2016). It does not mean that rules can be broken and it does not mean that no public interest is recognized. It simply means that one cannot assume that private and group interest can be presumed absent or wished away. It also means that transparency cannot be presumed or enforced, as nobody can be forced to be honest or show all her cards, in negotiations where demarcations and definitions of public goods always have consequences for private and group goods and where it is not always possible to achieve win-win situations.

The presence of actor strategies in governance does not make collective goods impossible to define or protect, to define as a community what to consider as natural resources, how to use them and how to divide public and private benefit in this. Moreover, it does not prevent the articulation of collective strategies for the pursuit of common goods. Such collective strategies ought to be articulated in governance and they will take the shape of new, overarching institutions which can coordinate other institutions, creating a direction in the development of the community and its resources. We develop this perspective in later chapters. For now, we can say that such strategy can amplify the power of a community over its own resources and its own future. Similar to other policy tools, they can be used and abused by elites or by certain actors promoting them actively or using them creatively, but this does not detract from their potential.

Another visit with Foucault: Power

Now we arrive at the point where Foucault's ideas on power can be introduced more productively. For Foucault, the commonplace understandings of power are mostly still valid, that is, he would not deny that knowledge is power, that people can have power, governments, that policies can exert power, that power can be used and abused, that governments can oppressive, corrupt, inefficient and that exercise of power can require strategy rather than direct imposition (Escobar, 1985).

Several of Foucault's insights which are useful for our own purposes, come under the label of dynamics of power. For Foucault, a balance of power is never entirely stable (Foucault, 2012). That is, even in oppressive regimes or relations, shifts are happening all the time and invisible micro movements might produce a sudden collapse later. It is also possible that the oppressor does not truly enjoy the oppressing and the oppressed finds benefits in maintaining the appearance of being oppressed. In the same line of reasoning, Foucault would not believe in any hierarchical pyramid of power, in any system of governance where supposedly all the important decisions are taken at the top and then simply handed down for development and implementation (Elden, 2007; Van Assche et al., 2011, 2017). For him, and this has been borne out by myriad empirical studies after him, all elements at all levels have to be involved before the hierarchy can work and this entails that many directions of power are entirely possible (Foucault, 2007, 2010; Richardson, 1996). Signals from the middle, the bottom, blockages at any point, actors at one level who are not supposed to be involved, all of it is possible in an interplay of routines, persuasion, coercion, tactics and strategy.

Power here comes out of routines which are institutionalized and this institutionalization and use of routines can be strategic or not, that is, with the real intention to maximize influence and that can be for private or public gain (Elden, 2007). Strategies go beyond the selective use of institutions and selective linking up with other actors and can include persuasion, maybe coercion, framing issues, problems, solutions in ways that look appealing to others expected to become part of the strategy, appealing to shared cultures, egos, flattering, appearing to be all powerful or entirely powerless (Escobar, 1985; Flyvbjerg, 1998; Hillier, 2002). Dissimulation, selective transparency, hiding facts, emphasizing others, appealing to certain experts and not others, stroking the ego of a particular expert group aligned with your ideas are all part of the classic tools of the strategist in and through governance (Latour, 2004). For Foucault, not all these tools in all cases are acceptable, moral, legitimate. He, as Machiavelli before, tells us to expect them in any environment where the stakes and rewards are real (Van Assche et al., 2016). And governance is such environment, as it promises influence over the taking of collectively binding decisions.

Foucault would also highlights that power triggers counter-power, as in resistance and possibly counter-strategies (Foucault, 2012). On the one hand, if strategies are observable, it makes them stronger in the sense that their visibility makes them more persuasive, that their mere existence and acknowledgment by others, by others in power and by people following them, makes a difference (Foucault, 2010). On the other hand, visibility makes it possible to attack, to resist and their unfolding in governance, their path of influence and implementation (their goal dependencies and reality effects, in terms of evolutionary governance theory) makes it possible to draw lessons regarding pros and cons for the community, for actors in governance and for potential counterstrategies (Flyvbjerg, 1998; Richardson, 1996).

In communist countries, strategies were often hidden and secret even the maps underpinning strategies were not public. Secrecy itself was elevated to the status of a public good. And this tends to leave legacies, as often, even now, new plans and policies are not readily accessible, while old plans and generally archival materials can be hidden or simply vanish with great regularity. Very ambitious plans were subjected to competing pressures, as they needed to involve more people and organizations, so they had to know something. However, if something went wrong, if resources were squandered, targets not met, quality controls evaporated, then many could be blamed, and the original plan could be dangerous in that blame game. Hence, a quiet evolution where the most important plans and policies could be the least visible ones, or, only visible for a short time. If an irrigation canal, a school, a factory or a polder ended up in the wrong place, in a different form, by actors pushing or pulling, by mere incompetence, or by smart adaptation, access to the original plan was a risk for all involved. Also maps, as basic inputs for strategy, and as witness of projects finished or unfinished, could conveniently disappear, could be 'under revision,' or could be labeled secret because of national interests, of a military or economic kind.

Niklas Luhmann would highlight that power in politics and administration can be anywhere and that the power of political leaders and administrative managers was highly overrated (Luhmann, 2018). Steering through governance was much more difficult than modernists assumed (see Chapters 8 and 9) and one of the reasons was the variety of mechanisms of resistance that could be observed in any administrative system. Even the humblest public servant, the one with one stamp, to stay in communist spheres, could strategically use that stamp to block the flow of administrative routines, could block, postpone, divert decisions and often resources. Even the most humble servant, say, the person with the coffee cart and cookies, could exert influence and push his version of an ideology or public good by connecting people and departments informally, by gossip, good and bad, in social gatherings after work and, who knows, by blackmail, since he knows more secrets than some of the managers.

Foucault and later actor network theory derived from his work would acknowledge that things can offer resistance and opportunity (Foucault, 2012; Latour, 2004, similar to the affordances idea discussed above). And, that clever strategy would take this into account; deep insight offered by the affordances of a building (who is sitting next to whom, which archives are in the basement, where is the bar, the interesting people, the exit where people don't see you leaving) can be helpful, even the nature of paperwork and papers (no space for long stories here, hiding tough points in footnotes there) can feature in micro-strategies which could have macro implications (Richardson & Weszkalnys, 2014).

Again, none of this means for Foucault that steering is not possible, that oppression cannot be denounced or that there is no strategy possible to pursue common goods. Foucault would consider power as an energy which is everywhere, which can be used for good and evil and which is there in absence of strategy (Flyvbjerg, 1998; Foucault, 2010). It is the fuel of governance, necessary to make governance work and necessary to give an impact to what is decided in governance; without power there is no resource management plans and no enforcement (Foucault, 2007). The energy is also not entirely controllable and can disappear or appear at a certain point without bystanders expecting it. Something in the context, in the system of governance or the community itself can shift, which endows something or someone with a new power, or which enables a strategy which heretofore was unimaginable. Something might change which makes a strategy which was objectively possible but cognitively difficult to grasp, suddenly easier to grasp, opening up new strategic possibilities (Van Assche et al., 2011, 2016, 2017).

Power/knowledge and strategy in resource governance

For Foucault, one key reason power is at the same time more important and less predictable and manageable than it appeared for previous theorists, is the entwining of power and knowledge (Flyvbjerg, 2011; Svarstad et al., 2018). Knowledge creates power and power creates knowledge, while power also relies on knowledge and vice versa. Foucault understands the world as discursively constructed, with discourses as conceptual structures which make parts of reality accessible and create it for those in the discourse (Escobar, 1985). Discourses are always selective understanding or constructions of reality, as those realities are always imperfectly understood and constructed by means of a limited set of concepts and relations, which could have been different (Richardson, 1996). Discourses are selective and contingent: there are always other ways to construct realities. Discourses highlight certain features and relations and move others to the background, or do not give them a place.

Discourses evolve, they can migrate, combine, dissolve, fragment, entirely disappear and they can integrate others, transforming them in the process (Bal & Marx-MacDonald, 2002). Evolution of discourse is in most cases co-evolution, as discourses shape each other over time (Cleaver & Whaley, 2018). Discourses on natural resource management are shaped by evolving discourses on the environment, biodiversity, sustainability, on democracy and commons (Biermann & Anderson, 2017; Rinfret, 2009). Discourses can have the character of narrative, or produce narratives, which make them more persuasive and they can form configurations which keep the constructed realities in place. Discourses on private property, neo-liberal ideology, resource exploitation can keep each other in place, while not highlighting the value of landscape, nature and sustainability (Descola & Palsson, 2003). One form of configuration is embedding, where broader narratives underpin or support more narrowly defined ones, where ideologies support ideas of common property and those enable the functioning of cooperatives but also the creation of public parks.

As discourses are never stable, their development cannot be predicted. They can be influenced from corners not foreseen. This does not preclude strategy; it means that strategy will have to adapt to changing discourses and that means also changing power relations (Armitage, 2005). As discourses produce what we understand as reality, it will influence our thinking and acting. Hence, power over discourse is power over others, their thinking and acting. Yet, the strategist is never entirely free, as discourse also holds power over her: one can start to believe the stories one is telling first for strategic reasons (corporate social responsibility) and one can believe them in the first place. The strategist can deliberately pursue a strategy of persuasion, or knowledge creation to convince others that what she wants is more real, or objectively the best course of action (fitting reality better), but at the same time she can be convinced by others in the same process of certain aspects of reality which modify strategy and, even if absence of that, the strategist might not be aware of assumptions in her own thinking which limit her strategy in ways not entirely visible to her. As all, including the strategist, live in discourse and as we are never entirely aware of the discursive structures enabling our thinking, the invisible limits to strategy are always manifold.

European coastal tourism developed rapidly in the 19th century, a development where entrepreneurs, local governments, but also strategically minded national governments played prominent roles. Whereas at first the sea itself was seen as medicinally important, the contact with the salty water and air, later the beach itself, up to that point a no-man's land and water, was discovered by the health tourists as a pleasurable place of recreation and socializing. Fishers, in many places prevalent on the beach, were relegated to new ports, built by governments. Later, tourists discovered beaches were rather small, and discovered the dunes for recreation, which led to planned developments, by the late

19th century, in the dunes itself, partly maintaining the sandy undulating landscapes in the (upscale) settlements. Those dunes, however, often gave way to development close to the sea, as the view of the sea was successfully sold by real estate developers as the key asset of a vacation place. In each step of this evolution, strategizing governments guided development in most European countries, but were also caught off-guard, or simply moved in a different direction, by qualities, assets, places 'discovered' by others.

That also means that it is impossible to discern the reality effects of a strategy, the effects in shaping the reality in the broader community, can never be observed from a neutral point of view by the strategist. It also means that those effects are more unpredictable than the strategist anticipates because shifts in discourse can occur in the community, which shed a different light on the strategy, the strategist, on the stories they tell and the results of the strategy that can be recognized (Flyvbjerg, 1998). A clean energy project can start to look like a scam quite easily. The effects of the strategy in governance itself, which EGT calls goal dependencies, are hard to observe, partly because of the inherent complexity and opacity of governance itself, partly because of the opacity of discourses and discursive configurations (Hillier, 2002; Van Assche et al., 2013).

Thinking and organizing thus become closely entwined for Foucault and this idea is also a tenet in this book. Power/ knowledge shapes how we see and comprehend things and how people try to shape each other's perspectives in governance (Newig et al., 2007; Van Assche et al., 2017). What looks like reality, will exert power and if things can be organized in such a way that they either seem to reflect reality or produce it, this gives the organizer power, as it gives the form of organization power. More directly, the way we understand things will determine how we organize things and this applies to individuals, organizations and to governance systems. Barbara Czarniawska and other organization theorists recognized that narratives on the world, on the identity and goals and environment of the organization shape its course, structure the way it structures itself and operates (Czarniawska, 2014). She added a meta-level by discerning narratives on the nature of an organization and of organizing itself, co-create the organization, in a process that is always one of self-organization and self-creation. This lines up well with systems theories on organization which emphasize this always contingent process of self-creation; narratives help organizations (and by extension governance systems) to find ground in this process (Luhmann, 2018).

Power/knowledge perspectives in governance are often used to analyze patterns of inclusion and exclusion, sometimes starting from the actors, sometimes from forms of knowledge, narratives, ideologies, kinds of expertise, which are allowed or not, dominating or nor, naturalized or not and, importantly, institutionalized or not, that is, encoded in policies, plans or laws, as well as in procedures of decision-making and organizational structures (Michael & Still, 1992; Van Assche et al., 2011). There might be a department of 'natural resources' but also a department of 'gold,' which is already telling about its importance. If the chief expert in an administration on natural resources has to be an engineer, that is telling about the role of engineering perspectives in that governance system (cf. Fischer, 2000).

The role of experts, the balance between participation and representation, between expert and local knowledges in governance, can fruitfully be studied through a power/knowledge, but also the procedures of decision-making, the way problems, topics and solutions are defined, the way other topics remain in the shadow or are simply not seen as a topic or a topic worthy of a place in governance, are by now classic Foucaultian topics (Fischer, 2000; Van Assche et al., 2017). All of those are relevant for an understanding of resource communities, as these (see Chapter 7) have a tendency to exclude actors and perspectives not associated with resource extraction and resource futures and to choose forms of organization which then make it harder to move in a different direction.

In the Soviet Union, natural resources were highly regarded as drivers of development and (resource-based) development was understood as the straight path towards a truly communist society. New resource communities were therefore founded across its huge territory, often in remote locations. Depending on the perceived importance of the resource, the location and the ministries advocating for the development, plans would take shape and responsibilities were divided. Economic planning preceded spatial planning and where local governments did not exist yet or were easily sidelined, the ministries backing the state resource companies involved, or the companies themselves would design and develop new villages, towns and even cities. The balance of power could shift later, as it did in Novosibirsk, where first Moscow-based actors took key decisions which resulted in impressive growth. Diversification of the economy and strengthening of local institutions led to a stronger local voice and lobby. In many Soviet resource towns, shifts in markets were not considered and as the USSR proved sensitive to world markets, the idea of scientifically predictable economic futures and the idea of engineering as central expertise, slowly lost ideological support.

Discursive constructions of resources and/in governance

In order to appreciate the value of Foucaultian perspectives on power/knowledge, it might be useful to come back to the basic concept of discourse. Discourses in governance do not simply 'sit together' around the table in governance. Nor are they simply associated with particular actors. Discourses in governance compete, collide, reinforce each other, recruit support, create new knowledge, bring in new actors that reinforce them; they can vanish, transform and new discourses can emerge. Conflict in governance for Foucault is not necessarily negative; conflict can bring real differences in perspective into the open, real sources of knowledge, hidden problems and opportunities for the community (Flyvbjerg, 2011; Van Assche et al., 2022). Conflict can also be productive. It can be productive in the sense that dialectical learning, learning through discussion, can take central place and something new can appear in governance (Van Assche et al., 2021). It is also possible that it simply leads to a better accommodation of interests and perspectives in governance, better reflecting the diversity of interests in the community, or better reflecting real adaptation options (Armitage, 2005).

Conflict and governance as such at slower pace, can generate new objects and even new subjects. New identity discourses can emerge through conflict, as others proved alienating, nor reflecting current values and sensibilities. Objects emerge more frequently in governance, as issues do not simply enter from the environment, but are often constructed in governance itself. When conflict erupts or simmers for a longer time, the pressure on actors to be creative is higher, the pressure to move their agenda forward or simply move governance forward by means of something new, which can be a new method, issues, but also a new object of governance which suddenly appears, as if it always had been there. Experience in governance can lead actors to redefine themselves, which can be restricted to a new agenda for a political party but it can also take the shape of a new organization, a new party, or a new subjective identity – as Sicco Mansholt, who invented European policies pushing industrial agriculture, but in the process changed his mind and turned environmentalist. A reinvention can be personal, as in such conversion, but it can also entail the creation of new subject positions, new narratives which could produce new organizations, identities, new roles in governance.

Coal extraction and transportation had a colossal impact in La Jagua (Colombia), in the early 2000s. A neighborhood revolted against local authorities on February 7, 2007, in the middle of the coal boom. The revolt represents a before and after in local power relations. After the revolt, government made sure royalties were collected, and used for improvements in education and health care. Air quality is monitored. The Companies launched social responsibility programs. Mining companies became active in cultivating local entrepreneurship, including financing, advice and procurement for their own operations. Company canteens tried to source their food from local farmers (whereas locals used to complain that the miners 'don't even buy yucca.')

Mining managers interviewed (Perez-Sindin, 2024) emphasized the need to think beyond the time horizon of extraction, so diversifying the local economy was the way forward. Besides the entrepreneurship support, farmers receive training in quality upgrading and control, in the short term to provision the company, in the longer term to grow their business. The two main Companies,

Swiss and American, are now a key source of municipal finances, but also central for local farmers, businesses and business development. One can say they structure the day-to-day life in the community, and function as a quasi-state. The conflict was productive, but the dependence on the companies is ambiguous. Economic development for post-extraction is encouraged, yet the dependence on private governance in the present makes it less likely that all aspects of self-governance can develop.

A person is not a discourse for Foucault and a person never 'makes' or controls a discourse by herself. Actors, if persons, are always shaped by a variety of discourses, some of which they are participating in. For natural resource governance, not only discourses about the resource or the resource town are relevant. Many discourses have implications for the observation, valuation, use of a resource, for their very definition. What is a resource in one perspective, is not for a different one. A discourse can have implications for one topic, which then has implications for the use of a resource (like oil, fish). A discourse can also become coupled to a different one, where the resource does figure prominently (if you are against the war, you are for oil).

Discourses can have indirect implications for the perspective of actors on a resource, while perspectives on a resource can have effects on many other discourses (I like oil thus also free markets). Discourses with broad influence on governance can have fine-grained and very indirect ramifications for the governance of a resource, e.g., discourses on efficient government, on public health, quality of life, social hierarchies, inclusion and exclusion. Thus, if elite attitudes change towards the resource because of their changing health perspectives and elites are prominent in governance, the governance of the resource could shift. If ideas on rule of law evolve, small scale illegal mining can be acted upon, while the same illegal miners can also be embraced as small entrepreneurs or as a downtrodden caste, when dominant discourses in governance move in a different direction.

The governance of gold mining is not only shaped by stories, ideas, images on gold. Indeed, if people dream of gold, if gold fever is a discursive construct which is normalized, this is important. If gold is a preferred material to express veneration of a Christian God, this will make a difference. If shells are valued more highly, as the medium of economic transactions, or potatoes, fish, bars of copper, this will affect the governance of gold mining if it is local. However, the more globalized the economy, the more stories about gold elsewhere become relevant (Romans come to Mauretania, Russians scrutinize Siberian rocks.) Yet, also very different discourses come into play, as well as institutions: narratives on economic development, resource endowments, as well as world markets for gold, and stock exchanges which might crash and drive people to gold markets.

We know that not all use of resources is coordinated through governance and this too can change through discursive shifts leading to redefined power relations. The lack of coordination, we know, is only partly a matter of choice, but changing discourses, changing forms of knowledge built into the governance system can lead to a new capacity to observe coordination options. Or it could lead to new ideas on what should and can be co-ordinated, in other words, on the preferred scope and limits of governance.

Some discourses are more likely than others to be included in governance (in a particular community, where they might be too different or disruptive) and some are broader than others, more ambitious than others in scope and ambition of explanation. Which means that the possibility to derive insights regarding resource use will differ. A perspective on health and environment offers many more potential conceptual connections with resource govern-ance than a discourse on sport and free time – though, an outdoor recre-ation version will find its way to discourse on preservation and wise use (Van Assche et al., 2017).

For one actor, a set of discourses can contribute to the perspective on one resource, while that same set can produce ideas on several others. These discourses can be primarily aimed at understanding the social, the ecological or their relation. In governance, several actors compete and collaborate, their perspectives on the resource, the environment, the community itself can evolve (Brosius et al., 2005). Other discourses will impinge on the preferred translation of the resource-related discourses into institutions which can then regulate their use.

In the Danube Delta, fish was the key resource, and could be exchanged for money, but also serve as a medium of exchange itself. In the 19th century, transboundary fishing took place, yet most fishing was for subsistence, and part of a livelihood which relied on other locales and resources. After the collapse of Romanian communism and later the USSR, the area, which was primed for agricultural and industrial development became, for the most part, a Biosphere Reserve, endowed with a unique form of regional governance. Environmental discourses replaced development discourses, and the previous fishing activities, subsistence and the few communist fish farms, now looked different. The (rather inefficient) fish farms were abandoned, while the fishers were first considered criminals, then, slowly, as part of 'sustainable development' solutions, which were, slowly, coupled with 'sustainable tourism' discourses, where the fishers and fish dishes became interesting for tourists, who were now also offered a more complete image of the cultural diversity in the wetlands, previously something of a problem for successive regimes.

The fish of value, meanwhile, still disappeared from the Delta, for many years, either illegally, or, legally, through a new system of fishing concessions, amenable to gaming by people with connections to national political or administrative elites. This was further enabled by the images eco-tourists expected to see (Pelicans, reeds) and the focus of conservationists (birds, otter, mink). Siphoning of valuable fish remained compatible with managing impressions and expectations of other actors, thus nothing had to change. The species of fish caught had changed several times over the last century, because of ecological changes and large Soviet infrastructure works, but this made little differences for many locals, as long as they tasted similar to the previously dominant species, and as long as catching them wasn't too difficult. For the high value species and their customers elsewhere, the species did make a difference, and at least for sturgeon, threatened and protected everywhere, stricter controls could interfere with the informally sanctioned flow of fish out of the reserve. The relatively peaceful coexistence of various (supposedly competing) discourses and (formal and informal) institutions in one governance system (de facto) centered around fish, is not perfectly stable.

Mediating discourses on governance itself, often with an ideological basis thus contribute to the shifting pattens of power/knowledge and thus to the continuing evolution of governance. Meanwhile, in the same governance evolution, other discourses, on other things, will lead to the production of other institutions, aiming to regulate something else, with possible implications for the use of resources, e.g., when resource policies encounter others in the use of land, or in the use of other resources (oil sands and fracking requiring a lot of water, where water management has many others goals and users in mind).

Resource governance and resource management

For resource communities, the Foucaultian perspective on power/knowledge in governance is thus relevant not only because it can shed a light on those discourses focusing on the resource, but also on the relation between actors, institutions and discourses and between resource related discourses and many others. In the following chapter, we deploy a largely Foucaultian analysis on evolving patterns of inclusion and exclusion in the governance of resource communities, which will highlight the patterns of simplification that can occur over time when exclusion becomes a more powerful mechanism than inclusion and when dissensus and conflict become gradually harder in a singularly focused community and its governance.

A final distinction to be made here is an elementary one, but one which might look different after the passages on Foucault and power/knowledge. Natural resource governance and natural resource management are often used interchangeably but we prefer to distinguish them, with natural resource management (NRM) referring to the more technical management of one resource, usually focused on optimization, using an economic and maybe engineering perspectives. Natural resource governance (NRG) then is actual governance, part of community governance, as the taking of collectively binding decisions on the use, valuation, extraction, circulation, processing of natural resources (Brosius et al., 2005). We know now that each term in this list will be the product and cause of power/knowledge relations in governance (Cleaver & Whaley, 2018; Van Assche et al., 2013). We know that in some ideologies and certain governance paths, NRG will be reduced to NRM, or that NRM will not develop into NRG. In both situations, there is no real resource governance, no discussion on the benefits and risks of resource governance, on the potential role of resources in the future of the community.

Here we do take a normative stance and argue that such a situation is nowhere desirable and that for resource communities it is highly problematic. Reducing natural resource governance to natural resource management makes it difficult to benefit maximally from the resource but also makes it hard to protect its environment and the options for future diversification. Developing the tools that might put the community on a different course is rendered more difficult.

References

Agrawal, A., & Gibson, C. C. (1999). Enchantment and disenchantment: The role of community in natural resource conservation. *World Development, 27*(4), 629–649. 10.1016/S0305-750X(98)00161-2.

Armitage, D. (2005). Adaptive capacity and community-based natural resource management. *Environmental Management, 35*(6), 703–715. 10.1007/s00267-004-0076-z.

Bal, M., & Marx-MacDonald, S. (2002). *Travelling concepts in the humanities: A rough guide.* University of Toronto Press.

Bevir, M. (1999). Foucault, power, and institutions. *Political Studies, 47*(2), 345–359. 10.1111/1467-9248.00204.

Biermann, C., & Anderson, R. M. (2017). Conservation, biopolitics, and the governance of life and death. *Geography Compass, 11*(10), e12329. 10.1111/gec3.12329.

Brosius, J. P. (2004). Indigenous peoples and protected areas at the world parks congress. *Conservation Biology, 18*(3), 609–612. 10.1111/j.1523-1739.2004.01834.x.

Brosius, P., Tsing, A. L., & Zerner, C. (2005). *Communities and conservation: Histories and politics of community-based natural resource management.* Rowman Altamira.

Bryant, R. L., & Bailey, S. (1997). *Third world political ecology.* Psychology Press.

Cleaver, F., & Whaley, L. (2018). Understanding process, power, and meaning in adaptive governance: A critical institutional reading. *Ecology and Society, 23*(2). https://www.jstor.org/stable/26799116.

Czarniawska, B. (2014). *A theory of organizing.* Edward Elgar Publishing.

Descola, P. (2013). *Beyond nature and culture.* University of Chicago Press.

Descola, P., & Palsson, G. (2003). *Nature and society: Anthropological perspectives.* Routledge.

Elden, S. (2007). Rethinking governmentality. *Political Geography - POLIT GEOGR, 26*, 29–33. 10.1016/j.polgeo.2006.08.001.

Escobar, A. (1985). *Discourse and power in development: Michel Foucault and the relevance of his work to the third world.*

Escobar, A. (1996). Construction nature: Elements for a post-structuralist political ecology. *Futures, 28*(4), 325–343. 10.1016/0016-3287(96)00011-0.

Fischer, F. (2000). *Citizens, experts, and the environment: The politics of local knowledge.* Duke University Press.

Flyvbjerg, B. (1998). *Rationality and power: Democracy in practice.* University of Chicago press.

Flyvbjerg, B. (2011). *Making social science matter: Why social inquiry fails and how it can succeed again* (S. Sampson, Trans.; 13. printing). Cambridge Univ. Press.

Foucault, M. (2007). *Security, territory, population: Lectures at the College De France, 1977–78.* Palgrave Macmillan UK.

Foucault, M. (2010). *The birth of biopolitics: Lectures at the Collège de France, 1978–1979.* Picador.

Foucault, M. (2012). *Discipline and punish: The birth of the prison.* Knopf Doubleday Publishing Group.

Hillier, J. (2002). *Shadows of power: An allegory of prudence in land-use planning.* Routledge.

Ingold, T. (2018). Back to the future with the theory of affordances. *HAU: Journal of Ethnographic Theory, 8*(1–2), 39–44. 10.1086/698358.

Latour, B. (2004). *Politics of nature: How to bring the sciences into democracy.* Harvard University Press. 10.4159/9780674039964.

Luhmann, N. (2018). *Organization and decision.* Cambridge University Press.

Madimu, T. (2022). 'Illegal' gold mining and the everyday in post-apartheid South Africa. *Review of African Political Economy, 49*(173), 436–451. 10.1080/03056244.2022.2027750.

Michael, M., & Still, A. (1992). A resource for resistance: Power-knowledge and affordance. *Theory and Society, 21*(6), 869–888.

Moreno, C. M., & Wilton, R. (2014). *Using space: Critical geographies of drugs and alcohol.* Routledge.

Newig, J., Voß, J.-P., & Monstadt, J. (2007). Editorial: Governance for sustainable development in the face of ambivalence, uncertainty and distributed power: An introduction. *Journal of Environmental Policy & Planning, 9*(3–4), 185–192. 10.1080/15239080701622832.

Perez-Sindin, X. (2024). Environmental conflicts around coal extraction in El Cesar, Colombia: from physical to symbolic violence. Under preparation.

Richardson, T. (1996). Foucauldian discourse: Power and truth in urban and regional policy making. *European Planning Studies, 4*(3), 279–292. 10.1080/09654319608720346.

Richardson, T. (2016). The politics of multiplication in a failed soviet irrigation project, or, how sasyk has been kept from the sea. *Ethnos, 81*(1), 125–151. 10.1080/00141844.2014.940990.

Richardson, T., & Weszkalnys, G. (2014). Introduction: Resource materialities. *Anthropological Quarterly, 87*(1), 5–30.

Rinfret, S. (2009). Controlling animals: Power, Foucault, and species management. *Society & Natural Resources, 22*(6), 571–578. 10.1080/08941920802029375.

Svarstad, H., Benjaminsen, T. A., & Overå, R. (2018). Power theories in political ecology. *Journal of Political Ecology, 25*(1), Article 1. 10.2458/v25i1.23044.

Van Assche, K., Beunen, R., & Duineveld, M. (2013). *Evolutionary governance theory: An introduction.* Springer.

Van Assche, K., Beunen, R., & Duineveld, M. (2016). Citizens, leaders and the common good in a world of necessity and scarcity: Machiavelli's lessons for community-based natural resource management. *Ethics, Policy & Environment, 19*(1), 19–36.

Van Assche, K., Beunen, R., Duineveld, M., & Gruezmacher, M. (2017). Power/knowledge and natural resource management: Foucaultian foundations in the analysis of adaptive governance. *Journal of Environmental Policy & Planning.*

Van Assche, K., Beunen, R., Verweij, S., Evans, J., & Gruezmacher, M. (2021). Policy learning and adaptation in governance; a co-evolutionary perspective. *Administration & Society*, 009539972110591. 10.1177/00953997211059165.

Van Assche, K., Duineveld, M., & Beunen, R. (2014). Power and contingency in planning. *Environment and Planning A, 46*(10), 2385–2400.

Van Assche, K., Duineveld, M., Beunen, R., & Teampau, P. (2011). Delineating locals: Transformations of knowledge/power and the governance of the danube delta. *Journal of Environmental Policy & Planning, 13*(1), 1–21. 10.1080/1523908X. 2011.559087.

Van Assche, K., Gruezmacher, M., & Beunen, R. (2022). Shock and conflict in social-ecological systems: Implications for environmental governance. *Sustainability, 14*(2), 610. 10.3390/su14020610.

Whatmore, S. (2008). Hybrid geographies: Rethinking the 'human' in human geography. In *Environment.* Routledge.

Zimmermann, E. W. (1951). *World resources and industries.* Harper.

7

CONCENTRATION PROBLEMS AND RESOURCE COMMUNITIES

Diversity and its values in governance and community

Diversity itself has diverse meanings. One can speak of cultural and ethnic and religious diversity in a community as well as of diverse inputs in governance or a diversity of forms and mechanisms of participation. Some academics speak of some communities as superdiverse. Diversity discourses can link to discourses of integration, of multi-culturalism, of inclusion and exclusion. We acknowledge the importance of diversity in these senses but intend to add an aspect which is derived from systems theories and which highlight certain problems when diversity is absent or reduced.

If we look at governance through a systems perspective, diversity can be beneficial in different forms (Van Assche et al., 2013, 2019; Von Bertalanffy, 1969). Diversity can be useful through a diversity of actors, where a set of actors can coordinate decisions which can together process environmental complexity better. This has benefits for adaptation to a particular environment and certainly to a changing environment. That environment can be external and physical but also internal, cultural, political (Van Assche et al., 2021; Von Bertalanffy, 1969). A smaller set of actors enables easy integration of ideas into policy and easy coordination but carries the risk of depending on the whims and vagaries of that group of actors (e.g., internal politics in one party or ministry) and its limitations (cf. Thielmann & Tollefson, 2009). Machiavelli already noted that the perfect prince was in fact not one prince but a group of people (and a set of organizations), as nobody had the skills and energy to provide answers to all challenges and the evolving conditions (Mansfield, 1998).

DOI: 10.4324/9781003332145-7

A larger set of actors however is only useful, from a systems perspective, if those actors are actually different (King & Thornhill, 2006; Luhmann, 2008). That is if they do not represent the same interests or perspectives. In that case, the adaptation difference is marginal. If a political party exists to give the impression of a viable opposition, while in fact being supported by the ruling party to perform democracy, this lack of diversity is not all too helpful for the quality of an existing democracy. Which brings us to the value of democracy itself, as the best-known system of politics which presumes to manage internal complexity and dissension, enabling it to adapt to changing circumstances, enabling it to transform itself without shocks to the larger system (Luhmann, 1990) – as opposed to rule by a few.

Diversity in perspectives, interests, in actor identities, is useful therefore to adapt and that same diversity can be used to maintain diversity (Van Assche et al., 2013). That is, once there is diversity in governance, it is easier to maintain because introducing it is harder since positions of power, organizational routines and structures, interests and entrenched perspectives and forms of expertise might have to be challenged (Duit et al., 2010; Schultz & Fazey, 2009). Organizational and institutional design can help in this maintenance of diversity, of difference (Chaffin et al., 2014). Democratic systems of checks and balances counteract tendencies to concentrate power, to reduce difference and homogenize perspectives in governance. Procedures of decision-making enable the inclusion of different actors and forms of knowledge at different points in time (Voß et al., 2006). Administrative structures, with specialized departments, enable the coexistence of different perspectives, forms of knowledge and multiplication of linkages with actors in governance and community (Brans & Rossbach, 1997).

Those structures and mechanisms have to be maintained, though, and if people do not pay attention, checks and balances can erode (Hillier, 2002; Luhmann, 2004). Systems theory would stress the usefulness of redundancy in the organization of governance. Not all forms of knowledge present in administration might be needed at every point in time (institutional memory and epistemic diversity have a value), not all departments have to be involved in all projects (During et al., 2022). Importantly, a degree of overlap in responsibility, in mandate, is not necessarily bad and several ways of regulating or coordinating for the same topic or problem might coexist (Broto, 2013; Fung, 2006). For new public management perspectives and generally neo-liberal perspectives emphasizing efficiency and lean government, this might sound odd or blasphemous.

Yet such redundancies can be considered to be different mechanisms and routes of adaptation to external change, as well as different routes to finding answers (During et al., 2022; Leydesdorff et al., 2018). When one route does not work, because of practical or political problems, a different procedure, leaning on other departments, community connections, other combinations of policies and plans, might work (cf. Nooteboom & Marks, 2010). In practice, one way of organizing is never perfect and obstacles can always arise. One can opt for continuous reform of a procedure or approach, or one can accept that within governance itself diverse paths towards adaptation might exist (Berkes et al., 2008; Duit et al., 2010). Even if this can lead to clashes, ambiguity and more complicated discussions. These discussions can be considered part of checks and balances, ways to control dominant perspectives and to maintain diversity and require an arena that embraces deliberation in a productive rather than confrontative or aggressive way (Van Assche et al., 2013).

In places with a singular focus and a homogenous identity, these considerations might sound even more inappropriate, as all agree on a direction, an identity, a form of organization and the resources and knowledges needed for that (Halseth, 2017; Hatzold, 2013). Many resource communities could serve as examples. A problem, then, is that democracy in these locales suggests that redundancies are wasteful and checks and balances unnecessary. This can undermine the quality of democracy in the longer run and especially its adaptive qualities (Luhmann, 1989, 1990). In new resource communities, this can be associated with a lack of diversity from the start, while older communities focusing on resource extraction later, can gradually lose diversity and the structures maintaining it in governance.

Systems theory analyzes problems also using the concept of feedback loops, where positive loops reinforce certain ways of thinking, acting, organizing and negative feedback loops weaken them (Valentinov, 2017; Von Bertalanffy, 1969). Communities dependent on cars tend to become dependent on oil and if infrastructures are built focusing on car use, several positive feedback loops will make it harder and harder to use other forms of transportation, to live in certain areas, to build in a certain way. Before one can speak of feedback loops, there needs to be feedback however and here the pattern of points and mechanisms of feedback in governance are important infrastructures for the development of feedback loops later, which put the community on a certain track.

The pattern of participation and representation in a democracy will differ per community, as will be the functioning of multi-level governance (Fung, 2006). The pattern of governance itself, the shape and functioning of the configuration of political, administrative and non-governmental actors involved, formally and informally, in collective decision-making (under the label of participation or otherwise), shapes the pattern of feedback, what governmental actors and the whole governance configuration hear and see and how much pressures associates with these observations (Kooiman, 2009; Voß et al., 2006). Civil society organizations in some places do not participate in governance but their protest will be heard directly or indirectly in governance circles, whether amplified through media or not (Folke et al., 2002).

Media might not participate but their editorial voice and ideological slant can be heard when actors anticipate that the community will be influenced by the voice, or when they believe the media voice already represents a common opinion which should not be ignored (Luhmann, 2000).

Through a complex pattern of feedback, a diversity of feedback loops can develop which does not necessarily gear the community towards one possible future (Valentinov, 2014). It can help to maintain a diversity within governance and within administration, which can help to avoid routines taking root which are not questioned anymore, possibly not observed anymore (Van Assche et al., 2013). If, within an administration, organizational identities develop which start from a unity of purpose in the community, translate this into decision-making premises and procedures, that are later not questioned anymore, in a system of poor feedback and little redundancy, then issues in the community will get the same scripted response over and over again and actors in governance will find it hard to consider even the possibility of change (Brans & Rossbach, 1997). The current form of organization is naturalized, looks like it is the reasonable and natural way to go, as one always did it, it always worked, nobody complained and it fit the general purposes of governance and general identity of the community.

Even complex patterns of feedback do not necessarily maintain diversity (Valentinov, 2014, 2017). Local politics might have a few parties, with different ideas but those parties might be tied to different roles in the mine, or to the union and management in the paper mill. Which means that both are tied to the same industry, to the same imagined future for the community. A critical local newspaper might exist, critical of management and unions, but always starting from the premises of a resource identity and a resource future. Later, when the newspaper is taken over by a conglomerate, the local content and voice might diminish and its function in the pattern of feedback in governance will diminish.

Niklas Luhmann, noted systems theorist, speaks of *de-differentiation,* when the processes of differentiation which led to the formation of complex governance arrangements come to a halt, or are partially reversed (King & Thornhill, 2006; Luhmann, 2004). Society marked by its slow, centuries-long march towards differentiation of politics, law, science, religion and economy as function systems and by its differentiation in specialized organizations, carrying out specific tasks, is not likely to take a path of wholesale de-differentiation (turning back the clock), but locally, this is indeed possible (Beck & Rosa, 2022). It is possible because communities, certainly if self-organizing (as municipalities) are never tightly coupled to their environment, that is, to their physical environment, to higher levels of governance. What happens locally is never entirely dictated by an economy, by nature, nor by what is said in the capital or what is happening at the neighbors.' Which means that there is always space for path creation at local level, degrees of freedom, of autonomy, in the development of the governance path (Duit et al., 2010; Van Assche et al., 2021). This leaves room for counter-productive processes of de-differentiation.

Diversity in governance, redundancy and checks and balances are all in peril when de-differentiation processes occur. De-differentiation can take the path of concentration of power and unification of perspective, but it can also take the shape of growing chaos and difficulty to coordinate. This is the case, e.g., when organizations expected to do something are in fact doing something else, so the pattern of specialization becomes blurred and it becomes less clear who can do what in coordination (Van Assche & Djanibekov, 2012). Which can be understood as a decrease in governance capacity, the capacity to organize *anything*. It is also possible that the boundaries between economy, law, politics become blurred, locally, to such an extent, that a dominant company, with political influence, can gradually undermine the rule of law. This is a problem in the ethical and political sense, but also in terms of practical adaptation, as it becomes less clear who can do what in response to a problem or opportunity and which policy tools can be used (Berkes et al., 2008; Schultz & Fazey, 2009). The 'teeth' of policy tools are likely to become less sharp under conditions of de-differentiation, as organizations using their identity, their ambition, tend to stop using the tools associated with their initial or official purpose and unused tools tend to become blunt (Luhmann, 1990; Van Assche et al., 2013).

These two faces of de-differentiation can occur at the same time, maybe counter-intuitively. Power and ideas can be concentrated, perspectives can become more homogenous, yet at the same time, governance capacity can decline. One can think of the collapse of the USSR, where it became increasingly harder to organize anything, at all levels, in a history of de-differentiation which was partly a history of ad hoc adaptations by governmental actors doing other things than they were supposed to do (Van Assche & Djanibekov, 2012). Self-transformation of the system as a whole became difficult because politics itself did not have clear mechanisms of change, tied to a pattern of hierarchy and ideology and as signals coming from law could not lead to political change (Luhmann, 1990, 2008).

Our considerations on the value of diversity and the dangers of de-differentiation serve as an introduction to the next passages, on the concentration problem in resource communities. Concentration problems can develop slowly, can be described as de-differentiation, decreasing diversity in governance, with serious implications for the understanding of changing environments, for the articulation and implementation of alternative futures. The following passages build on the introductory chapter, where we mentioned the concentration problem briefly and links closely also to the previous chapter on power/knowledge.

The concentration problem

Resource communities are not unique in every respect and their problems are not entirely unique. Some problems are quite closely associated with resource communities. We know from previous chapters that they can be rife with symbolic violence, trauma, that a variety of social and economic problems can occur in them, both during boom and bust periods. When the industry is in decline, a separate set of issues appears, some of them similar to those of other places in decline, to remote and small places, now more left to their own devices, or simply similar to poor places with low education levels. Resource addiction can lead to other addictions and youth with few options can either leave or give up (Freudenburg, 1992; Marais, 2022; Van Assche et al., 2021).

Once again, context matters, every place and every resource economy are slightly different, but the similarities are still striking. In the introductory chapter, we introduced the concept of the 'concentration' problem to synthesize ideas on a set of recurring problems in resource communities, to make them understandable in their cohesion. Here, we intend to develop this concept further, leaning on ideas discussed in the previous chapters. Concentration problems indicate problems with pattens of feedback and feedback loops, both positive and negative. Everything related to an industry focus can be gradually reinforced, all other things can be slowly marginalized, undermined or simply forgotten (Perez-Sindin & Van Assche, 2020; Van Assche et al., 2020).

Capital and employment can concentrate in one activity, even one company, to the detriment of anything else. Knowledge in governance and the community can revolve around the industry and what is useful for it. Narratives on past, present and future can be reshaped through the lens of a now dominant industry. Power can be concentrated in the hands of the company and those aligned with them in governance, even in democratic settings (Gunder, 1981; Halseth, 2017; Hayter, 2017). Interests and perceived interests can be interconnected tightly, in such a way that other interests are not perceived or not around the table in governance (Fung, 2006). People living in the community, after a period of industry dominance, tend to share many ideas and perspectives, on the good community, on life, environment, on the uselessness of pursuing alternatives, the treacherous character of those trying to regulate the industry or imposing limits on extraction (Van Assche et al., 2017).

Other people, other activities, can be filtered out slowly, because they do not fit, they are not supported, they are not profitable enough. The next generation can either leave to pursue schooling and jobs elsewhere or stay and reproduce the political and economic relations in the community. Over time, more similar people will flock to the community and people in the community will tend to become and think more alike, in a striking version homogenization which is bound to trigger local de-differentiation. Such homophily can stifle innovation and, more elementarily, self-transformation in the community. It can make reinvention highly unlikely, except possibly after a radical collapse of the industry, with no possible revival in sight (see above).

This cluster of feedback loops can gradually close the community and its governance system off from new ideas and different people, but also from its environment. New connections and collaborations with non-resource towns, higher level governments, civil society organizations and companies in other sectors, or even more innovative ones in the same resource sector, become harder to establish, harder to see as relevant and viable. The community can slowly become trapped in a closed cycle of decision-making which appears transparent to insiders, but in fact turns more and more aspects of governance into unquestioned routines and structures, thus a form of black box.

The concentration problem thus undermines checks and balances, reso-nating with our observations earlier in this chapter. Moving towards more local participation, on more topics and less relying on representation, on local politicians and on local administrations and its experts, will not solve much, as the perspectives in administration, politics and the community at large have become remarkably similar. Conflict is possible, as noticed before, but usually revolves around different positions in and on the same industry, without questioning its centrality. Even when the industry is gone, this situation can remain the same for a long time, as only in rare cases is there a new industry that is able to shape the community and its governance with such force.

Power/knowledge relations in governance make it difficult to develop, present, defend alternative futures for the community, to develop and maintain the expertise that might be involved and the policy tools (policies, plans, local laws) that might enable reinvention. Identity narratives render governance more rigid and if industry or community feel threatened, con-sidering alternatives can look as betrayal. Even remembering existing tools that might have had implications for alternative futures becomes difficult and institutional memory, in the case of older communities, tends to be rewritten so as to render older and more diverse histories as precursors of the 'real' destiny of the community, for the period when the community finally came into itself.

Social and cultural life in the community can be structured by the key activity, sometimes directly by the industry itself. Times might have gone when the mine established a local theater or even opera, when the mill built a skating rink, when unions had their own music bands and cultural associa-tions and now few would accept the pervasive influence of the company in the old-style company towns, get their groceries in the company store, but many gladly accept the cultural norms that emerged out of a paternalistic and dominant industry. For example, the provision of food, holiday trips and sponsorships of children during the mining boom in the Free State Goldfields were all embedded in the social and cultural life of the community and losing these things was hard to accept.

In As Pontes, Spain one can clearly recognize a version of the concentration problem. The coalmine was closed and flooded, meaning that another coal boom cannot be expected. Yet, in interviews, media analysis, in surveys, a new identity is now recognized, associated with a broad category 'industry,' particularly heavy industry or energy. Even if the scale of former extraction created many environmental and social divisions, alternatives to 'big industry' are systematically not considered. Alternative futures, different from 'industry' are hard to see, because the industrial identity narrative is deeply entrenched in governance and widely shared in the community. It is easier to sell and believe because the problems of the boom (1970s–90s) are largely gone, restructuring social memory, downplaying the former power and impact of the Company. Alternative economies are hard to imagine because of the long dominance of the Company, and because of young people leaving. While identities and economies predating the boom were thoroughly erased during industrialization.

The concentration problem and governance

The concentration problem is not merely a problem of governance but one of the whole community, of a community which is so focused on and shaped by its main industry, that anything else than perpetual industry dominance becomes hard to grasp and organize. The effects on governance deserve special attention, however, because here the conditions are created for co-ordinating change in the future. If the tools to change things, the cognitive tools to observe change, the expertise to understand change, are allowed to atrophy, implementing a change in direction later is difficult.

We dwell on this because simply having policies or plans does not mean that they can be implemented and simply having the authority to formulate strategies for change, does not mean that this will happen and there is no relation with the quality of observation, of policy and of policy integration necessary (Thielmann & Tollefson, 2009; Van Assche & Djanibekov, 2012). Existing strategic documents, if not immediately in line with industry priorities, will not have been used and after a while, they will lose their coordinative power, their 'teeth.' This is the case because trust in their potential to coordinate is lost, because their legitimacy will be doubted and because in practical terms, things will have evolved differently, with other tools of coordination taking precedence and other priorities in terms of what requires coordination.

This last statement is not of merely theoretical interest, as not only capacity to integrate policy into strategy tends to atrophy, but also the belief in the need and validity of any strategy (Van Assche et al., 2021). Governance capacity is thus likely to dwindle, which is not strange if we consider that, in a simplified future revolving around the resource, especially if private actors take the lead, the community does not have to think much about its future and does not need to create and maintain the policy tools needed for more comprehensive strategy. Nor is it impelled to discuss change, to create and maintain arenas for discussion and debate on such topics.

The concentration problem can thus also be described as a gradual shrinking of observation, a narrowing of reflection (cf. Harste & Laursen, 2021). Or, to put it more bluntly, of not thinking about certain aspects of present and future which then has implications for the possibilities to organize for those aspects (Berkes et al., 2008; Duit et al., 2010). If expertise gradually disappears from governance, or when new expertise, new roles, new policy tools, are only there to promote the key industry or to mitigate damage done by it, this will further erode the quality of observation and problem solving in governance. It will reduce the chances that future strategies will have the required substance to understand its own possibilities and limitations and it will reduce the diversity of knowledges which can be used in internal discussions to test ideas for possible futures (Hillier & Gunder, 2003). Meanwhile, the channels from where truly different signals could enter governance, shrivel.

In terms of evolutionary governance theory (EGT; Van Assche et al., 2013), one can say that the concentration problem is a description of a situation marked by very strong path dependencies and interdependencies (Perez-Sindin & Van Assche, 2020). Fewer actors, fewer forms of knowledge remain in governance and they become tightly coupled, meaning that they co-evolve and make it hard for others to enter governance. The whole community can be dependent on one company and community politics can be reduced *de facto* to the internal politics of that company. But these dependencies can also stem out of ineffective government level policies and approaches imposed at a local scale and are not able to address local issues (Marais, 2013). Path dependencies of cognitive and organizational entwine, as certain forms of organization in governance, a light administration and the structure of that administration, the role of a chamber of commerce, of unions, keep certain forms of knowledge, certain narratives and perspectives in place and vice versa (Van Assche et al., 2013).

Goal dependencies under the concentration problem tend to be weak (Van Assche et al., 2020), that is, new institutions which envision the future of the community will have limited impact in governance. They will be ignored, fall between the cracks, the proponents will be vulnerable to marginalization. Only policies and plans which align with a resource-dominated future stand a better chance at finding a route towards implementation, or at least create more different responses within governance (Van Assche et al., 2021). Yet, even so, one needs to bracket this assertion, as the idea itself of complex institutions moving the community in a self-chosen direction, is likely to be alien and key decisions about the community future are likely to be taken elsewhere, at higher levels of governance or by private actors or coalitions thereof – think of 'the Alberta oil patch' as a set of networked organizations promoting oil extraction. Which means that strategies affecting the community future are likely to be someone else's strategy and that local influence is likely to be limited (Folke et al., 2002). The afore-mentioned rescaling of resource economies (due to globalizing capitalism), the disentangling of companies from the local context, does not help in this regard; the input by local politicians, civil society organizations and unions on visions for the future will be limited (Halseth, 2017; Hatzold, 2013).

This does not mean in all cases that local effects will be weak, including the effects in governance we called goal dependencies. It is just that we are dealing with someone else's goals and not simply a somebody, but an industry that is the lifeblood of the community. Thus, a distance is created between industry and community, yet a distance that is not great enough to cause much resistance, in most cases, as the power of identification and dependence is too great (Gunder, 1981). The distance is also likely too small to force a collective reflection on alternatives; rather, what one can observe more commonly is an increasingly passive attitude towards community futures (Herrfahrdt-Pähle et al., 2020). This is especially true when globalization also means few jobs, lower salaries, more unpredictability because of more direct exposure to the vagaries of international markets and less sheltering by companies with at least some local loyalty (Perez-Sindin & Van Assche, 2020; Van Assche et al., 2020).

Material dependencies (we return to this in Chapter 8) tend to be stronger than in other communities, but the awareness of these dependencies – thus the capacity to manage them – very selective. The material preconditions for successful resource extraction, including infrastructures but also features of the environment, above or below the surface or the sea, tend to be sharply observed, by industry workers, managers, local politicians and residents alike, with the associated form of local knowledge become widely shared, common knowledge, visible in common parlance, in public discourse. What might be useful for other activities, in the environment, recedes to the background. How the functioning of governance is shaped by the environment, by its reshaping in an extraction history, becomes less clear, as such meta-reflection is not of the order of the day (Hillier & Gunder, 2003; Voß et al., 2006). While the focus of governance and everyday life might be on certain aspects of the environment, that does not mean that the limiting effect of this singularly focused physical environment on governance is understood (Burnham & Kingsbury, 2021). In general, the presence of concentration problems makes the observation of concentration problems harder.

Trauma can result from material dependencies in communities marked by concentration problems. Living between tailing dams and mining dumps can leave traumatic legacies and shape governance in ways that weakens adaptation. Failure of tailing dams is a global concern. The Brumadinho tailings dam failure in Brazil in 2019 was one of the world's largest, and the Merriespruit disaster in 1994 was the largest in South Africa. More than 50% of South Africa's approximately 400 tailings dams do not have a current owner. This reality holds many risks for nearby communities. On the morning of September 11, 2022, there was a catastrophic dam failure at a diamond mine near Jagersfontein in the Free State Province. Several people died, many were injured, and extensive damage had been done to houses, infrastructure and farmland. A commission of enquiry determined the reasons and pointed to the lack of appropriate mine closure policies, legislative uncertainty, failure to obey regulations and structural problems in the design of the tailings facility.

One can understand the concentration problem as a simplification of governance in all its aspects, with in some communities, some paths of its development, some aspects becoming more extremely simplified, some of the effects more outspoken. This is rather natural in the perspective of EGT, where each governance path is necessarily unique, a unique outcome of a particular set of co-evolutions (Van Assche et al., 2013). In one community, a diverse economy can be overtaken by an exceedingly profitable resource extraction, elsewhere a community established for extraction can first see a dozen smaller enterprises, then a wave of consolidations, after which the remaining company is bought out by a foreign competitor. In one place, an appreciation of the local landscape, its agricultural and tourist potential, can be quickly displaced in local politics, by overriding economic interests which require dramatic landscape change, while elsewhere, concentration problems seep in more quietly, through gradual acquisition of land by one industry and slow replacement of labor in other sectors by jobs in the more profitable resource sector.

Memory and the concentration problem

The concentration problem and memory can entangle in various pernicious ways. People can leave in large numbers, being replaced by others more directly associated with a new resource industry, which directly alters social memory and makes for an easier restructuring of identity and from there governance. Or they can simply leave, without being replaced, when the industry is declining or offering less attractive jobs (Gill, 2023; Luloff, 1990). When the industry is gone but people stay, social memory and resource identities can linger for generations (Perez-Sindin & Van Assche, 2021). Social memory in a ghost town is not much to speak about.

Increasing self-similarity in a community will reinforce social identity and hence a particular structuring of social memory. Memories from pre-resource times will be simplified, forgotten and possibly ridiculed. Nostalgia might exist in the margins but is not comparable to the overriding nostalgia which can mark former resource communities, especially places where the concentration problem was strong and industry collapsed all of a sudden. When identities and memories are closely tied to an industry, a company and then it disappears, this will cause shock and often trauma (as we discussed earlier). What gave sense and organizational cohesion to the community collapses and those remaining find it hard to orient themselves in life and towards the future. The past then comes to dominate the present and this is the well-known nostalgia of former resource towns.

If schooling is largely on the job training and locally, few higher education options are available (a special interest in local diversification by higher level governments is typically needed for that), young people tend to leave or become enrolled in the existing jobs, identities and memory narratives (Freudenburg, 1992). Young people do not bring in truly different experiences into the community and this forms an obstacle for the natural self-transformation of social memory and identity one can find elsewhere (Barthel et al., 2010). Schooling thus is not merely a conservative force; schools do not simply reproduce existing narratives and social orders. They offer opportunities for people and places to reinvent themselves, for young people to get other opportunities and reinsert themselves in the social fabric (if jobs can be found) in new roles, carrying new versions of the identity narrative and new capacities for community adaptation (Chaffin et al., 2014; Perez-Sindin & Van Assche, 2020).

Moreover, schools can be natural places of reflection on community identity and history, carriers of more complex forms of social memory and places of discussion, of connecting those memories to different possible futures (Gill, 1991). To fulfill such function, schooling cannot be reduced to what can be immediately applied in the current version of the dominant industry. The choice here is not between theoretical versus practical education and our argument is not in any sense directed against vocational schooling. Schooling and schools should contribute to an alleviation of the concentration problem, not its perpetuation.

Media also potentially function as carriers of reflections but also places to discuss and question social memory and identity. Local media, if truly interested in the local community, if truly well-informed and with local readers or listeners, can similarly be conservative or progressive, reproducing concentration problems or softening them (Luhmann, 2000). Media can be a mouthpiece of industry, of unions, of local politics, or they can be more critical, open-minded and engaged. Local newspapers can be arenas for substantial discussion, providing local politics with information and arguments, or they can simply reflect political positions already taken. In order to dislodge concentration problems, the 'memory work' that local media can do is substantial but needs to be organized (Esmark, 2009). If truly local, journalists, editors and owners do not escape the forces that created the concentration problem in the first place. Taking a critical position, by questioning social memory, presenting alternative interpretations, can be easily taken as an outsiders' position, with unpleasant implications (Berkes et al., 2008; Hatzold, 2013).

The concentration problem can be reinforced through social memory if resource work becomes multi-generational, when grandparents do not have different stories to tell their grandchildren and when no generation can imagine a different future, or can generate a different version of the past, maybe one reconsidering the problems associated with resource extraction. Of course, this is never entirely the case, since even in stable resource communities one cannot turn back the clock. Nonetheless, the cohabitation of generations working in the same mine or trying to catch the same fish can create cohesive communities through shared social memory, and at the same time, it carries the risk of reinforcing concentration problems in governance.

In a more technical sense, memory within governance can reproduce or loosen the grip of concentration problems. The memory of the governance system itself, the sharing of experiences within circles of actors participating in governance, stories of success and failure, of relevant and irrelevant topics, of legitimate and illegitimate roles of government, shapes the current functioning of governance in a direct manner (Esmark, 2009; Kooiman, 2009; Van Assche et al., 2020). Once a community and a governance system are in the grip of the concentration problem, the pressure to reinterpret past success and failure through the lens of the resource will grow and reinserting alternative interpretations of success and failure in governance will become more difficult (Beunen et al., 2013). This might be the case and reinforced by the afore-mentioned tendency to not reflect, to routinize governance, to reduce the scope of governance, but, in principle, it remains possible to bring back a more deliberate reflection on the history of governance *in* governance. Especially when this history is not restricted to a knowledge of routines and standard explanatory narratives but also considers success and failure and scope and ambition of governance in the past, this cultivation of governance memory can increase reflexivity in governance and increase adaptive capacity (Chaffin et al., 2014; Voß et al., 2006).

At the level of organizations in governance, such effort at memory work can be undermined or supported. Each organization participating in governance has its own memory, its own archive, its own sites of recollection and discussion of memory, its own connections between memory and identity.

Administrative actors can be important here as they tend to be more stable, more amenable to maintain their own institutional memory and as they can institutionalize and legitimize certain memories. they can keep official documents and distinguish between what happened and what didn't, what was decided, what was tried and what wasn't. Administrative instability, mobility of key figures, shrinking and abolition of roles and departments in administrative reform, all likely to happen under concentration problems and symptoms of them, tend to erase institutional memory of many administrative actors and such loss will trigger a loss of memory in the governance system as such – with consequences pointed out above (Van Assche et al., 2020). Histories of informality, of neo-liberal sub-contracting (consultants), of local politics thwarting its own administration (if perceived as ideologically different, as too closely tied to other levels of government, etc.), all common in resource communities, tend to aggravate the situation (Gunder, 1981; Halseth, 2017).

Futures and the concentration problem

The construction of futures under the concentration problem is a real problem. The concentration problem is a futures problem, as the closed systems of governance and community, the simplified and less diverse systems, produce simplified futures. Seeing alternatives becomes harder and when it does happen, their testing, their implementation turn into real problems. In Chapter 8, the effect of legacies on the construction of futures will be discussed in broader terms, but in our discussion of the concentration problem, the symptoms of this syndrome in the construction of futures require some emphasis and repetition.

Indeed, it is the interplay of the different forms of concentration and simplification in governance that affects the construction of futures rather than one feature of resource communities, or one mechanism at play under the concentration problem. It is the web of feedback loops which caused and expresses the concentration problem that makes it so hard to take a distance from the present, from the resource, from current asset definitions.

The undermining of checks and balances, the impoverishment of public discussion and of expertise in administration renders the testing of constructed futures shallow (Van Assche et al., 2021). The resources for such futures and the reasons to diverge from a current situation perceived as satisfying stem from observation, in governance and in the community and under the concentration problem, these observations are also less diverse, prone to de-differentiation (cf. Luhmann, 1989; Voß et al., 2006). The signals from the environment that could encourage a community to change course are scarce, as feedback mechanisms are scarce and codified in terms of resource interests. The narratives of identity which might inspire new activities are rarely flexible, as few opportunities exist for the narratives to evolve and diversify, given the homogeneity of experience and the difficulty of staying rooted while living a different life, sparking new experiences which could possibly seep into public discourse and governance.

The first step when considering alternative futures, the doubt about the present situation, or the doubt about its possible extension into the future, is already questionable under the concentration problem, as the standard shared perception of the situation is rooted and anchored in so many ways (cf. Hillier, 2002). Shared stories, administrative routines, political discourse, minimized expertise in governance, rooted identities, all conspire to not go beyond current observations and frames of observation. If, against all odds, an alternative interpretation of the situation comes through, the same set of dependencies puts pressure on the drawing of inferences, on the drawing of conclusions in terms of alternative futures which might be needed. Doubting can also be questioned from a moral perspective and can even be felt as betrayal (Fisher & Smith, 2012).

Under the concentration problem, the negative effects of extraction are often not observed, or only grudgingly so – as when other levels of government, or civil society organizations repeatedly draw attention to it (cf. Harste & Laursen, 2021; Luhmann, 1990). This non-observation constrains options for future development, as, e.g., environments become polluted, forests cut, roads are cut through the most attractive wilderness areas and unique forms of agriculture or crafts are forgotten. Similarly, the non-observation of alternative assets can lead to their neglect, or simply to their non-inclusion in alternative futures. Indeed, crafts might be an order of magnitude less profitable than the central resource of the moment, but if the writing is on the wall that the timeframe for resource extraction is limited, such assets ought not to be ignored. The landscape itself, certain infrastructures (think fishing port) can be assets in other narratives on the future, but this will only become imaginable if there is a moral permission and practical possibility to detach from the present preoccupations. A clear sign of concentration problems is when resource companies themselves are more aware of the limited timeframes of extraction, of the need to recognize alternative assets and build them into alternative futures, than the community where they operate. At the same time, this relative openness of perspective is easy to understand, as its decision-making is nimbler and as its identity is not tied to a resource future for the place.

The idea of the palimpsest is useful to understand the traces of different histories in the landscape. A landscape is almost never a product of one period, one activity, one ideology and political regime. A palimpsest is a manuscript where traces of older writing, erased but imperfectly so, can shimmer through the writing that is visible on the surface. The discovery of an older script reduces the dominant writing to one layer among others and can direct the eye to the discovery of more histories, more stories written into the landscape.

In resource towns dominated by one activity, and in the grip of the concentration problem, the understanding of a landscape as palimpsest can draw the attention to traces of other stories, and possibly break open the narrative dominance of the resource. Mining might be central to the social memory of Crowsnest Pass, Alberta, but streams survived the scarring of the landscape, streams reminding people of natural beauties, of fly fishing, of possible tourism futures. In places where the resource industry vanished, it can leave traces in the landscape which can be forgotten but could also be unearthed as a narrative asset. In Edmonton, Alberta, a history of coal mining is legible only indirectly, and a history of oil structures current self-understandings, while older indigenous histories are selectively made visible in the landscape.

Vanishing resources, lingering futures and the Big Other

When resource extraction leaves a place, the concentration problem does not necessarily leave. Nostalgia for the past, especially when there is faint hope of a resource revival, can keep resource futures alive so the only good future remains a return to the past, to the centrality of the resource. Once again, observation in governance and community is a problem, as the actual functioning of the industry, the downsides for the community and the actual power relations in governance are easily forgotten.

If the industry collapses, thoroughly and it is utterly clear that no return to the past is possible, the shadow of the past can still linger (Dennis, 1956). The company might be gone, the mayor supported by company management might have been replaced and the company salaries might have evaporated. but a legacy of the concentration problem is the difficulty in imagining alternatives, a difficulty which is present, as we know, both at a discursive and an organizational level. The cognitive and organizational resources are not there to easily discern the negative legacies of extraction, nor to easily recognize other assets, or even to discuss what might work.

When young people leave and a generation stays which is deeply invested in a resource identity, such process is reinforced (Fisher & Smith, 2012; Marais, 2022). When the community is small and isolated, when the local newspaper closed its doors, when grudges are held against other places, against environmentalists, tourists, higher-level politics, this tends to close the minds and reinforce attachments to the resource past and fantasies of a resource future (see Chapter 9). Newcomers might arrive, propose alternatives, yet, in a context marked by concentration legacies, this can easily lead to polarization of discourse and of politics with the possible effects of swings between newcomers in power and old-timers, between old futures and new futures. What contributes to the swings is the problem with testing futures diagnosed before, a problem leading to disappointment when new futures do not deliver fast enough, after which people find consolation in old identities and dreams of old futures.

Before broadening our perspective in Chapter 8, we like to introduce one more concept: the Big Other. The Big Other is a concept from Lacanian psycho-analysis (see also Chapters 5 and 9) and can only be dealt with summarily here. Yet, for the understanding of post-collapse resource economies, it is useful. Lacan himself said that 'the Big Other does not exist,' which meant that it has no existence outside the community of people saying that it exists (Hook, 2017). But the fact that people act as if it exists makes it real. The Big Other is the normative face of the symbolic order (see Chapter 5), the voice that tells us how to behave, even if there is no voice; it is the Lacanian version of the Freudian super-ego, but amplified because it is everywhere (Burnham & Kingsbury, 2021).

In the Free State, a region in South Africa, gold was the master and the mining companies functioned as Big Other. When mining declined, the internalized voice of the mines and mining futures lingered on, but the new South Africa, after apartheid, represented a new collective, a new voice, a new potential Big Other. The post-apartheid government articulated many plans for the Free State, aiming at diversification and finding a new path. Cargo airports, innovation industries and other ambitious initiatives, never materialized, alas. Still, the new superego demands new initiatives, and less reflection on the failure of the previous ones.

The Big Other, for Lacan, is a source of authority and a power around which things become organized. The Big Other can be present in a little other, especially when this is not so little, when it is a large company in a small community, a company around which everything is organized and which is the de facto center of authority. Once the real company is gone, the actor that sparked the development of a resource identity, of concentration problems, of resource futures, the structure remains, the stories remain, the limited means of coordination and orientation remain (Burnham & Kingsbury, 2021). The Big Other, in other words, remains and it is of little relevance whether he is dead or alive. Alternative structures to give meaning to self and community, to past, present and future are not available and simply tearing down the old symbolic building without credible plans for a new one is utterly destabilizing (cf. Stavrakakis, 2002).

The tight couplings between individual, community and company in many resource communities, as well as the oversized meaning *and* power of the company make for a tight grip of this Big Other on the life of the community. It makes for a series of interconnected obstacles for change which are not only located in governance but also in the psychic life of the community. Trauma might be part of this history as can also be symbolic violence, but not necessarily so. The centrality of the company, the symbolic value of the resource, the tight weaving of life around it can create circumstances where it is nearly impossible to restructure the imaginary and symbolic orders in such a way that new meanings of self and new ways to navigate the environment and the future emerge (Van Assche et al., 2021a).

In the Canadian Province of British Columbia, the community of Kitimat was established by a government-owned corporation after the second World War for the smelting of aluminum. The ore came from elsewhere, but the energy needed to transform bauxite into aluminum was plentiful. Hydro-electric works made it possible to provide cheap energy, yet the actual impetus came from higher level governments, both the Province of BC hoping to develop its northern regions and a federal government thinking in cold war terms, trying to secure strategic autonomy in the production of planes and weapons. Aluminum was seen as the metal of the future, and the geopolitical future was one of competition with the USSR.

Clarence Stein, famous American planner and designer was hired in 1951 to design the new town which would be built by Alcan, the crown corporation, afterwards sold. The town would become self-governing yet the company dominated life in every possible way, with company hierarchies reflected in the spatial organization of the town and union conflicts spilling over into town politics. As neighboring Terrace developed more commercial activity, what existed in Kitimat slowly shriveled, as salaries at the smelter made locally small business ventures look less attractive. When Alcan, the crown corporation, was sold to a private company with headquarters outside Canada, this caused a shock locally as the staff numbers went down but also as the town felt 'cut loose.' without many alternatives in sight. The new owner was less interested in being the Big Other yet remained so in the collective imagination, expected to fulfill the roles of the previous company.

References

Barthel, S., Folke, C., & Colding, J. (2010). Social–ecological memory in urban gardens—Retaining the capacity for management of ecosystem services. *Global Environmental Change, 20*(2), 255–265. 10.1016/j.gloenvcha.2010.01.001.

Beck, U., & Rosa, H. (2022). The transformation of modern society through processes of cosmopolitanization, acceleration and increasing global risks. In B. Bornemann, H. Knappe, & P. Nanz (Eds.), *The Routledge handbook of democracy and sustainability*. Routledge.

Berkes, F., Colding, J., & Folke, C. (2008). *Navigating social-ecological systems: Building resilience for complexity and change*. Cambridge University Press.

Beunen, R., Van Assche, K., & Duineveld, M. (2013). Performing failure in conservation policy: The implementation of European Union directives in the Netherlands. *Land Use Policy, 31*, 280–288. 10.1016/j.landusepol.2012.07.009.

Brans, M., & Rossbach, S. (1997). The autopoiesis of administrative systems: Niklas Luhmann on public administration and public policy. *Public Administration, 75*(3), 417–439.

Broto, V. C. (2013). Review: Adapting institutions: Governance, complexity and socio-ecological resilience. *Environment and Planning C: Government and Policy, 31*(1), 182–183. 10.1068/c460wr1.

Burnham, C., & Kingsbury, P. (2021). *Lacan and the environment*. Springer Nature.

Chaffin, B. C., Gosnell, H., & Cosens, B. A. (2014). A decade of adaptive governance scholarship: Synthesis and future directions. *Ecology and Society, 19*(3), 56.

Dennis, N. (1956). *Coal is our life: An analysis of a Yorkshire mining community.* Eyre & Spottiswoode.

Duit, A., Galaz, V., Eckerberg, K., & Ebbesson, J. (2010). *Governance, complexity, and resilience.*

During, R., Van Assche, K., & Van Dam, R. (2022). Relating social and ecological resilience: Dutch citizen's initiatives for biodiversity. *Sustainability, 14*(7), 3857. 10.3390/su14073857.

Esmark, A. (2009). The functional differentiation of governance: Public governance beyond hierarchy, market and networks. *Public Administration, 87*(2), 351–370. 10.1111/j.1467-9299.2009.01759.x.

Fisher, S. L., & Smith, B. E. (2012). *Transforming places: Lessons from Appalachia.* University of Illinois Press.

Folke, C., Colding, J., & Berkes, F. (2002). Synthesis: Building resilience and adaptive capacity in social-ecological systems. In *Navigating social-ecological systems: Building resilience for complexity and change* (pp. 352–387). Cambridge University Press.

Freudenburg, W. R. (1992). Addictive economies: Extractive industries and vulnerable localities in a changing world economy 1. *Rural Sociology, 57*(3), 305–332.

Fung, A. (2006). Varieties of participation in complex governance. *Public Administration Review, 66*(s1), 66–75. 10.1111/j.1540-6210.2006.00667.x.

Gill, A. (2023). *Respecting context in northern resource town planning: The case of Tumbler Ridge.*

Gill, A. M. (1991). An evaluation of socially responsive planning in a new resource town. *Social Indicators Research, 24*(2), 177–204. 10.1007/BF00300359.

Gunder, R. J. M. (1981). *An analysis of the stable single resource mining community in British Columbia (T).*

Halseth, G. (2017). *Transformation of resource towns and peripheries.* London and New York: Routledge.

Harste, G., & Laursen, K. B. (2021). Niklas Luhmann's anti-totalitarian observation of systems. *Kybernetes, 51*(5), 1710–1723. 10.1108/K-04-2021-0328.

Hatzold, M.-E. (2013). Social conflict, economic development and extractive industry: Evidence from South America. *Community Development Journal, 48*(3), 501–505. 10.1093/cdj/bst026.

Hayter, R. (2017). Single industry resource towns. In *A companion to economic geography* (pp. 290–307). John Wiley & Sons, Ltd. 10.1002/9781405166430.ch18.

Herrfahrdt-Pähle, E., Schlüter, M., Olsson, P., Folke, C., Gelcich, S., & Pahl-Wostl, C. (2020). Sustainability transformations: Socio-political shocks as opportunities for governance transitions. *Global Environmental Change, 63*, 102097. 10.1016/j.gloenvcha.2020.102097.

Hillier, J. (2002). *Shadows of power: An allegory of prudence in land-use planning.* Routledge.

Hillier, J., & Gunder, M. (2003). Planning fantasies? An exploration of a potential Lacanian framework for understanding development assessment planning. *Planning Theory, 2*(3), 225–248. 10.1177/147309520323005.

Hook, D. (2017). *Six moments in Lacan: Communication and identification in psychology and psychoanalysis.* Routledge.

King, M., & Thornhill, C. (2006). *Luhmann on law and politics: Critical appraisals and applications*. Bloomsbury Publishing.

Kooiman, J. (2009). Governance and governability. In *The new public governance?* Routledge.

Leydesdorff, L., Johnson, M. W., & Ivanova, I. (2018). Toward a calculus of redundancy: Signification, codification, and anticipation in cultural evolution. *Journal of the Association for Information Science and Technology, 69*(10), 1181–1192. 10.1002/asi.24052.

Luhmann, N. (1989). *Ecological communication*. University of Chicago Press.

Luhmann, N. (1990). *Political theory in the welfare state*. De Gruyter.

Luhmann, N. (2000). *The reality of the mass media*. Stanford University Press.

Luhmann, N. (2004). *Law as a social system*. Oxford University Press.

Luhmann, N. (2008). The autopoiesis of social systems. *Journal of Sociocybernetics, 6*(2), 84–95.

Luloff, A. E. (1990). Small town demographics: Current patterns of community change. In *American rural communities*. Routledge.

Mansfield, H. C. (1998). *Machiavelli's virtue*. University of Chicago Press.

Marais, L. (2013). The impact of mine downscaling on the free state goldfields. *Urban Forum, 24*(4), 503–521. 10.1007/s12132-013-9191-3.

Marais, L. (2022). *The social impacts of mine closure in South Africa: Housing policy and place attachment*. Taylor & Francis.

Nooteboom, S., & Marks, P. (2010). Adaptive networks as second order governance systems. *Systems Research and Behavioral Science, 27*(1), 61–69. 10.1002/sres.985.

Perez-Sindin, X., & Van Assche, K. (2020). From coal not to ashes but to what? As Pontes, social memory and the concentration problem. *The Extractive Industries and Society. 7*(3), 882–891. 10.1016/j.exis.2020.07.016.

Pérez-Sindín, X. S., & Van Assche, K. (2021). "Coal [from Colombia] is our life". Bourdieu, the miners (after they are miners) and resistance in As Pontes. *Resources Policy, 71*, 102006.

Schultz, L., & Fazey, I. (2009). Effective leadership for adaptive management. In C. Allan & G. H. Stankey (Eds.), *Adaptive environmental management: A practitioner's guide* (pp. 295–303). Netherlands: Springer. 10.1007/978-1-4020-9632-7_16.

Stavrakakis, Y. (2002). *Lacan and the political*. Routledge.

Thielmann, T., & Tollefson, C. (2009). Tears from an onion: Layering, exhaustion and conversion in British Columbia land use planning policy. *Policy and Society, 28*(2), 111–124. 10.1016/j.polsoc.2009.05.006.

Valentinov, V. (2014). The complexity–sustainability trade-off in Niklas Luhmann's social systems theory. *Systems Research and Behavioral Science, 31*(1), 14–22.

Valentinov, V. (2017). Materiality in natural resource management: A systems theory view. *Journal of Environmental Policy & Planning, 19*(3), 323–326.

Van Assche, K., Beunen, R., & Duineveld, M. (2013). *Evolutionary governance theory: An introduction*. Springer.

Van Assche, K., Beunen, R., Duineveld, M., & Gruezmacher, M. (2017). Power/knowledge and natural resource management: Foucaultian foundations in the analysis of adaptive governance. *Journal of Environmental Policy & Planning*.

Van Assche, K., & Djanibekov, N. (2012). Spatial planning as policy integration: The need for an evolutionary perspective. Lessons from Uzbekistan. *Land Use Policy, 29*(1), 179–186.

Van Assche, K., Gruezmacher, M., & Deacon, L. (2020). Land use tools for tempering boom and bust: Strategy and capacity building in governance. *Land Use Policy, 93*, 103994–103994. 10.1016/j.landusepol.2019.05.013.

Van Assche, K., Gruezmacher, M., & Granzow, M. (2021a). From trauma to fantasy and policy. The past in the futures of mining communities; the case of Crowsnest Pass, Alberta. *Resources Policy, 72*, 102050–102050. 10.1016/j.resourpol.2021.102050.

Van Assche, K., Verschraegen, G., & Gruezmacher, M. (2021b). Strategy for collectives and common goods: Coordinating strategy, long-term perspectives and policy domains in governance. *Futures, 128*, 102716–102716. 10.1016/j.futures.2021.102716.

Van Assche, K., Verschraegen, G., Valentinov, V., & Gruezmacher, M. (2019). The social, the ecological, and the adaptive. Von Bertalanffy's general systems theory and the adaptive governance of social-ecological systems. *Systems Research and Behavioral Science, 36*(3), 308–321.

Von Bertalanffy, L. (1969). *General system theory; foundations, development, applications* (Revised Edition, Issue 1968, p. 40). George Braziller.

Voß, J.-P., Bauknecht, D., & Kemp, R. (2006). *Reflexive governance for sustainable development*. Edward Elgar Publishing.

8

LEGACIES AND FUTURES IN THE GOVERNANCE OF RESOURCE COMMUNITIES

Memory and legacies in governance

Myriad relations exist between the past of a community and its possible futures. The past is remembered and this is a process of continuous reinterpretation and reconstruction. Some versions of the past are codified and become *history* and that history can play a role in the formation of policies, plans, future strategies. Other versions circulate as local knowledge and as institutional knowledge in governmental and other types of organizations. This knowledge of the past, this version of memory is also likely to play a role.

For the understanding of the linkages between the various legacies in the community and the way they affect the construction of futures, we need to go through governance, where collectively binding decisions are taken. This also means that the concepts of evolutionary governance theory which were introduced earlier, are useful especially when they speak of the rigidities introduced in governance paths (Van Assche et al., 2013). We must remind ourselves that futures are stories of a particular nature, with a particular status and well placed to be represented in strategies, as we will analyze later.

History as micro-history can play a role in governance, as the history of administration and politics itself can play a role in guiding decision-making and in identity formation in governance (Flyvbjerg, 1998; Howell et al., 2019). It is possible that transitions or shocks in governance lead to a re-examination of the past and maybe new production of official or academically approved history. It is also possible that emerging insight in academic history ends up on the political agenda or seeps into minds and discussions in governance (Sanz-Hernández, 2020; Van Assche et al., 2009).

DOI: 10.4324/9781003332145-8

Much more than history, *memory and* its twin *forgetting* play a role in governance. The social memories circulating in the community, their processes of transformation and competition exert continuous pressure on politics and administration, especially in democratic polities (Flyvbjerg, 1998; Legg, 2007). The more those polities hinge on participation and on localism, the more relevant this will be and the more the governance system will have to adapt to this type of pressure. New pasts can be suddenly conjured up, in relation to dissatisfaction with the present, or in relation to a new image of the future (and vice versa) (Borer, 2010). The memory of the political and administrative systems, will also play a role in the reproduction of the governance, providing identities which can help in orientation and coordination (Sandercock, 1998). One can add here the memory (and forgetting) of individual organizations, of ministries, departments, institutes, chambers of commerce, non-governmental organizations, which play a role in their self-understanding and ideas of their actual and ideal role in governance.

A governance system is not an organization, yet it relies on organizations. Those organizations can lose memory easily. Research in small communities in Alberta and British Columbia, many of them former resource communities, underscored the importance of administrative capacity and institutional memory for broadening the horizons, for discerning alternative paths. Local administrators come and go, lured away by higher urban salaries, jobs for the spouse, by more amenities for a growing family, and sometimes pushed away by a social environment felt as unwelcoming. When there is no money for full time staff, consultants are hired when money is available, often provincial money, with strings attached, also in terms of preferred consultants.

Thus, people come and go, their knowledge of the facts as well as the rules of the game also go. What remains is a neglected, understaffed, overburdened, sometimes systematically thwarted local administrations that pays less attention to the paperwork and that in addition must generate a later institutional history and underpin legitimacy of new decisions by historical reference. In some cases one administrator stays forever, over time dominating politics and acting as gatekeepers of memory for new staff, as well as for local politicians and residents. The attitude can be entirely unselfish, an adaptation to a low resource environment, with the motto 'I have to do everything myself.' In some cases the attitude can be less benevolent; the creation of a turf that has to be defended. In both cases, one of over-stability and one of transience, institutional memory is simplified and institutional capacity weakened.

Legacies of the different sorts mentioned earlier, can be present in the community *and in the governance system itself.* Material, cognitive and organizational (or institutional) legacies will affect the construction and use of official histories, the relation to academic and alternative histories and they will shape the types of social memories defined above, as well as their interplay (Grabher, 1993; Halseth & Sullivan, 2004). Memory and history, as mechanisms of binding time, can be seen as mechanisms *reinforcing* path dependencies. Restructuring memory and history, however, can also be interpreted as enabling *path creation* in governance. Discursive production of this sort never stops, as sensibilities, problems and values in the community continuously evolve, so this potential for path creation never disappears completely (Jakes et al., 2015).

Groups identify themselves by means of shared histories, futures and often place associations, just as place identities tend to incorporate memories, sometimes official histories and references to groups of people (Neill, 2003). Within the governance system, this means many things. It means first of all that place, history and group identity can be politicized and can have re-percussions for the evolution of governance. Many social memories will compete, combine, transform each other in partly unpredictable patterns. Legacies from the past influence how this pattern of relations between different memories plays out (Perez-Sindin & Van Assche, 2020).

Unraveling those legacies can be useful when reorientation in governance is expected; hence, the cultivation of reflexivity in governance, an increased awareness of the diversity of memories and legacies at play (Feindt & Weiland, 2018; Voß et al., 2006).

Forms of knowledge associated with certain stories once institutionalized can keep governance on a particular track (Clapp, 1998). These institution-alized stories can make it harder to produce new institutions which embody a different direction of development, perhaps incompatible with the institu-tionalized story, or make it harder to institutionalize other forms of knowl-edge which are similarly incompatible (Marais et al., 2021; Storey, 2016). Some stories are easier to doubt than others, easier to question, refute and change (Blomquist & Ostrom, 1985). On the knowledge side or discursive side, one can speak of *discursive configurations* or sets of discourses, entangled or embedded, which keep each other in place. Which means that they tend to be naturalized, that their truth tends to go unquestioned (Throgmorton, 2003). Institutionalized narratives reflecting an old ideology might still exert a strong pressure on the direction of governance, even when identity narratives and ideologies in the community are changing (Jordan, 2006).

In the United States (US), mining moved from east to west in the course of the 19th and early 20th centuries. From Appalachian coal to Michigan copper, Minnesota iron, and Montana metallic diversity, a similar collection of ethnic groups moved west, groups with histories in mining and stonecutting. Cornish roots remained visible in certain dishes, and hierarchies within the mines (with Anglo managers and foremen). The combination of Slovaks, Polish, Italians, Greeks can be traced from east to west, fed by new immigration from Europe but also by families maintaining both an ethnic and a miners' identity.

Social life in the mining towns remained organized along ethnic lines, later also per union or religion but the conglomerate of ethnicities remained similar and reinforced the new place identities of young mining towns. Place and social identity thus kept each other in place, despite short histories of mining. When people assimilated into American culture, when educational opportunities increased, and other industries popped up, this fragile set of relations unraveled.

Interdependence between actors and institutions and between institutions, is affected by discursive shifts, as actors can embrace new stories but institutions not readily. That is, actors can reinterpret existing institutions, can select other ones, but the institution itself, both its normative side and substantive aspect, cannot be reinterpreted at will, as most instances, concepts, intentions, goals, assumptions are spelled out. Therefore, interdependence between institutions further reduces this space for reinterpretation, take for example a constitution which cannot be easily changed while being implied in the production of other laws.

Legacies and futures

For the construction of futures, we know that remembering and forgetting in the community and in governance are fundamental. What is remembered about the community, what it identifies with, will naturally shape its construction of visions of the future (Van Assche et al., 2009; Welzer, 2010). Those memories that are interwoven with identity narratives are most likely to influence visions of the future (Neill, 2001). If that identity is linked to a strong and idealized version of the past, a return to that past is in the cards, meaning the construction of futures which appear as a resurgent past. If the identity is connected to a resource extraction which does not exist anymore, a return to the past is even more emphatically impossible, at the same time, the desire to do so might be stronger (Antze & Lambek, 2016; Howell et al., 2019).

Cognitive, organizational and material legacies will delimit the construction and functioning of futures in governance. For resource towns, these legacies, as we know, can entail the lack of development of alternative development scenarios, as the future was only conceived in terms of the resource (Busse & Gröning, 2013; Halseth & Sullivan, 2004; Lockie et al., 2009). We know that when people came to a place for a resource future, because the money to be made was much better, this tended to marginalize other activities. If the development takes place in a remote area and all infrastructure needs to be developed, the inclination to save cost and improve 'efficiency,' narrowly defined by providing only the basics for residents and focusing entirely on the resource activity, is even stronger. This creates material legacies which are hard to shake off.

The normalization of Rietspruit in Emalahleni, South Africa, was praised as best practice but it was not long before this optimism crumbled. The municipality's inability to maintain and manage the infrastructure that had been installed by the mining company has created local resistance. Many households did not want to own a house in Rietspruit. Elsewhere in Emalahleni, the closing of 17 company towns has increased the number of people in informal settlements (van der Watt & Marais, 2021). *In both cases, the mining companies transferred their long-term liabilities to the local municipality, and, in line with government policy, the Emalahleni Local Municipality was keen to take responsibility. However, this has put severe pressure on the infrastructure of a fragile municipality* (Campbell et al., 2017).

Once people share a certain mentality, a set of expectations regarding quality of life and environment, the situation becomes naturalized and alternatives are harder to imagine. A self-select process emerges, where newcomers are those attracted to economic incentives and the lifestyle and those locals not identifying with either move to the margins of community life or move out altogether. Those who stay have a chance to make good money but at the same time if things go sour, alternatives are hard to pursue (Venables, 2016).

Fort McMurray, Alberta, has long been the epicenter of oil extraction in Canada bringing workers from far and close. Although oil and oil extraction are a constant reference for the community, many have tried to imagine alternatives that could perhaps exist alongside the main economic activity. A young entrepreneur organized a canoeing business and for 10 years took visitors, mainly family and friends of oil workers, on trips up and down the Athabasca River. Accepting he was having difficulties in keeping his business afloat, he finally called it quits and took a job in the oil sector. In 1 year working there he made more money than in the previous 10 with his canoe bussiness.

Places identifying with fisheries for several centuries, where education is a fishing education, a job is a fishing job and administration is mainly the administration of the fish plant, have great difficulties in bringing in new voices in local government and governance, great difficulties in convincing voters that a more substantial and expensive administration might be needed. They have great difficulties in imagining something else beyond the fish, as their infrastructure, their location itself, their family and community identity, are tied up with the fisheries (Clapp, 1998; Hayter & Barnes, 2008; Venables, 2016).

Larger communities might be more tied to the extraction by more and more powerful interests, yet, they might have the resources and the internal variety to move in a different direction (Hayter, 2000). Specialization and institutional memory are likely stronger and this can help to discern signals in the environment that change might be needed.

Boom and bust and nostalgia

Many resource communities share an entrenched belief that trying to look into the future is useless and second, that whatever short term action or initiative comes up should be embraced, regardless of the long-term consequences or compatibility with existing strategies (Markey & Heisler, 2010). This pressure on time horizons in governance makes it more difficult to entertain long-term perspectives, further eroding the capacity to rethink existing futures or to construct new ones or to seek the space for such activity (Van Assche et al., 2020). The cycles of boom and bust often lead to a glorification of the past, of one boom period or a generalized 'good period' where things were supposedly better than in the current period. That does not mean that the period from which this past is observed is objectively a bust. It only means that there is a construction of a period that was supposedly better. We know from previous chapters that such golden period can become constructed as 'reality,' as reflecting the real character and the real potential of the community and everything that deviates from it is seen as unworthy and quite possibly, unreal (Hibbard & Davis, 1986).

The longing for a glorified past can be strong, while the actual functioning of the place in that past is not well-understood. This forgetting is a product of the loss of status and centrality and it makes it less likely that a return to anything resembling that past might be possible (Van Assche & Teampău, 2015). Such *deep forgetting* makes the construction of realistic futures in governance and community more difficult (Legg, 2007). When places are relegated to the economic and cultural margin and this happens easily in resource towns on a downturn, also because they are often located in a spatial and political margin to begin with, they easily forget the conditions of remembering and forgetting. The infrastructures to bring back what is forgotten are gone or crumbled and these infrastructures can be varied (Van Assche et al., 2009). The narrative of a glory period can take away responsibility for those in the present, while engendering resentments that are bound to have difficult implications in local politics (Liu & Hilton, 2005; Welzer, 2010).

Trauma and symbolic violence

We have mentioned in previous chapters that resource communities can be marked by trauma. Trauma at community level for us follows psychoanalysis, a non-remembering, a non-observation, because of experiences which were hard to incorporate in the collective memory and identity (Antze & Lambek, 2016; Borer, 2010; Erll & Nünning, 2008). What is observed is partial and only partially explained, barely connected to an accurate interpretation of the past and this in turn, puts pressure on the construction of past, present and future. A collapse of the economy, of the resource underpinning the economy, as well as the pains of extraction itself, can further prepare the ground for trauma, for further constraints in the construction of futures (Erikson, 1994; Renes, 2022). If identity is tied to a resource economy, that identity will be affected when the resource is gone, or the profits and lifestyles based on it are gone.

We know that a deeply troubled history, a deeply ambiguous relation *vis a vis* the leading companies, *vis a vis* political leadership, does not mean that more critical perspectives on the resource economy itself are likely to emerge. The centrality of the resource in identification makes it hard to find different ways to relate to the environment, to the future and painful histories are routinely whitewashed, as the central figure of the resource or resource company is needed to maintain the validity of community identity (Assmann & Czaplicka, 1995; Neill, 2003). Latent fear of collapse, in physical sense and in terms of community identity, blocks systematic questioning of the old authority, even if the relation was deeply problematic and leading to a series of symptoms affecting well-being in the present and a clear-headed view of future possibilities (Flyvbjerg, 2004).

Crowsnest Pass, a municipality in Alberta, Canada, was a booming coal mining area in the early 20th century and experienced several ups and downs until the last mine closed in the 1983. By then four towns had merged into the new municipality of Crowsnest Pass. In the neighboring communities of the province of British Columbia mining continued offering jobs to some Crowsnest residents and offering hope for a revival of mining locally. A history of weak local governance in the smaller mining towns preceding the merger, a communal life dominated by the mining company offering work to several generations in the same families, with a cultural life organized along ethnic and religious lines, led to a nostalgic new municipality, seeing the only desirable future as a return to the golden days of mining. At the same time these communities were being suspicious of alternative interpretations of past and future and dismissive of governance for the long term.

The Big Other of the mining company, which had structured life and imagination in the separate communities stayed alive after mining died and giving meaning to present and future without reference to a mining company was difficult. Local governance capacity was slowly enhanced, partly because of support and regulations emanating from the Provincial level, partly because some new residents did arrive, looking for mountain scenery and a more rural lifestyle. Yet, when in the years after 2010 a new narrative took over local politics for a while, the backlash with the next elections was serious, and in 2014 a new council took over, disappointed in the new and hoping for a return of the old.

In our interpretation, trauma left Crowsnest Pass scarred in the sense that extraction and closure created a dependence on an unacknowledged problematic behavior of the mining companies (and railroad companies, and provincial government). Thinking about alternative futures was blocked in governance and a repetition of moves in governance consists of dismissing planners, dismissing alternatives, glorifying the mines, hoping for a return of the mine. The trauma, in our view, is visible in this repetition but also in a different aspect of fantasy. It is visible when cracks in the nostalgic façade appear, a new vision might come through but there is not enough reflection on this new future, one can say it isn't tested but simply accepted. Both the collective imagination and the tools of governance show legacies of the mining past, creating difficulties imagining and organizing for the future. When swindlers show up with entirely unrealistic tourism development ideas for example, it is hard to recognize these ideas as fantasies.

Resource communities are prone to histories of symbolic violence. Symbolic violence can appear, as we noticed, in different manifestations, one of them being the silent acceptance of the suffering coming with resource extraction and living in a resource community (Borer, 2010; Burawoy, 2019). Silent acceptance can still lead to trauma, however, and it can also lead to creative re-appropriation, to the construction of new identities incorporating elements imposed from elsewhere into a new frame. The diversity of forms of symbolic violence in resource communities can only be understood by widening our perspective, beyond the community and to the broader society that establishes resource communities and demands resources, as we illustrated in Chapter 4. If people are forced to work in a mine, the violence is not symbolic anymore. If their only option for employment is in a mine and their previous identity is expected to fade quickly, this is symbolic violence. The power relations in and around the community thus produce an array of potentialities for symbolic violence (Marais, 2013, 2022).

Symbolic violence has implications for the functioning of memory, as new memories are created under its pressure. Behaviours in resource communities, especially if dominated by a few players and especially if expected to serve higher purposes (e.g., supporting a regime, a dominant group), are expected to adjust quickly to the functioning of the community which at the same time is firmly placed under the master signifier of the resource. Long working hours, a simplified social and cultural life, limited tolerance for expression of alternative views, or of alternative identities, contribute to the pervasiveness of symbolic violence in resource communities (Hayter, 2000; Lockie et al., 2009). In places where workers are not allowed to participate in local governance, for instance when they are flown in and out or live in camps at the margins or as foreigners with a poor immigration status, they become subject to a form of symbolic violence, further aggravating the concentration problem in governance (Campbell et al., 2017; Douglass, 1998; Markey et al., 2011).

The Ruhr region was the industrial powerhouse of Germany for almost a century. Prussia acquired it after the Napoleonic Wars and started with coal mining and steel industry right away. By the late 19th century the region had become the most densely populated region in Germany, but in a deconcentrated pattern that can only be explained by the location of coal mines and steel mills.

The intensity of activity and the pattern of infrastructure development and waterways made for pervasive pollution. These were yet more reasons to run away when industries started to collapse in the 1960s. A combination of federal and regional investment plus stricter environmental regulation in the 1970s was used to clean up pollution and to seize this as an opportunity to develop expertise which could be sold to other places later and also used to develop related expertise on green energy and sustainability transitions. Thus, a material legacy triggered a response in governance (material dependency) which proved adaptive. Note that even in this success story, the numbers of jobs in the new industry (in the tens of thousands) did not match the old industry (in the hundreds of thousands).

Thus, governance reflects memory processes in the community and it also enables the creation of memory in the community (Assmann & Czaplicka, 1995; Hoelscher & Alderman, 2004). This can happen piecemeal or in a concerted strategy, aiming at promoting some identities, pasts and futures and weakening others. Organizational and cognitive legacies put pressure on the processes of remembering and forgetting, influence their selectivity, while material legacies, including the state of the built environment and the landscape, make it easier to promote certain histories than others (Butters et al., 2018). A conscious and collective effort at examination of the past can move a community in a different direction, can break open the deadlock in the construction of community futures. The past shapes what can consciously drive decisions in the future, but also the unconscious dimension of governance (Van Assche et al., 2009).

In the Romanian Danube Delta, a variety of natural resources have been used for centuries: not only fish but also reed and many other things nature has offered. When Romania became communist after World War II, the Delta offered promise for fishing, fish farming, fish processing, reed cultivation, and extraction of fine sand. In a less overtly way it also offered a suitably inaccessible place for political prisons. After seeing the Dutch polders, strongman Nicolae Ceaucescu believed that the 'useless' parts of the Delta should be turned into agricultural land and what was first a collection of mostly uncoordinated projects now had to coalesce into a 'complex plan' for the Delta.

The narrative was one of communist economic development, of unused potential of the land, and the tool was that of a highly ambitious and integrated plan, developed mostly by engineers, and mostly kept secret in its entirety. An institute was established in Sulina just outside the Delta, to produce the expertise and detailed plans to make it possible. Yet, failures were not reported, resources diverted or simply not sufficient, and internal power tactics made coordination even more difficult. The low soil quality agronomists found under the wetlands was kept secret, and engineering problems postponed but never solved. The result was that by the collapse of communism (1989) the complex plan was not fully implemented, which then left an opening for nature conservation to take over as the policy focus afterwards, with the establishment of the DDBRA, Danube Delta Biosphere Reserve Authority (1993).

The authoritarian character of planning for the Delta, its perceived importance for the nation, did not take local opinion into account, nor other experts, nor anyone contradicting the unrealistic ambitions of the leader. Meanwhile, people were moved in to urbanize some villages and the rich and multi-cultural history of the area was almost erased, as was the natural history. As actual governance capacity was limited, and further diminished because of competition and secrecy, the plan largely failed and damaged social and ecological systems so much that only a small base for reinvention remained. With recent policies under the flag of 'sustainable development,' neither sustainable nor development were well understood locally, local governance capacity was not fully restored, so the legacies of communist strategy left behind severe limitations for strategy afterwards, aiming at different goals.

Futures in resource communities

Futures are narratives, imaginations of the futures which play out in governance, some of them produced in governance, others entering from the outside. We know that futures, in order to have an effect, are about thinking and organizing and that thinking is about analyzing and imagining (Beunen & Barba Lata, 2021; Doganova & Kornberger, 2021).

We understand now that futures in resource communities are under a particular set of pressures, some of which we summarized under the heading of 'concentration problems.' We also know that the concept of the concentration problem does not cover all possible and typical relations between past and present in resource communities. We do know now that resource communities are prone to develop concentration problems. We know that they are prone to histories of trauma and symbolic violence. Concentration problems, trauma and symbolic violence, modify the relations between past, present and future in resource communities. In a place where the resource economy is dominant and where that has been the case for a long time, we can expect a greater pressure to focus on that particular activity and therefore we can expect the concentration problem to persist.

Futures will have to *pass through* governance, in order to be endowed with legitimacy, become the subject of discussion and deliberation in legitimate arenas and become coupled to policy tools. It is in governance that futures will acquire a form which makes it possible to couple futures and policy tools making them implementable through policies, plans and laws guiding the community towards a more open future (Feindt & Weiland, 2018; Voß et al., 2006).

Both the imagining and the organizing of futures need to have a secure place in local governance, this cannot simply be a process of accepting and implementing futures which emerged in the community. One can add a third aspect of the process here; *testing* futures. In this regard both deliberation in the political sphere and the critical analysis in the administrative sphere are important (Van Assche et al., 2020; Voß & Bornemann, 2011). Imagining, organizing and testing futures are all subjected to learning processes and this learning takes place in governance. Critical discussions in politics and administration, in the broader circles making up governance, can produce new futures and if this is at the same time a reflexive process of learning, it can make the next discussion more productive. In other words: a discussion on a possible future can teach everyone about that future but can also teach about the process of constructing futures (Dunlop & Radaelli, 2020).

In resource communities, marked by the problems we discussed at length, the imagining, organizing and testing of futures, the reflexive learning processes which could make this easier, can all be affected by a history of a single focus; focusing on one thing. Focusing on one thing means learning for that single thing, maintaining the tools, the imagination for that single thing and therefore not testing and relying on the tools of coordination for that single purpose. This also explains why, when, against all odds and maybe after a shock, an alternative future is considered, this future is often at odds with the real options available, why it often has the character of fantasy (Glynos & Stavrakakis, 2008). Which then leads to disappointment and to a loss of trust and interest in governance and its capacity to artic-ulate policy for the longer term and to move the community in a different direction. A bad experience with a certain idea in combination to a lack of internal deliberation, imagination, testing and coordinative capacity, makes for a poor assessment of the experience.

On the Halsnaes Peninsula, Hundested is a harbor town in North Zealand, Denmark. Around the harbor were a number of businesses, including the Hundested Motor Plant, which through many generations produced dependable engines for Danish fishing cutters, as well as the coal import, fish auction, smokehouse, canning factory, boatyard, and fish auction. With the addition of a new ferry port in 1969, a cargo port in 1987 and a container port in 1995, port expansions continued. Many businesses, including those in the metal and plastic industries, were founded in an industrial area east of the city in the 1960s and 1970s. Hundested was severely impacted by the 1980s collapse in fishing and allied industries, and the ferry service Hundested-Gren failed in 1996. Yet, the population did not stop growing. The community managed to reinvent its own economy through internal deliberation, imagination, testing and a healthy coordinative capacity. A fishing port, a ferry port, a cargo port, a container port, and a yacht port may all be found in Hundested Harbor today. In the harbor, there are several fishmongers but also a glassblowing facility. A few artists are contributing to the revitalization of the waterfront, including those organizing the yearly sand sculpture festival. Interest in the town grows and with *it more enterprises have come to the port like a brewery opened in the former blacksmith shop. The Fisheries and Harbor House chronicles the history of the port. Also, a maritime experience center is being built in new structures at Hundested Harbour. (Hundested\ lex.dk, 2017)*

Towards a bridging synthesis

In the previous sections of this chapter, we re-introduced and re-connected the key ideas from the preceding chapters in a narrative manner. Now, we will further condense the argument, and, as a concise synthesis, present this as a bridge to the next part of the book, which is dedicated to looking forward, to visioning and strategizing. We structure this section as a series of theoretical vignettes, each providing a partial synthesis of ideas already encountered.

1 Past and future are created in the present. It is in the present, that memories and history are constructed, and futures assembled. Preoccupations of the present are essential, as well as legacies from the past, in shaping the construction of futures and pasts. Some memories coalesce into an official history, others do not. A diversity of social memories with a presence in governance is helpful in furthering resilience and adaptive capacity. Some futures can coalesce into visions and strategies.

2 The past of a community produces memories and identities which mutually shape each other. Social identities stabilize memories and vice versa. They can produce and link to other narratives, which can then gain greater prominence in governance through such association. Once ideas, often derived from narratives, are encoded in institutions, their more rigid pattern of change gives the ideas and narratives a longer leash on life. They can become unexamined assumptions or remain a topic of discussion in governance.

3 Social identity has a double nature, as narrative identity and autopoietic identity, yet each aspect of this nature serves to stabilize the community and its governance. Governance itself further serves to both stabilize the community and give it options to transform. Neither narrative nor autopoietic identities are entirely transparent, but it is practically and theoretically possible to unearth the narrative underpinnings of community and governance, while the autopoietic reproduction of governance can per definition not be entirely elucidated.

4 Legacies (e.g., of a history of resource dominance) can be found in the community and its governance system. A central legacy in the case of resource communities is the formation of a resource identity which is present in local governance and other aspects of community life. A resource identity can shape futures and pasts, and influences the observation of the physical, economic and cultural environment. Legacies of

extraction histories affect both autopoietic and narrative identity, with each shaping memory and future. Identity and memory form a tight coupling, which stabilizes governance.

5 Legacies (of resource dominance) in governance deserve special attention because it is in governance that possible transformation of the community has to be decided. Evolutionary governance theory helps us in giving us an image of governance and the enablers and constraints for self-transformation. Resource legacies can thus be found to affect power relations (including patterns of inclusion and exclusion), selectivity in knowledge and narratives present in debates, in administration, encoded in institutions (policies, plans, laws). Resource legacies can be visible in the use, articulation, forgetting, implementation of institutions, in the relation between formal and informal institutions.

6 Still in terms of EGT, resource legacies can shape, often through the mediation of memory and identity, the pattern of dependencies in governance, which means that the possibilities of transformation will be affected. The balance between path dependence and path creation, the pattern of interdependence, unobserved material dependencies, goal dependencies, all of this can be molded through a history of resource centrality. Understanding the history, the alteration of dependencies and the resulting options for self-transformation is helpful. Goal dependencies will have to be maximized, rendered transparent, and guided towards intended reality effects, in order to make any future strategy work.

7 One can summarize the effects of resource legacies on future governance as limitations on the imagination and organization of possible futures. Some legacies pertain more to the domain of imagination (effects on narratives, identities, observation), some more on the organization, on creation of strategies and their implementation (institutions, patterns of inclusion and exclusion, materiality, resources).

8 In the case of resource communities, many effects or legacies of a history of dominance can be analyzed as *observation* problems. Or, the pattern of transparency and opacity is altered, the possibilities to observe self, governance system, community, and environment, and hence to understand functioning, (lack of) integration, and realistic futures. This can be seen as limited observation, limited diversity of memory, of knowledge and topics in governance, and limits to the testing of ideas, especially ideas about the future, when they do come up. The options to discern the contingent nature of identities, memories, policies, economies and environment are reduced as diversity and redundancy are lacking, as few mechanisms of correction, adaptation and enrichment survive the pressures and selectivities of a history of resource dominance.

9 For resource communities, this can lead to a variety of situations where opacity of past, present and future lead to problems. Some have been

FIGURE 8.1 Legacies in governance and community futures. Different types of legacies in governance shape the organizational futures as well as the imagined futures of a community.

labeled as concentration problems, where simplification in co-evolution is the essence, others as community trauma and legacies of symbolic violence, where inaccessible pasts and invisible legacies of those pasts create trouble. One other path leads to what we can call weak governance, to few options to coordinate action, and to corruption, crime and disillusionment. Another path leads to the dissolution of the community, if governance, either formal or informally based, cannot provide for basic services, for basic levels of identification and trust, for elementary levels of economic prosperity and social support. (Figure 8.1)

It is important to note that the analyses which led to our discerning of such sad possible futures, also indicate that none of those paths is entirely autonomous, mechanically self-reproducing or self-reinforcing. What makes them look natural in some cases is the activity of people, of individuals, groups and governance systems which *naturalize through narrative* that a certain future is unavoidable, a certain identity fixed forever, and a certain past perfectly remembered.

References

Antze, P., & Lambek, M. (Eds.). (2016). *Tense past* (0 ed.). Routledge. 10.4324/9781315022222.

Assmann, J., & Czaplicka, J. (1995). Collective memory and cultural identity. *New German Critique, 65*, 125. 10.2307/488538.

Beunen, R., & Barba Lata, I. (2021). What makes long-term perspectives endure? Lessons from Dutch nature conservation. *Futures, 126*, 102679–102679. 10.1016/j.futures.2020.102679.

Blomquist, W., & Ostrom, E. (1985). Institutional capacity and the resolution of a commons dilemma. *Review of Policy Research, 5*(2), 383–394. 10.1111/j.1541-1338.1985.tb00364.x.

Borer, M. I. (2010). From collective memory to collective imagination: Time, place, and urban redevelopment. *Symbolic Interaction, 33*(1), 96–114. 10.1525/si.2010.33.1.96.

Burawoy, M. (2019). *Symbolic violence: Conversations with Bourdieu.* Duke University Press.

Busse, M., & Gröning, S. (2013). The resource curse revisited: Governance and natural resources. *Public Choice, 154*(1), 1–20. 10.1007/s11127-011-9804-0.

Butters, L., Okusipe, O. M., Eledi, S. B., & Vodden, K. (2018). Engaging the past to create a new future: A comparative study of heritage-driven community development initiatives in the Great Northern Peninsula. *Journal of Rural and Community Development, 12*(2–3), 186–209.

Campbell, M., Nel, V., & Mphambukeli, T. (2017). A thriving coal mining city in crisis? The governance and spatial planning challenges at Witbank, South Africa. *Land Use Policy, 62*, 223–231. 10.1016/j.landusepol.2016.12.027.

Clapp, R. A. (1998). The resource cycle in forestry and fishing. *The Canadian Geographer/ Le Géographe Canadien, 42*(2), 129–144. 10.1111/j.1541-0064.1998.tb01560.x.

Doganova, L., & Kornberger, M. (2021). Strategy's futures. *Futures, 125*, 102664–102664. 10.1016/j.futures.2020.102664.

Douglass, W. A. (1998). The mining camp as community. In *Social Approaches to an Industrial Past.* Routledge.

Dunlop, C., & Radaelli, C. (2020). The lessons of policy learning: Types, triggers, hindrances and pathologies. In G. Capano & M. Howlett, *A modern guide to public policy* (pp. 222–241). Edward Elgar Publishing. 10.4337/9781789904987.00024.

Erikson, K. (1994). *A new species of trouble: Explorations in disaster, trauma, and community.* Norton.

Erll, A., & Nünning, A. (Eds.). (2008). *Cultural memory studies.* Walter de Gruyter GmbH & Co.KG. 10.1515/9783110207262.

Feindt, P. H., & Weiland, S. (2018). Reflexive governance: Exploring the concept and assessing its critical potential for sustainable development. Introduction to the special issue. *Journal of Environmental Policy & Planning, 20*(6), 661–674. 10.1080/1523908X.2018.1532562.

Flyvbjerg, B. (1998). *Rationality and power: Democracy in practice.* University of Chicago press.

Flyvbjerg, B. (2004). Phronetic planning research: Theoretical and methodological reflections. *Planning Theory & Practice, 5*(3), 283–306. 10.1080/1464935042000250195.

Glynos, J., & Stavrakakis, Y. (2008). Lacan and political subjectivity: Fantasy and enjoyment in psychoanalysis and political theory. *Subjectivity, 24*(1), 256–274. 10.1057/sub.2008.23.

Grabher, G. (1993). The weakness of strong ties; The lock-in of regional development in Ruhr area. In *The embedded firm; On the socioeconomics of industrial networks* (pp. 255–277). Routledge. https://ci.nii.ac.jp/naid/10030364606/en/

Halseth, G., & Sullivan, L. (2004). From Kitimat to Tumbler Ridge: A crucial lesson not learned in resource-town planning. *Western Geography, 13*(14), 132–160.

Hayter, R. (2000). Single industry resource towns. In E. Sheppard, & T. J. Barnes (Eds.), *A companion to economic geography* (pp. 290–307). Blackwell Publishing Ltd.

Hayter, R., & Barnes, T. J. (2008). Canada's resource economy. *The Canadian Geographer / Le Géographe Canadien, 45*(1), 36–41. 10.1111/j.1541-0064.2001.tb01165.x.

Hibbard, M., & Davis, L. (1986). When the going gets tough: Economic reality and the cultural myths of small-town America. *Journal of the American Planning Association, 52*(4), 419–428. 10.1080/01944368608977114.

Hoelscher, S., & Alderman, D. H. (2004). Memory and place: Geographies of a critical relationship. *Social & Cultural Geography, 5*(3), 347–355. 10.1080/146493 6042000252769.

Howell, J. P., Kitson, J., & Clowney, D. (2019). Environments past: Nostalgia in environmental policy and governance. *Environmental Values, 28*(3), 305–323. 10.3197/ 096327119X15519764179809.

Hundested | lex.dk. (2017, May 4). Den Store Danske. https://denstoredanske.lex.dk/ Hundested.

Jakes, S., Hardison-Moody, A., Bowen, S., & Blevins, J. (2015). Engaging community change: The critical role of values in asset mapping. *Community Development, 46*(4), 392–406.

Jordan, J. A. (2006). *Structures of memory: Understanding Urban change in Berlin and beyond.* Stanford University Press.

Legg, S. (2007). Reviewing geographies of memory/forgetting. *Environment and Planning A: Economy and Space, 39*(2), 456–466. 10.1068/a38170.

Liu, J. H., & Hilton, D. J. (2005). How the past weighs on the present: Social representations of history and their role in identity politics. *British Journal of Social Psychology, 44*(4), 537–556. 10.1348/014466605X27162.

Lockie, S., Franettovich, M., Petkova-Timmer, V., Rolfe, J., & Ivanova, G. (2009). Coal mining and the resource community cycle: A longitudinal assessment of the social impacts of the Coppabella coal mine. *Environmental Impact Assessment Review, 29*(5), 330–339. 10.1016/j.eiar.2009.01.008.

Marais, L. (2013). The impact of mine downscaling on the free state Goldfields. *Urban Forum, 24*(4), 503–521. 10.1007/s12132-013-9191-3.

Marais, L. (2022). *The social impacts of mine closure in South Africa: Housing policy and place attachment.* Taylor & Francis.

Marais, L., Nel, V., Rani, K., Rooyen, D. van, Sesele, K., Watt, P. van der, & Plessis, L. du. (2021). Economic transitions in South Africa's secondary cities: Governing mine closures. *Politics and Governance, 9*(2), 381–392. 10.17645/pag.v9i2.4032.

Markey, S., & Heisler, K. (2010). Getting a fair share: Regional development in a rapid boom-bust rural setting. *Canadian Journal of Regional Science, 33*(3), 49–62.

Markey, S., Storey, K., & Heisler, K. (2011). Fly-in/fly-out resource developments: Implications for community and regional development. In *Demography at the Edge.* Routledge.

Neill, W. (2001). Memory, spatial planning and the construction of cultural identity in Belfast and Berlin—An overview. In H.-U. Schwedler (Ed.), *Urban planning and cultural inclusion: Lessons from Belfast and Berlin* (pp. 3–23). Palgrave Macmillan UK. 10.1057/9780230524064_1.

Neill, W. (2003). *Urban planning and cultural identity.* Routledge.

Perez-Sindin, X., & Van Assche, K. (2020). From coal not to ashes but to what? As Pontes, social memory and the concentration problem. *The extractive industries and society, 7*(3), 882–891. 10.1016/j.exis.2020.07.016.

Renes, H. (2022). Landscapes of conflict and trauma. In H. Renes (Ed.), *Landscape, heritage and national identity in modern Europe* (pp. 63–69). Springer International Publishing. 10.1007/978-3-031-09536-8_7.

Sandercock, L. (1998). *Making the invisible visible: A multicultural planning history.* University of California Press.

Sanz-Hernández, A. (2020). How to change the sources of meaning of resistance identities in historically coal-reliant mining communities. *Energy Policy, 139,* 111353. 10.1016/j.enpol.2020.111353.

Storey, K. (2016). The evolution of commute work in the resource sectors in Canada and Australia. *The Extractive Industries and Society, 3*(3), 584–593. 10.1016/j.exis. 2016.02.009.

Throgmorton, J. A. (2003). Planning as persuasive storytelling in a global-scale web of relationships. *Planning Theory, 2*(2), 125–151.

Van Assche, K., Beunen, R., & Duineveld, M. (2013). *Evolutionary governance theory: An introduction.* Springer.

Van Assche, K., Devlieger, P., Teampau, P., & Verschraegen, G. (2009). Forgetting and remembering in the margins: Constructing past and future in the Romanian Danube Delta. *Memory Studies, 2*(2), 211–234. 10.1177/1750698008102053.

Van Assche, K., Gruezmacher, M., & Deacon, L. (2020). Land use tools for tempering boom and bust: Strategy and capacity building in governance. *Land Use Policy, 93,* 103994–103994. 10.1016/j.landusepol.2019.05.013.

Van Assche, K., & Teampău, P. (2015). *Local cosmopolitanism: Imagining and (re-) making privileged places.* Springer.

van der Watt, P., & Marais, L. (2021). Implementing social and labour plans in South Africa: Reflections on collaborative planning in the mining industry. *Resources Policy, 71,* 101984. 10.1016/j.resourpol.2021.101984.

Venables, A. J. (2016). Using natural resources for development: Why has it proven so difficult? *Journal of Economic Perspectives, 30*(1), 161–184. 10.1257/jep.30.1.161.

Voß, J.-P., Bauknecht, D., & Kemp, R. (2006). *Reflexive governance for sustainable development.* Edward Elgar Publishing.

Voß, J.-P., & Bornemann, B. (2011). The politics of reflexive governance: Challenges for designing adaptive management and transition management. *Ecology and Society, 16*(2). https://www.jstor.org/stable/26268901.

Welzer, H. (2010). Re-narrations: How pasts change in conversational remembering. *Memory Studies, 3*(1), 5–17. 10.1177/1750698009348279.

9

TRIPPING OVER THE REAL

Why strategies often do not work in resource communities

Introduction

This chapter forms a transition towards the sections on strategizing. We will be approaching obstacles to strategizing before discussing strategizing because in our view many of these obstacles emerge from the legacies discussed in the previous chapters. Now that we have discussed the issues of memory and legacy, of remembering and forgetting, it is good to discuss the implications of these patterns in community and in governance for the creation of obstacles for implementation. Sometimes, these will be visible in earlier stages, in strategy formulation and visioning, as might seem logical already, given the ideas presented in Chapter 8.

We can distinguish between two categories of issues, which are often not distinguished. First, there are the issues of implementation, of translating futures to reality. These are issues of steering, of path creation, where we need to deal with unacknowledged complexity and unacknowledged dependencies and systems relations (Barrett, 2004; Hood & Peters, 2004; Leong & Howlett, 2021). Unanticipated side effects of policy and planning that have certainly been observed for a long time and classics have been written on this topic. There is the importance of contingency, which is often not observed, the dynamics of discourse and the interplay between power and knowledge, which performs the function of a driver in governance (Van Assche et al., 2014). These ideas will be briefly elaborated below but are summarized now because they can all be seen as belonging to the category of *not seeing reality*. They are all obstacles to implementation stemming from a non-observation (for a various of reasons) of what *could have been observed* without many problems by an uninterested outsider who takes the effort to ask and combine

DOI: 10.4324/9781003332145-9

a variety of sources to reconstruct the path of governance and the relation between governance, community and environment (van de Mosselaer & Duineveld, 2021). This does not mean that the outsider could have foreseen or prevented all problems or that he or she could have formulated a procedure where all problems could have been avoided.

A second type of obstacles, harder to analyze but with observable effects, stem from what we call, following the psychoanalysis of Jacques Lacan, encounters with the Real (Eyers, 2012; Stavrakakis, 2002; Zizek, 1992). We encountered Lacan in Chapter 5, where the Real already appeared. We can thus speak of tripping over reality and tripping over the Real. Speaking of tripping over the Real implies limits of observation which cause governance systems to miss things which come back with a vengeance (Roberts, 2009; Valentinov et al., 2019). This must be unraveled, analyzed and on the other hand reconciled with empirically attested cases where realities are successfully ignored for a very long time, where the tripping can be postponed for a very long time. Stacked support mechanisms, in institutions, in power/knowledge relations, enable the system to maintain its course, against growing resistance, which is still not observed, or otherwise explained away. The underlying distinction is therefore between the Real, as a concept derived from Jacques Lacan's work and reality, where reality can be understood as discursively constructed, or not, but where that reality can suddenly show cracks, shifts, ruptures, slow erosions of persuasive quality. Those we consider, following Lacan, intrusions of the Real (Eyers, 2012; Fink, 1995).

The Real has to be understood as both an external and an internal limit, where outside forces and occurrences can suddenly intrude and the frameworks of meanings have to accommodate them. And where our own observational capacity as individuals and as administrative organizations, is structured and limited by a history of interactions, forgotten but leaving an imprint, with external environments (Gunder & Hillier, 2009; Hillier & Gunder, 2003). Tripping over the Real thus has a double sense from the start. Both internal and external environments partly elude observation and understanding, and this has effects not only on the old question of 'implementation' later on in the governance process, but on other aspects of governance as well, including the formation of futures, the strategies of negotiation and interaction, the images of roles, competition over resources, patterns of inclusion and exclusion, of policy integration (Moyaert, 1996; Pressman & Wildavsky, 1984).

Implementation obstacles and reality

Let us first discuss, briefly by necessity, some of the key insights emerging from the literatures on tripping over reality, after which we can return to Lacan and the Real. In this, we need to establish general principles, but also to look what might be special here for resource communities. Why is the tripping different for resource communities? The answer cannot be complete, but partial answers do appear, linking to the insights of Chapter 8, on their particular relation between past and future.

Hood and Peters (2004) helpfully summarized three traditions of 'surprise' in studies of policy administration. They highlighted the importance of culture, in the organization and the community, for unexpected results of policies, plans, even laws. In line with systems theories, they recognized unrecognized complexity as a second source of surprise, arguing that complex systems cannot be predictable because their pattern of feedback loops does not allow for linear responses. Third, they recognized the Mertonian tradition of understanding unanticipated and unintended consequences as stemming from a set of factors reflecting configurations of power and knowledge. Some factors stem from lack of information or wrong information, others from intentions, power relations and strategies and then there are those clearly reflecting power/knowledge interactions, such as overly focusing on the short term (driven by other's strategies and one's own).

One can rephrase the problem of surprise as a problem of steering in governance, a rephrasing which brings us to a different landscape of literatures. Better steering means less tripping and better steering, we argue, comes from an understanding of governance paths (Boston, 2021; Nair & Howlett, 2017; Van Assche et al., 2021). That is, a better understanding of the co-evolution of governance, community and environment can give a better idea of the effect of a policy or plan, of a vision or strategy. Understanding these co-evolutions means an understanding of the dependencies introduced earlier. If one is familiar with the pattern of dependencies in governance and the couplings with community and environment, then it is easier to see what could happen when a policy is enacted, without ever taking away all contingencies and uncertainties. Any steering attempt will trigger responses and adaptations that are partly unpredictable, but the deeper the insight in systems relations, the less unpredictable these responses will be.

In a deeply unpopular regime we can expect new rules will likely not be followed. If they are, maybe due to coercion, people might vent their frustration in other ways, maybe by breaking other rules, or undermining the regime in spots perceived as weaker. Conversely, if people are used to planning and trust it, they are likely to comply with planning rules and critiques will not start from a fundamental disbelief in the power of planning. If a government is not trusted at all, if their version of the public interest is perceived as private interest, then grand visions coming from that government are likely to be dismissed and if the visions are pushed, counterpressure and resistance will probably build.

The nature of the object of steering is relevant, in understanding the potential for tripping. Is this object recognized in the community?

Is it found important and clearly connected to a problem or desire they identify or identify with? Was it a product of governance itself? Was it promoted by one actor? Or was it a result of co-construction in governance, or maybe in a more participatory process endowing it with stronger legitimacy? Or, maybe there is a material dependency at play and the object was quickly constructed as a response to an environmental change. The resources available to governance and community to understand the object and its receptiveness to steering, are factors to consider.

A history of disappointment in steering makes it harder to steer later. A history of tripping makes it more likely new strategies will trip over reality. This is the case, we know now, because the thing one is tripping over is not the same anymore, it is changing in response to the making of plans and it is changing in response to the observation of those plans by people who can act and think unpredictably and cynically (Perdue & Pavela, 2012; Perez-Sindin & Van Assche, 2020). A history of failed plans makes planning very unlikely, unless a new set of actors emerges in conjunction with a shift in discourse, maybe identity. Yet, a history of non-planning makes for a similarly formidable obstacle.

Recent trends in theory and practice towards decentralization and participation in governance have many benefits, discussed elsewhere, but come with drawbacks as well. Steering remains possible but the predictability of governance is reduced because more people and organizations become involved, because procedures will be longer, more ideas and stories will be included. In general, steering under decentralization and multi-level governance is more difficult (Kooij et al., 2014). This does not entail that path creation is impossible, simply that rapid decision-making and implementation become less common. The task of coordination which is central to governance but even more in strategy for change, will become more formidable.

The centralization of power which makes it easy to connect expert and political perspectives has many problematic sides, but implementation is indeed easier. Thinking and organizing are easier to couple in centralized systems of governance, democratic or otherwise. Decentralized systems relying on more participation offer the potential for longer-term stability because of continued support and legitimacy (Luhmann, 1990). A local focus of governance can however mean that local communities do not have the support, the expertise, the perspective and understanding of problems and opportunities, which might be necessary. Organizational tools might be missing and the insight that they are missing. Localized realities will be richer in some ways yet simplified in others; while central steering can trip over local knowledge and feelings, localism can trip over unobserved environments, bigger issues and silent assumptions.

Not all resources are associated with communities, and, even when this is the case, their capacity to strategize might be limited. Rare earth minerals are a case in point. They are essential to modern technologies. Seventeen minerals are usually classified as rare earths and a distinction is made between light ones such as lanthanum, neodymium and others and heavy ones such as terbium and gadolinium. Rare earths extraction is a laborious and environmentally costly process requiring large mines, extensive tailing ponds with polluted sludge and the used of toxic products involved in the separation of the minerals. Workers and residents can therefore get sick in various ways, leaking tailing ponds being just one of them. The US, in particular one Californian mine, was the main global producer of rare earths from the 1940s to the 80s. Chinese industrial policy boosted the national production since the 1990s, leading to a global dependence on Chinese rare earths. Since 2010 there has been a contentious debate on export tariffs and a frantic search in the rest of the world for alternative reserves. Meanwhile, the Californian mine closed due to environmental problems (leaking waste water). In 2022, Swedish deposits were discovered in Kiruna, while Canada was already known to hold 40–50% of world reserves and known for not doing much with it.

Rare earths 'communities' are hard to find as their extraction is largely a recent matter, the locations tend to be remote and unrelated to previous patterns of agriculture and habitation. Only in some cases, significant rare earth deposits are associated with resources which were already extracted and associated with communities (such as Kiruna, Sweden). The location of processing plants is more relevant for the idea of 'rare earth communities' and those plants can be more easily associated with existing metallurgical operations and their skilled workforce. As these minerals are so directly tied to geo-politics the communities which are equipped to process (or new ones) will be under increased pressure and will likely see a reduced autonomy as they play a central role in national or transnational strategies.

Less tripping and more adaptation

Better steering, less tripping, also means that there are options for adaptations. And this means that, for longer term and more ambitious endeavors like the sort that might be needed for reinvention of resource communities, implementation cannot be understood as a matter of pushing a button and then hoping for conformity with the stated intentions of policy or strategy. Blueprint planning in modernist style might have worked sometimes in the sense that a large project was built, but in the time it took to design and build, it often became clear that the plan or design was not the best one. In regional design projects, or land consolidation project, the timeframe can be decades and optimizing a landscape for a certain agricultural production, for a certain pattern of settlements, might make no sense anymore after project implementation (Pressman & Wildavsky, 1984). Lack of adaptation and adaptation mechanisms in governance is hence another reason for tripping over reality.

A perfect design of the governance system does not exist. One aspect of such unavoidable imperfection is that an optimization for one aspect of governance entails problems for other aspects. One can speak of tradeoffs, the kind of tradeoffs familiar to engineers and designers, who know that no car can be designed for speed, price, robustness and beauty at the same time. A balance must be struck. In governance, steering and adaptation are similarly impossible to optimize at the same time. This does not mean that they are incompatible; steering can happen through adaptive mechanisms, relying on feedback inside and outside governance. Yet, there are necessary limits to the feedback and its integration, as what comes back might contradict other elements of feedback and might contradict basic assumptions or goals of the policy or strategy (Van Assche et al., 2021).

In order to find a desirable balance between adaptation and steering, a balance which enables observation of the changing environment and minimizes tripping over reality, it is useful to distinguish between different forms of adaptation. Some forms are unintentional, a result of the routines of the governance system and the informal institutions in the community. Others are intentional and short term and among those some are part of a longer-term strategy while others are truly *ad hoc* adaptations. Some *ad hoc* adaptations require political intervention while others rely on staff, on administration. Sometimes, adaptation needs a long-term perspective in governance and a longer-term strategy to move in a desired direction or to mitigate a problem which can hamper the community in the longer term (Howlett, 2009; Nair & Howlett, 2017). Climate change is of course an example, but volatile energy and resource prices are relevant for us, as well as the shifts in technology for one resource and the shifts from one resource to others. Long-term trends can be cultural and ideological as well. For example, the dawn of neo-liberal resource economies and local governance ideas in the 1980s is a key example for resource communities; they were not prepared to observe the implications of these trends and to articulate responses to them.

Adaptation, moreover, cannot be adaptation to everything. Not everything is observed, observable, relevant and important. A focus on one thing can make some other things invisible and others only blurry, or partially visible. A policy focus derived from such always imperfect observations of reality will inevitably imply that other policy issues receive less attention, or never really become an issue. A focus on climate risk might obscure the persistence of rather corrupt elite rule and obscure persistent issues with property rights and good governance, which could be aggravated if the climate plans are blind to them.

Fort McMurray, in Northern Alberta, is not a young settlement. A trappers post in the late 18th century, it survived as a small community until the 1960s when oil, abundantly present but mixed with sand and other deposits, could be extracted profitably. A boom in the 1970s followed, two busts and two more booms. The settlement was administratively upgraded a few times, until it received city status in 1980. An informal shift in policy at the Provincial level and the bust of the late 1980s led to a downgrading of Fort McMurray in the sense that in 1994, it was integrated in the new regional municipality of Wood Buffalo, and in the sense that the province clearly chose for industry-built camps, rather than the development of Fort McMurray.

Despite struggles with the province and difficulties with the oil industry, as neither was interested in investing in and giving space to Fort McMurray, a strong shared oil identity kept the interdependent players together and a growth narrative dominated local governance. These two path dependencies were productive in that they kept the community going through struggles and doubts, but they made also for limited reflexivity and limited adaptive capacity. A dramatic fire in 2016, during a bust, and later a unprecedented flood did not cause a rethinking of either the growth narrative or the oil identity. Technological innovation (thus fewer workers) and a doubling down on the camp model by industries did not leave the benefits of higher oil prices for Fort McMurray itself. Yet, adaptation was limited, given the path dependencies mentioned, given the limited autonomy since 1994. A discourse on fiscal 'responsibility,' de facto on saving and efficiency, was a very limited response to bust periods and a serious policy focus on sustainability, since 2012, could only be limited in ambition because of the oil sands operations outside Fort McMurray, and because the rebranding operation had to counter an overwhelmingly negative (environmental) image. On a positive note, one can say that the sustainability orientation of local strategy did succeed in reducing several blind spots in previous policies, making the community more attractive for families.

Tripping in resource communities

For resource communities, tripping over reality in policy making for change or for the longer term is easier than for many others. The pattern of dependencies often found there, including the distinct possibility of finding a version of the concentration problem, limit the transformation of governance, the options for steering. The dependencies in resource communities will make it difficult to observe certain problems and opportunities, for instance, problems are seen and policy responses formulated however the response might trip over itself, or slowly reveal to be focusing on the wrong problem (Furnaro, 2019; Gruber & Orihuela, 2017). In other words, for resource communities, general problems of observation in governance can make it hard to implement policy and at the same time the policies formulated might not be the most appropriate ones. We refer to our earlier reflections on the coupling of past and future in resource communities, the difficulties in envisioning alternatives.

Path dependencies, interdependencies and goal dependencies (see above) in resource communities do not only affect the formulation of alternative futures but they also create implementation obstacles for what is formulated. For some communities, an alternative future does emerge in governance, or a new way of benefiting from the old resource becomes apparent, but the awareness of the environment and of policy tools, resources and needed infrastructures might be underdeveloped. One might imagine oneself a new tourism destination, but the observational capacity might not be there to see that the existing assets are not unique, not substantial enough, that the connectivity with more densely populated areas is not there.

Cognitive path dependencies and material dependencies can make for a problematic combination in resource communities. The combination of narrow visions of the future, of the environment and a deep dependence on that material environment, can easily trap a community in a false opposition of either trying to repeat the past, or trip over reality when trying something new. A history of disillusion breeds more disillusion, a history of tripping leads to more tripping, and in some cases to stop trying. That could be the case unless something changes and new forms of observation are introduced and the concentration problems can be tackled.

For resource communities, dependencies entangle in particular manners. The dependence on a material environment, on resource extraction, is held in place by identity narratives, probably economic ideologies, by local cultures which formed over time, around identity narratives (Bell & York, 2010; Glynos, 2011; Seidl, 2016). Discursive constructions of the environment then inspire observation of that environment, which can become institutionalized, normalized and hard to change. If a creek is near a dump, it can be seen as part of the dump and not a natural asset or a potential tourism destination for flyfishing.

Material dependencies are never entirely transparent to the community itself. This might sound strange in the case of resource communities, as the resource is so central and transparently so. Yet, we would argue that the effects of the environment on governance, on the community and the effects of the activity, supported by governance, on the environment, are often *less* transparent for the community in such cases. This lack of transparency is the case because of the concentration problem, because of the extraordinary focus of observation and coordination. Water pollution will be imposed as an object of observation by outsiders, or by insiders when they are hindered in their daily activities or affected in their health in a visible manner that is hard to explain away.

Resource communities tend to struggle with reflexivity in governance and with a diversity of perspectives in the broader community. This reduced diversity of observations finds its way into governance meaning that the quality of observation and self-observation in governance are hampered aggravating the risks for tripping over reality later one (Gunder & Hillier, 2009). We brought up the point already that the risk of tripping when trying to implement strategy cannot be disconnected from the difficulties in coming to the appropriate policy in the first place. The same set of observations underpin both.

In the Soviet Union, natural resources were highly regarded as drivers of development and (resource-based) development was understood as the straight path towards a truly communist society. New resource communities were therefore founded across its huge territory, often in remote locations. Depending on the perceived importance of the resource, the location and the ministries advocating for the development, plans would take shape and responsibilities were divided. Economic planning preceded spatial planning and where local governments did not exist yet or were easily sidelined, the ministries backing the state resource companies involved, or the companies themselves would design and develop new villages, towns and even cities. The balance of power could shift as it did in Novosibirsk, where first Moscow-based actors took key decisions which resulted in impressive growth, then diversification of the economy led to a stronger local voice and lobby. In many Soviet resource towns, shifts in markets were not considered and as the USSR proved sensitive to world markets, the idea of scientifically predictable futures and the idea of engineering as central expertise, slowly lost ideological support.

Lacanian insights into the opacities of governance and community

Opacity for communities can be deep. In the previous paragraphs we encountered several reasons why observation of self and environment is always limited, why the observation and understanding of governance in governance is always limited. Observation from within the system never fully elucidates that system (Brans & Rossbach, 1997). Furthermore, if the system is fully geared towards one activity and, as community, simplified and homogenized, then the obstacles for rich observation and self-observation are layered. The community was intended as a tool to do something in the environment, not in a full sense as an organism that can continuously rethink itself in ongoing discussion as most communities, at least in recent decades.

In the chapter on trauma, we encountered another manifestation of opacity, causing a community to trip. We referred to psycho-analyst Jacques Lacan and his ideas on the Real, as distinct from reality. for Lacan Reality we know is underpinned by an entanglement of the Real, Symbolic and Imaginary orders (Bailly, 2012; Hook, 2017). The Real is the least knowable of them, yet can strike back, as an obstacle or a force, as an unexpected event. We refer to our earlier discussion and we will develop the idea also further in this chapter. Trauma, we know, can up well in communities when they least expect it. Connecting what happened in the past with a current problem, behavior, fantasy, is often not possible for the community itself (Hillier & Gunder, 2003). Something could not find a place in the symbolic order and emerged in the form of symptoms which might not be observed and, if observed, are not easy to explain.

In Chapter 8, we approached the Real from a different angle, where we noticed that the entanglements of a community and its environment but also its past, leave marks that are not understood. Current entanglements are not seen or understood. An inside and an outside are entwined in manners not grasped by the inside (the governance system, the community itself), leading to a difficulty for the inside to see what belongs to itself, what is inside, what is outside or a mark or effect of it. The Real here shows itself as the obstacle, the difficulty in attribution and the systematic mistakes made. This can build up to self-aggrandizement and tripping up, disillusion (Copjec, 2015; Stavrakakis, 2002).

Lacan distinguishes between the Real Real, the symbolic Real and the imaginary Real. The symbolic Real is easiest to grasp, as that which cannot be grasped (Zizek, 1992, 2011). That which resists symbolization, or shatters seemingly safe and stable meanings after a while. The meaning of something can seem stable of a place, a community, a landscape, a resource, yet, suddenly it shifts, different images, affects, meanings erupt, an eruption of the Real. In other cases something might seem safe and stable, but staring at it long enough, especially at its materiality, makes it uncanny, produces unease, disorientation.

The Imaginary Real, for Lacan, is the unfathomable in its imaginary intimations. The staring leads not just to uneasiness but to a new experience, maybe a suggestion of the sublime. A new experience can also appear out of nowhere, without much staring, without reflection or focus (Hook, 2017). The Imaginary Real can disturb meaning and it can disturb images and feelings. As images trigger feelings and structure identities, the imaginary Real can upset identities, the individual ego and, we argue community identities. An intervention of the imaginary Real can shake up our idealized identities, our comfortable homes made of image and discourse (as both symbolic and imaginary orders are involved in identity construction) (Bailly, 2012; Zizek, 2011).

The Real Real then is the Real of horror, of deep anxiety, of nothing working anymore, nothing being normal anymore, of a hard barrier to make sense, feel at home and feel real at all. This can be a matter of small things, of little triggers collapsing the world of a community, when these little things are keystones in the identity construction of the community. Big shocks can also invoke the Real Real, an unexpected trembling of all that is known, an earthquake that turns a village into rubble, rocks crumbling, the ground turning into an abyss, all that is solid melting into air (Zizek, 1992).

Our reality, as individual and community, does not hold very well without some support. Indeed, one can imagine, as Lacan, reality as upheld by the three orders, but the presence of the Real there is both supporting and disruptive. It is necessary for our sense of reality and it also never entirely fitting that reality. Following Lacan, other supports are needed to make our life world inhabitable. Fantasy is one of them, master signifiers are others (Glynos, 2011; Hook, 2017).

Lacanian fantasy

Fantasy is not unreality for Lacan, but imaginary elements which can be perceived as real or unreal. Our sense of reality, including our sense of self, is underpinned by fantasy, by images and aspirations, while other fantasies, products of desire, are clearly recognizable as not real, but wished for (Glynos & Stavrakakis, 2008). For Freud, dreams were expressions of wishes and wish fulfillment, betraying fantasy self-images. While the collective does not dream the same dreams in a literal sense, communities do desire things, have idealized self-images and can produce shared visions, stories, images, mythologies, fables and histories that represent such idealized and fantasized self (Turner, 2022). Fantasy, we see, can have many productive effects (Hillier & Gunder, 2003).

Which brings us to the idea of productive fictions. Communities need fiction, even if they are able to recognize it as such. The fiction can be linked to fantasy, or not. It can be a matter of small things being glossed over to make the community function and it can be a matter of guiding stories which cannot be entirely true, but nevertheless move and connect people (Van Assche et al., 2021). Planning for the long term, strategy for reinvention can be considered productive fictions, in the sense that literally, they are not possible; perfect coordination is not possible, perfect integration of knowledges and policies and people do not perfectly follow rules (Roberts, 2009). Moreover, reality is never entirely predictable and knowable (McConnell, 2010). Nevertheless, they serve functions, they can be highly productive fictions. Without coordination and collective action, the collective would not be the same and cannot become itself, one could argue. A collective does not simply express itself but creates itself through the fictions it produces. After which those fictions can come to resemble reality, while reality itself can be partly structured by fictions (Turner, 2022; Žižek, 2018).

Finally, there are Master Signifiers, signifiers which can mean many things, are open to interpretation, but at the same time serve a precise function like pinning down of otherwise fleeting discourse. Ideology and religion can provide master signifiers, but also science and culture (Zizek, 1992). Master signifiers like 'sustainability,' or 'justice,' can connect various signifiers otherwise merely juxtaposed and 'pin them down,' to the rest of perceived reality, by providing a general framing which endows all the parts with sense. Communities and individuals have their master signifiers but might be interpreted by others through different master signifiers. For example, place promotors might speak of a place as a 'ski paradise' while locals think of it as a 'former coal town' and some outsiders of a calm family resort. At the same time, master signifiers unify and divide (Kooij et al., 2014). They unify signifiers and can unify people using the same master signifiers to gloss over differences, or to remain unaware of differences. Meanwhile, as said, the same place, situation, can be framed through different master signifiers and divide people or communities in this way. New ideologies can emerge, providing new master signifiers which can divide a previously harmonious community.

When the industry leaves town and people feel lost, when local governance is not used to thinking in a different direction a handful master signifiers offer themselves. Canadian research showed that 'innovation' and 'tourism' are common shorthands for alternative futures which still have to be articulated, indicating a new direction, while 'resource town' or 'service hub' might be similarly open to interpretation, yet suggesting that existing identities do not have to be questioned as much, that similar activities offering similar lifestyles might continue.

Such process is natural, and master signifiers are part and parcel of our functioning as community, yet in the case of former resource communities, where not only the articulation but also the internal testing of new futures is not strongly developed, an automatic shift towards common master signifiers, present in media and presented by consultants, can be problematic. Especially as tourism and innovation potential are not uniformly distributed, they might hinge on qualities and assets that are easily overlooked or overestimated in communities that are not used to paying attention to these qualities and assets and are desperate for new prosperity (ambiguously desperate for reinvention).

Tripping and desire

Master signifiers, productive fictions, fantasies are part and parcel of the human repertoire of communication, of community building and identity construction. They are neither good or bad per se, rather necessary with necessary side effects. They are necessary because the Real, symbolic and imaginary orders do not hold together perfectly. Both individuals and communities have to adjust their understandings, self-images, expectations continuously; they have to adapt and put together the pieces again, to navigate bigger and smaller social and physical worlds.

Communities, when they try to give direction to themselves, operate in that same world and the systems of governance they devise to do this, cannot escape this world either, the world of fantasy, master signifiers, productive fictions. In the first part of this chapter, we summarized basic insights in the 'tripping' of communities over their own plans and policies and pointed out some special reasons for the tripping in resource communities. The Lacanian ideas briefly presented here and encountered a few times before, harmonize with these insights. They might stem from a theoretically different perspective but the insights themselves do not contradict what could be gleaned from the more mainstream literatures.

As suggested earlier, Lacanian insights can add layers to the opacity of a community to itself. For Lacan, none of the tricks people use to tell themselves the world is an unproblematic unity or an unproblematic home and that their individual and communal identities are stable, that their ideologies are real and substantial, are perfect. At some point, any identity shows cracks, any master signifier will show slippage, will divide where it united (or vice versa).

Lacan helps to see how what is not consciously observed, what happened in the past, can come back to haunt communities. Some of the reasons added for imperfect transparency, observation, communication in a Lacanian perspective add up to a return of the repressed, of the disavowed, of the Real in all its manifestations. One can speak of an imperfect digestion, or metabolization, of certain events, in social memory, in governance, in the way the environment is understood and managed. In terms of Chapter 8, an empirical boundary can be encountered, but also a repressed memory. The Real can haunt us as individuals and as communities in unique ways, as we constructed ourselves in unique ways out of materials where the provenance is not entirely clear (Copjec, 2015; Zizek, 1992). We might aspire to something because someone else aspires to it, because we aspire to a new identity and often, we do not know why.

In Lacanian speech, the real object of desire is usually not known but something in our reality can come to embody it. One could hope to be young forever but instead buys a sports car; in Lacanian speech the car would be called the *objet petit a* (Bailly, 2012; Hook, 2017). What attracts us in people is not a feature we are supposed to like but an *objet petit a* which does not exactly coincide with a feature which we could express in words, as the *objet petit* is of the order of the Real. For communities, the same can apply, as communities desire and do not know what they desire or why. Why is 'innovation' the magical word for so many? Why is something in an innovation park the embodiment of desire? Lacan would say that the *objet petit a* cannot be perfectly stabilized, as desire tends to move on and attach itself to other objects or features. A person might be attractive for a supposed reason, but the attraction might disappear, even if, objectively nothing changed. The same applies to communities, their desires expressed in policies, the *objets petits a* pursued, the futures envisioned and endowed with desire.

Because the future is unknown, it does not offer much resistance against projection of desires and expectations. Fantasy can reign more freely, trauma can be imagined absent, while wholeness, unity and harmony assumed. Of course, this is bound to create traps for the future as well as unfulfilled expectations. Yet this does not mean that visions, plans, strategies for communities are only self-delusion, problematic products of the imaginary ego of the community (Gunder & Hillier, 2009). We know that visions, plans, policy in general can change reality, bring reality closer to the dream and bring the community into being. They can be performative. The point for communities is to capitalize on the productive sides of fictions and to avoid a haunting by the Real later. We know the common reasons for tripping over reality are common enough.

In former or declining resource communities, change might be under way, but not observed. Individual observations might emerge, but without finding resonance in governance. If imaginary and symbolic cohesion are not fundamentally challenged, communities can continue for a long time to deny that the industry is in decline, that alternatives are needed. It might also take a long time to realize that there might be viable alternatives already realizing themselves. Understanding this might come indirectly, through eruptions of the Real in unexpected moments. One can realize, individually and then collectively, that people leave, that at the same time newcomers are doing something different, new. At first they might be ignored and deemed harmless but when they become more integrated in the community they might open the eyes of old-timers; for example by pointing at the landscape and heritage as means to have desirable lifestyles and new economies and emphasizing that self-organization is happening and that it can be amplified in its economic importance.

The Real of these futures, as they are already present, can suddenly appear and this is a rather common occurrence. In the Canadian Province of British Columbia, the communities of Revelstoke and Nelson, both had resource histories that left a heritage which could be reused, a landscape that was not in ruins. New arrivals seeing the place with new eyes allowed for a gradual reinvention, where what was previously a simple background or even an annoyance (old stuff) became seen as an asset and as symbol for a new future. In both cases local strategy built on such eruption of the Real, and a new narrative materialized. In Revelstoke, a rediscovery of ski opportunities became central to this narrative and in Nelson an idea of alternative lifestyles, healthy and mindful living, of an eco-friendly model community provided master signifiers.

Fantasy and desire in resource communities

In resource communities, past, present and future are connected in unique ways, as we know. This brings about a set of obstacles for the formulation and implementation of strategies for change. Even where the concentration problem is not clearly present, these obstacles can be observed and can cause a tripping over reality and a tripping over the Real. In the first sections of this chapter, we outlined reasons for tripping over reality which are recognized in mainstream policy literature and which are often magnified in resource communities (cf. Bloom & Cederstrom, 2009). We argued that their mono-functional nature deprived them, partly from the outset partly in evolution, of some of the cognitive and organizational tools to reduce the chance of tripping over reality.

In terms of Chapter 8, these limitations in resource communities are visible in the phases of imagining, testing and coordinating futures. A meager presence of alternative narratives makes for a meager testing exercise and that holds true as well for an impoverished diversity of forms of expertise in administration and a limited understanding of system-environment relations (Hood & Peters, 2004). A focus on local resource extraction might be complemented easily by international networks associated with the same resource, so other places do enter the picture in local governance, but those are essentially similar places, or places in a hierarchy defined by the resource (Halseth, 2005). Comparisons with places that transitioned, or places who diversified or found different paths of development, occur more rarely. Such comparisons can even be seen as threatening, as taking away from a singular focus on the resource future, as undermining the resource identity, as possibly admitting to cracks in the façade of certainty and perpetual resource-based prosperity.

In such situations, when comparison to places 'that made it' is perceived as an insult, it becomes hard to distinguish viable from non-viable strategies for change and difficult to recognize obstacles that might cause the community to trip up (cf. Zizek, 2017). It is hard to distinguish productive from non-productive fiction and it becomes hard to distinguish between 'fantasy and vision,' it becomes very difficult to observe when master signifiers are turning into liabilities and rigidities in thinking and governance that are non-adaptive are maintained (Glynos, 2011).

Traversing the fantasy, in psychoanalytic parlance, might be necessary; meaning a gradual deepening of self-understanding which reveals the reasons for and functions of the fantasy. Such an effort, which we will later argue must be part of a self-analysis, as self-therapy in the community, can take away the attractiveness of certain goals, objects, collective imagined futures. At least, it can attenuate the libidinal investment, reveal some of the risks, limitations, open up the focus of exploration of community futures. The inescapability of a certain future, as well as the inescapable attraction of one alternative solution (tourism, innovation) can start to look less firm, can start to lose their grip on collective imagination and, from there move on to undermine governance (Marais et al., 2021).

A conscious collective traversing of the fantasy can be accompanied, in self-analysis by a deconstruction of master signifiers (Fink, 1995; Hook, 2017). A community might have lived in the sign and in the shadow of a very limited but tightly coupled set of master signifiers. Self-analysis can focus on each signifier separately, or on a particular coupling, but this, will only work if there is a willingness to scrutinize these infrastructures of the collective self-understanding. Following Slavoj Zizek, one can recognize here the circularity of ideology and the circularity of identity: ideologies and identities only 'work' if there is a belief in them and undermining that belief is only possible when it is already slipping. Or, in the other direction, the construction of an identity and ideology is only possible when it is already there (Zizek, 1992, 2011).

The *objets petit a* for resource communities are often circling around the resource itself, where the mine, the port, the derrick, the road to the mine, the bar next to the mine, can be invested with desires and aspirations of the community and be equated to prosperity can be taken to mean not worrying about the future or for community cohesion, they can strand for a blissful non-reflexivity (Bailly, 2012; Hook, 2017). There is no need to think, just work, just support what supports us all. Long after a mine is closed, a well is abandoned, buildings, infrastructures, even ruins and slag heaps can function as *objets petit a,* can become the place of projection of desire, then tinged with nostalgia. The physical presence of reminders of the good old resource days can then maintain the circle of desire, around the *objets petit a*. The presence of resource jobs not far away, yet outside the community, can keep the desire alive and a shared ideology, in the region, maybe the country, can do the same thing. Ideology and its master signifiers (say of neoliberalism, or localism) can stabilize and structure the fantasy produced by the desire that does not let go of its *objets petit a.* Once it is forced to let go the limited tools in governance to imagine, test, coordinate alternatives, increase the chance that a new fantasy will take its place (Ruti, 2008).

The Real of resource communities, the Real that can make it trip when trying to change, is not a phenomenon which coalesces into one hard obstacle for change. It is also not something that has a purely negative presence. Just as unobserved dependencies in governance, the Real is obstacle as well as enabler; it is negative not in a policy sense, only in an epistemological sense (Copjec, 2015). Which means that it is negative only in the sense that it shows up as cracks, stains, unintelligible or anxiety-provoking anomalies in the imaginary and symbolic orders. These cracks and stains can work out positively and negatively when trying to imagine a community future and a strategy and a way to move in that direction, a community strategy. They can provide support and they can make us trip.

Concluding

For resource communities, there is a lot of tripping and we argued that the Real enters the equation in particular ways in these communities. The non-observation of limits imposed by the past, by legacies and memories on imagining and organizing futures, can be considered a haunting by the Real that, under the unfavorable conditions of a declining and less locally governed resource economy, leads to more tripping than unacknowledged support (Eyers, 2012). The same applies to the silent interweaving of community and environment. Being shaped by an environment and not being aware of it leads to blind spots, as marks of the Real, which can be supportive or problematic, but when conditions have changed and those conditions are not observed or disavowed in the community. What was formerly supportive or at least non-resistant, can turn into lumps and lumps that become the obstacles that make one trip when trying to move in a different direction, or even in the same direction (Fink, 1995).

The notions expounded above can, we believe, be useful in the analysis of resource communities. Ideally, they can play a role in their self-analysis, as such therapeutic process might be necessary to make space for a new interpretation of self in resource communities in uncharted waters. Such new interpretation cannot come out of an outsider analysis, that is, only when the community itself comes to a new understanding of itself, can this be the basis of transformative change. We develop this line of thought in the following chapters where we will discuss community strategy, but also the necessary self-analysis preceding the formulation of such strategy.

References

Bailly, L. (2012). *Lacan: A beginner's guide*. Simon and Schuster.

Barrett, S. M. (2004). Implementation Studies: Time for a Revival? Personal reflections on 20 years of implementation studies. *Public Administration, 82*(2), 249–262. 10.1111/j.0033-3298.2004.00393.x.

Bell, S. E., & York, R. (2010). Community economic identity: The coal industry and ideology construction in West Virginia. *Rural Sociology, 75*(1), 111–143. 10.1111/j.1549-0831.2009.00004.x.

Bloom, P., & Cederstrom, C. (2009). "The sky's the limit": Fantasy in the age of market rationality. *Journal of Organizational Change Management, 22*(2), 159–180.

Boston, J. (2021). Assessing the options for combatting democratic myopia and safeguarding long-term interests. *Futures, 125*, 102668–102668. 10.1016/j.futures.2020.102668.

Brans, M., & Rossbach, S. (1997). The autopoiesis of administrative systems: Niklas Luhmann on public administration and public policy. *Public Administration, 75*(3), 417–439.

Copjec, J. (2015). *Read my desire: Lacan against the historicists*. Verso Books.

Eyers, T. (2012). *Lacan and the concept of the "real"*. Palgrave Macmillan.

Fink, B. (1995). *The Lacanian subject: Between language and Jouissance*. Princeton University Press.

Furnaro, A. (2019). Hegemony and passivity in mining regions: Containing dissent in north-central Chile. *The Extractive Industries and Society, 6*(1), 215–222. 10.1016/j.exis.2018.07.009.

Glynos, J. (2011). On the ideological and political significance of fantasy in the organization of work. *Psychoanalysis, Culture & Society, 16*(4), 373–393. 10.1057/pcs.2010.34.

Glynos, J., & Stavrakakis, Y. (2008). Lacan and political subjectivity: Fantasy and enjoyment in psychoanalysis and political theory. *Subjectivity, 24*(1), 256–274. 10.1057/sub.2008.23.

Gruber, S., & Orihuela, J. C. (2017). Deeply rooted grievance, varying meaning: The institution of the mining canon. In E. Dargent, J. C. Orihuela, M. Paredes, & M. E. Ulfe (Eds.), *Resource booms and institutional pathways: The case of the extractive industry in Peru* (pp. 41–67). Springer International Publishing. 10.1007/978-3-319-53532-6_2.

Gunder, M., & Hillier, J. (2009). *Planning in ten words or less: A Lacanian entanglement with spatial planning*. Ashgate Publishing, Ltd.

Halseth, G. (2005). Resource town transition: Debates after closure. In S. J. Essex, A. W. Gilg, R. B. Yarwood, J. Smithers, & R. Wilson (Eds.), *Rural change and sustainability: Agriculture, the environment and communities* (1st ed., pp. 326–342). CABI Publishing. 10.1079/9780851990828.0326.

Hillier, J., & Gunder, M. (2003). Planning fantasies? An exploration of a potential Lacanian framework for understanding development assessment planning. *Planning Theory, 2*(3), 225–248. 10.1177/147309520323005.

Hood, C., & Peters, G. (2004). The middle aging of new public management: Into the age of paradox? *Journal of Public Administration Research and Theory, 14*(3), 267–282.

Hook, D. (2017). *Six moments in Lacan: Communication and identification in psychology and psychoanalysis*. Routledge.

Howlett, M. (2009). Policy analytical capacity and evidence-based policy-making: Lessons from Canada. *Canadian Public Administration, 52*(2), 153–175. 10.1111/j.1754-7121.2009.00070_1.x.

Kooij, H.-J., Van Assche, K., & Lagendijk, A. (2014). Open concepts as crystallization points and enablers of discursive configurations: The case of the innovation campus in the Netherlands. *European Planning Studies, 22*(1), 84–100. 10.1080/09654313.2012.731039.

Leong, C., & Howlett, M. (2021). *Policy learning, policy failure, and the mitigation of policy risks: Re-thinking the lessons of policy success and failure*. Administration & Society, 009539972110653. 10.1177/00953997211065344.

Luhmann, N. (1990). *Political theory in the welfare state*. De Gruyter.

Marais, L., Nel, V., Rani, K., Rooyen, D. van, Sesele, K., Watt, P. van der, & Plessis, L. du. (2021). Economic transitions in South Africa's secondary cities: Governing mine closures. *Politics and Governance, 9*(2), 381–392. 10.17645/pag.v9i2.4032.

McConnell, A. (2010). Policy success, policy failure and grey areas in-between. *Journal of Public Policy, 30*(3), 345–362. 10.1017/S0143814X10000152.

Moyaert, P. (1996). Lacan on neighborly love: The relation to the thing in the other who is my neighbor. *Epoché: A Journal for the History of Philosophy, 4*(1), 1–31. 10.5840/epoche1996417.

Nair, S., & Howlett, M. (2017). Policy myopia as a source of policy failure: Adaptation and policy learning under deep uncertainty. *Policy & Politics, 45*(1), 103–118. 10.1332/030557316X14788776017743.

Perdue, R. T., & Pavela, G. (2012). Addictive economies and coal dependency: Methods of extraction and socioeconomic outcomes in West Virginia, 1997–2009. *Organization & Environment, 25*(4), 368–384.

Perez-Sindin, X., & Van Assche, K. (2020). *From coal not to ashes but to what? As Pontes, social memory and the concentration problem.* The Extractive Industries and Society. 10.1016/j.exis.2020.07.016.

Pressman, J. L., & Wildavsky, A. (1984). *Implementation: How great expectations in washington are dashed in Oakland; Or, why it's amazing that federal programs work at all, this being a saga of the economic development administration as told by two sympathetic observers who seek to build morals.* Univ of California Press.

Roberts, J. (2009). No one is perfect: The limits of transparency and an ethic for 'intelligent' accountability. *Accounting, Organizations and Society, 34*(8), 957–970. 10.1016/j.aos.2009.04.005.

Ruti, M. (2008). The fall of fantasies: A Lacanian reading of lack. *Journal of the American Psychoanalytic Association, 56*(2), 483–508.

Seidl, D. (2016). *Organisational identity and self-transformation: An autopoietic perspective.* Routledge.

Stavrakakis, Y. (2002). *Lacan and the Political.* Routledge.

Turner, K. (2022). *Lacanian fantasy: The image, language and uncertainty.* Taylor & Francis.

Valentinov, V., Verschraegen, G., & Van Assche, K. (2019). The limits of transparency: A systems theory view. *Systems Research and Behavioral Science, 36*(3), 289–300. 10.1002/sres.2591.

Van Assche, K., Duineveld, M., & Beunen, R. (2014). Power and contingency in planning. *Environment and Planning A, 46*(10), 2385–2400.

Van Assche, K., Gruezmacher, M., & Granzow, M. (2021). From trauma to fantasy and policy. The past in the futures of mining communities; the case of Crowsnest Pass, Alberta. *Resources Policy, 72*, 102050–102050. 10.1016/j.resourpol.2021. 102050.

Van Assche, K., Verschraegen, G., & Gruezmacher, M. (2021). Strategy for collectives and common goods: Coordinating strategy, long-term perspectives and policy domains in governance. *Futures, 128*, 102716–102716. 10.1016/j.futures.2021.102716.

van de Mosselaer, F., & Duineveld, M. (2021). Strategic openings: On the productivity of blended long-term perspectives in spatial strategy. A Dutch case study. *Futures, 130*, 102752. 10.1016/j.futures.2021.102752.

Zizek, S. (1992). *Looking awry: An introduction to Jacques Lacan through popular culture.* MIT Press.

Zizek, S. (2011). *How to read Lacan.* Granta Books.

Žižek, S. (2018). The seven veils of fantasy. In *Key concepts of Lacanian psychoanalysis* (pp. 190–218). Routledge.

10
STRATEGY AND COMMUNITY IN RESOURCE COMMUNITIES

Introduction: Thinking about strategy

Strategy, as a vision for a desirable future and coupled to an idea of how to get there is a compelling way for actors to assert they will make a difference. What made modernist agendas attractive in the post war period still holds attraction to politics and administration today: the promise of steering, of comprehensive planning, rational knowledge integration and grand strategy (Hillier, 2002; Scott, 2020). However, what many refer to as strategy is usually not more than a check list of activities or actions thought to improve the future. It lacks a coherent goal and reasoning of what might happen in the future if a certain path is followed. These check lists or plans allow for more control and predictability; things can be traced and followed; targets can be met. Strategy, as opposed to a plan, requires a leap of faith, requires accepting uncertainty. Strategizing is more of a journey in which success is difficult to prove or guarantee, benefits and risks are enormous (Carter et al., 2008; Mintzberg, 1987). Risks and benefits of strategy, of linkages between long-term perspectives, strategy and certain forms of policy coordination and integration must be assessed per case (Golsorkhi et al., 2010).

Strategy, as we defined it in our introductory chapter, has three dimensions. First, we see it as narrative, a narrative is more persuasive than a list or framework and provides cohesion and logic. Second, a strategy also needs to be seen as an institution, a tool of coordination in governance, which leads us to the third dimension; strategy helps to coordinate other institutions. Strategies cannot function if they exist in isolation, isolated from the narratives important for the community and separate from the other institutions as they exist in the community (Czarniawska, 1997; Van Assche et al., 2020;

DOI: 10.4324/9781003332145-10

Van Assche et al., 2021). If a strategy does remain isolated, it will be less effective and less legitimate and supported in the community. An ambitious strategy, one aiming at reinvention of a resource community for example, will have to be comprehensive, it will touch not only existing policies but also require a dialog, in fact a form of coordination of several policy domains (environmental policy, economic development, infrastructure, etc.) (Kornberger, 2022). In order to bring the vision for the future closer, coordination of existing institutions and policy domains might still not be enough, as new institutions might have to be created, which then can be connected and coordinated with existing ones and with the driving narrative behind the strategy (Kornberger et al., 2021).

Resource communities and strategy

For resource communities in particular, the need for strategy is immense and at the same time so are weaknesses in the capacity to organize and coordinate action, in other words, the capacity to strategize. Such situation might tempt communities or well-meaning outsiders to adopt grand strategy, requiring enormous steering power and giving central place to predefined technical solutions or perceived best practices. A modernist engineering mindset is quite common, in the practice of 'saving' or 'fixing' resource communities. We know by now that this steering of power in many communities does not exist, cannot be assumed (Meyer et al., 2020). Which means that either the strategy can fail, when local implementation derails local governance even more, or that it can be imposed by external actors, which keeps the community in a dependent state, keeps governance weak (Schuftan, 1996; Whittington, 1996). Moreover, there is a real chance that checks and balances in local governance, already fragile due to the concentration problem and other issues, will be further undermined (Van Assche et al., 2020).

Another common response, in resource communities, is to assume that nothing is possible, that strategizing makes no sense. One can point at the weak demographic and financial base, assuming that strategizing is mostly about spending money, about building things or giving away things which cost money. Ideological obstacles to spatial planning, for example, can then be reinforced by ideas that planning. A form of strategizing can be interpreted as mostly being about doing extra things, about embellishing spaces and elaborating processes (Caine et al., 2007; Scott, 2020) while 'we know' how things are most easily and logically organized in this place. Discursive closure, pride of place, possibly linked to a tightly controlled social identity thus form a third obstacle to strategy.

Yet, for us, strategy does not have to be expensive, or grand, nor something dominated by technical expertise and driven by modernist assumptions. And certainly, it cannot be reduced to a checklist of activities or goals. Strategies can exist in many forms, scopes and time frames. Strategizing needs to be understood as a process whereby a community can, on a continuous basis, reflect on itself and try to give shape to its future (Czarniawska, 2014). We will elaborate our perspective on strategy in the following pages as an adaptive process, meaning that certainty is neither an assumption nor a goal and that strategizing is also a matter of managing certainty. Outcomes and assumptions will have to be assessed on a regular basis and both narratives and institutional dimensions reconsidered every now and then. A narrative might lose its persuasive power, an institution might lose its coordinative power and if the strategy itself fragments in a set of disconnected goals where cohesion is not considered, it will either stop working, or move the community in a direction it never desired (Whittington, 1996; Williamson, 1999).

Following Henry Mintzberg, strategy is thus considered as emerging, as something requiring crafting and following David Seidl and others, we understand it as a practice (Golsorkhi et al., 2010; Mintzberg & Lampel, 1999; Mintzberg & Waters, 1985; Whittington, 1996). The process of strategizing will be more complex in communities than in organizations, as the goals are more diverse, internal complexity higher and the uncertainties involved more substantial. When communities are in trouble and when communities are equipped with a simplified or atrophied governance system, this will be even more complicated and it means that the stakes are higher in the process of self-analysis that precedes the actual crafting of strategy (Van Assche et al., 2013; Voß et al., 2006). In such self-analysis, the effects of a history of extraction, possibly of violence, trauma and concentration problems, on the community and its governance system will have to be unearthed, together, positively, with the more hopeful narratives about the future, about assets and opportunities, which exist in the community. The self-analysis will have to reveal the pattern of dependencies in governance and the difficulties and enabling factors for the transformation of governance itself. In all likelihood, strategy will have to transform governance itself (Van Assche et al., 2021).

We reiterate the importance of starting the process of crafting strategy with a thorough self-analysis process, one that attempts to reveal legacies, dependencies and other challenges inherited from the past that might be weakening the capacity to organize and coordinate action. Self-analysis and strategizing will allow for the discovery of possibilities and options for a new development path and at the same time it will reveal the community's limits and obstacles. For some this might appear as daunting, a discouraging endeavor that will likely end in disappointment and that will leave the community with a feeling that it has no control over its future. We believe this might be the case when self-analysis has not gone far enough. We must recognize that self-analysis won't be easy and that is especially true for resource communities, with troubled pasts and burdensome legacies, nonetheless it is a step that must be taken. We will discuss what self-analysis entails and ways in which it can be undertaken that might help in relieving some of the pressure of this undertaking. In Chapter 12, we derive a method of self-analysis which can lead to a vision, as unified narrative and from there, a strategy.

Self-analysis

Self-analysis is a process of reflecting about the past, about the events and decisions that have led to the current state of affairs. It is intended to untangle paths of development with the hope of learning about the past to understand how avoid problems, manage challenges and capitalize on achievements for the future. As we have pointed out already, for resource communities, re-visiting the past will be a tough and likely painful experience. Self-analysis might be something resource communities hesitate to jump into and are intimidated to begin, however it is unavoidable if strategy is to succeed. The quality of self-analysis will be reflected in the quality of strategy.

An understanding of the context in which the strategy will be embedded is a necessary starting point for self-analysis, certainly as that context might have to be changed as part of a strategy. We have argued that central to this context is the community's system of governance, the main relationships between the different elements in the system and how they change and shape each other. Without an understanding of the particularities of the local governance system, it is hard to change it and hard to use it to effectuate change in the community (Aal, 2022; Mintzberg & Lampel, 1999; Van Assche et al., 2019).

It is through governance that collective actions are coordinated and that interactions between the society and the environment are mediated. Governance systems thus are welding social and ecological systems together; it is through governance that a society engages with its natural environment and defines acceptable interactions with its elements. From this perspective we can agree with a functional approach to defining natural resources, where natural resources come into being and evolve as a result of human-nature interactions (De Gregori, 1987). The arrangement of actors and institutions and the power relations in the system, the different types of knowledge structure the system and are responsible for shaping its interactions with nature.

Self-analysis thus entails a reconstruction of:

- the functioning of governance,
- the governance path and
- the embedding of governance in the community,
- its couplings with material, including natural, environments.

Governance establishes many of the couplings and aims to manage most of them. If much is ungoverned, then strategizing is difficult and both the potential and risks of certain interactions with the environment cannot be assessed, nor managed.

As a strategy requires a binding narrative, about the future and as such narrative is not likely persuasive if it is not connected to existing narratives in the community, a mapping and understanding of narratives will have to be part of the self-analysis. Simply collecting narratives will not be sufficient, as it is the connections between narratives that might keep them in place, might make a situation or approach look like it is natural or unavoidable (Boje et al., 1999; Czarniawska & Gagliardi, 2003; Jessop, 2002). We spoke earlier of governance configurations.

Such configurations, as we know, are not only about the future. Narratives about the present, the past (social memory) and the future can shape each other, as narratives about one thing can determine attitudes, images and narratives about other things. For our resource communities, where the functioning of social memory is an issue in many ways, this mapping of social memory is crucial, as it can be a starting point for an interrogation of social memory and identity, after which new futures can appear more easily in the collective imagination (Clegg, 2006).

Roblin City (Manitoba, Canada) never became a reality. The Scottish architect William Bruce, who moved to Winnipeg in 1906, was ambitious, prolific, and eager to ingratiate himself with the regional elites. He felt the political winds and the grand narrative of the economic boom of Manitoba, which needed a port to export its agricultural bounty. Bruce named his dream city on the Hudson Bay, Roblin City, named after a provincial Premier, and derived its design largely from then popular neo-baroque City Beautiful forms, most notably embodied in the recent Chicago plans. Bruce intended Roblin City to be self-governing and large, up to half a million people. The prewar economic bust, the short shipping season and shallow waters of the Hudson Bay made sure that political enthusiasm dwindled, even if similar plans were revisited in later decades. One can add that local observation, local knowledge as well as useful forms of expert knowledge were missing in the plan, which would have been extremely costly to implement, and would have made for a non-adapted and adaptive, and unpleasant living environment. One can say that a narrative was briefly persuasive, but neither knowledge or policy integration were con- sidered (Burns & Goldsborough, 2012; Van Assche et al., 2022b).

Narratives

Narratives or stories are at the heart of any attempt at strategy and under- standing existing narratives is essential. As a new strategy will require a new narrative, the enabling and constraining factors are to a large extent in the realm of narrative. People are not able to see 'a mess' because they see tidiness, or they do not believe in corruption because they believe in justice (cf. Douglas, 1966). They more easily see or believe something when it connects to shared beliefs, values, hopes, which tend to be embodied in narratives.

Narratives therefore are not just a rhetorical tool, to make a policy work better; nor are they loosely held discourses which can all be shed easily when conditions require. Indeed, sometimes this is true, as not all stories are pertinent to identity and as the telling and creation of stories is part and parcel of everyday life, stories serve many purposes, including tactical and strategic ones (Brown & Augusta-Scott, 2006; Lockhart, 1982). They can be used and abused in many ways. Nevertheless identity is largely a matter of stories told about self, others, environment, about past, present and future and about ways such narratives are entangled, we addressed this from several angles in previous chapters.

Narratives thus steer the community's path, they play a role in representing but also defining the desires, hopes and fears of the community. This can happen directly, speaking about a fear or hope directly visible in an interpretation of present or future and it can be indirect, where, through myriad pathways analyzed by psycho-analysis, they help to create identities, which then serve as new crystallization and catalyzing points for new hopes, desires, fears, etc. (Pigg, 2002; Wertsch, 2008). Identities, as such, are narrative constructs which affect the future in several ways, but which can, in general, be understood as stabilizing perspectives, stabilizing the moods of the community and rendering affects more predictable and manageable. (The same possible future will not inspire hope one day, fear the next day, from the same identity perspective.)

Narratives create and dissolve conflicts, problems, define the response to shocks. When narratives become encoded in governance they gain power over the community, even if they are not observed anymore. This could happen in many ways, for example through actors identifying with certain narratives and through old and new institutions showing the traces of certain narratives and the implied assumptions, the forms of knowledge or methods they favor. The mapping of narratives, as part of self-analysis, thus, in many cases, extends to a mapping of mappings with a presence, possibly a quiet presence, in the institutions used right now and in new institutions created to guide the community towards the future. Old assumptions can be built into new tools, therefore making a truly different future harder to achieve.

Uncovering stories can thus be considered part of self-analysis and becomes fundamental in understanding the context in which strategy will be embedded and in understanding the past as well as the possibilities for the future (Boje et al., 1999; Brown & Augusta-Scott, 2006). It will also help in recognizing both obstacles and materials for strategy and it will be useful in realizing what current assets are and what future assets could be. As said, important narratives for our purposes are those narratives which motivate collective decision-making (Czarniawska & Gagliardi, 2003). This process should allow for ways of discussing and confronting the stories or narratives that have defined the community and its path of development.

Unearthing or uncovering are good words to describe this process, which cannot be seen as a purely technical exercise. What is hidden is sometimes so because of contingent histories, simple forgetting but it can also be hidden because people do not want to remember or because they *cannot* remember. Hence, the comparison with therapy, where new interpretations of self, environment and future might emerge by a new confrontation with the past (Kapitan et al., 2011). As in therapy and we hinted at this before, the actual work needs to be done by the client, here the community and not the therapist, in our case an advisor of some sort. Self-analysis, therefore, must be persuasive for the community and must be carried out in a process owned by the community. It must be something that is perceived as urgent, a real need has to be recognized and circumstances have to be felt as exceptional; the routine forms of reflexivity (if existing) do not work, the routine processes do not offer guidance and lost their appearance of reality.

The mapping (which will be spelled out in some more technical detail in Chapter 12) is therefore not an exercise to be delegated lightly, as it is an integral part of the therapy which can create space for new futures, for strategy. It must be integrated in the consideration of futures and it has to be carried lightly. If the results, however painful, do not resonate within the community, if the response is denial, an anger which collapses conversations, blind fear, or disillusion, then its value is limited (Besio & Pronzini, 2011; Caine et al., 2007; Gaventa, 2004). What is rather normal, to be expected, is strong emotions, as some of the stories deeply held might be recognized as part of the problem and as some stories not acknowledged, but structuring thinking and acting, might be associated with affects previously not well understood (Gunder & Hillier, 2007; Scott, 1998). In addition, the mere mapping and unearthing of narratives can be felt as tinkering with identity and this can be felt as a threat and as illegitimate -especially in cultures where identity is understood as a natural core, which should be expressed and never questioned. Self-analysis can be hard when the self is expected to question many of its own assumptions and structures; resistance against such form of interrogation will likely show up in the form of seemingly rational arguments, as questioning of the legitimacy and morality of the exercise and likely resistance will be expressed as strong emotions, either positive or negative.

Outsiders, insiders and leaders

Thus, the self-analysis might not be entirely carried by the self. A small group, or an individual, might be appointed or simply acknowledged as taking on a quasi-therapeutic role. Which, of course, bestows power on those people. Questionable as this might be we recognize that such delegation of power and such projection of all-knowingness, is the bread and butter of politics and certainly the business of consultants. One can speak of productive fictions, of suspension of disbelief and one can refer to the facts that communities cannot and should not be forced into a trenchant process of self-analysis. One can expect, pragmatically, that only communities where some realization of deep problems already occurred, will be inclined to submit themselves to it. Paradoxically, but not strangely, this reiterates the point that those who need such therapy the most, do not see the need for it. Histories of trauma, violence and serious forms of the concentration problem might make it hard to see any problem at all and if problems are recognized, it will likely be somewhere else.

Because uncovering certain narratives might be challenging for resource communities to do on their own, considering support from outsiders might make sense. Outsiders can play a significant role in self-reflection, bringing up questions that might be uncomfortable for locals to bring up, locals avoiding digging deep into troublesome memories. Outsiders can also fill a gap in local expertise and can avoid overemphasizing intractable conflicts, differences, identifications or other obstacles for productive deliberation (Lockhart, 1982). Careful balancing between insiders and outsiders will allow for self-analysis to take place and to avoid polarizing discussions (Caine et al., 2007). Importantly, such balancing will make it easier to work within existing governance arrangements without replacing or overriding them immediately, thus giving less weight to calls for unrealistic change as a precondition for further analysis and deliberation (Staples, 2001). Outsiders, in other words, might be helpful in getting the process going, in clearing obstacles for self-analysis stemming from some of the things that ought to be uncovered through self-analysis (in psychoanalytic terms; overcoming resistance) (Quigley et al., 2019).

In the end, all answers will have to come from the locals. Which means that it might be necessary to shift the balance between insiders and outsiders during the process. If a particular advisor or facilitator, or process manager, triggers so much resistance, or shows so little understanding or empathy that the self-analysis derails, or, if it emerges that the presence of *any* outsider at some point is unproductive, one might have to reconsider. Conversely, even if locals prod the outsider for answers, about a better future, a better process of governance, or about other ways to interpret themselves, their social memory and identity, the outsider must resist the urge to be useful, as her input can easily block the process of self-analysis under way.

In this balancing act, between insider and outsider perspectives, leadership plays a prominent role (Staples, 2001; Voß, 2007). In any community, leadership will need to balance perspectives within and beyond the governance system. It will need to adapt and steer based on imperfect information and relying on much creativity. Community leaders decide on decisive issues, choose which battles are worth picking, which conflicts are worthwhile confronting and which are best left alone. These tough decisions rely on the leaders' ability to balance strategy and tactic (Hidle & Normann, 2013; Uhl-Bien & Arena, 2017). This ability will be enhanced after a self-analysis took place. Self-analysis helps leaders to know which tools to embed in other tools, to make short term responses useful for the long-term (Jones, 2009).

Italian sources from the Middle Ages and the Renaissance, including well-known authors such as Bruno Ladini (13th century), and Niccolo Macchiavelli, (16th century), speak of the figure of the 'podesta,' mostly its manifestation in the 12th and 13th centuries. This original version of the podesta was an outsider, a 'foreigner,' meaning a person not from the city state. Usually, the podesta was still an 'Italian,' meaning he could speak Italian, and either a nobleman or cleric. Later, successful merchants, who tended to have experience in city administration as well, were elected. A podesta could be a recurring role, similar to a mayor, but in many cases, it was an occasional role, when the political and administrative routines, in a system of several councils, did not work anymore, due to internal strife.

Factions could evolve in cities, associated with families, with the merchant class, with particular professions, or around a grievance or aspiration. These factions could lead to never-ending conflict, even urban warfare, and to the collapse of governance and real threats to the economic and political survival of the polity (Martines, 1988). Hence, in times of crisis, the leaders of factions could get together, push the alarm button, and elect a 'foreign' podesta for a limited term. The idea being that the outsider status, plus relevant experience, could get them through the crisis, restore a form of good governance, and then move on, or possibly be re-elected. The term could be short, even shorter than a year, and the hope was that clear-headed technocratic government could help to solve problems but also to remain accountable and to hold powerful citizens accountable. This did not always work, as the Villola chronicle writes for 1195: 'Lord Guidottino da Pistoia was podestà of Bologna and he was wounded during his time in office (…). Some of the greater men of Bologna seized him and tore out his teeth, because he had fined a great number of them.' (Sabapathy, 2011)

Returning now to that process of self-analysis, one can see a double role for leadership: managing the insider/outsider balance, the role of the analyst and second, playing that role herself. Again, leadership can be distributed and leadership can also be intentionally limited in scope and time, similar to an interim manager. A mayor can choose to run only once, a chief of administration can tie his fate to one transition process.

Leadership can also notice, in a unique way, the need for reform, the problems mounting, the problematic nature of some legacies in governance and community. If we assume leadership in a community is attempting to keep a constant eye on the collective good and is continuously reminding themselves and their team why they are doing what they are doing, who is really benefiting, how all pieces and actions in governance fit together and benefit the community, how it helps the community to transform in the way it envisions for itself, then it is easy to assume leadership *might have been involved in self-analysis before it became a collective effort* (cf. Voß et al., 2006). Leadership can, if endowed with reflexivity itself, enhance the reflexivity of governance and community. It can help to see whether a full-fledged self-analysis is realistic and whether outsiders might be needed to facilitate the process (Alvesson et al., 2009; Alvesson & Sveningsson, 2013).

Leadership, in other words, is not just about steering but also about seeing, to make it effective in complex transition processes of resource communities. Leaders might be required to see things that the rest cannot and does not want to see. One can say that in many instances leadership within a resource community will need to act as *both insider and outsider*. Local leaders will need to have strong local knowledge and enough knowledge of how things work beyond the community, in higher levels of government or in other communities or parts of the world, to be able to temper expectations, avoid getting trapped in wars of small differences and assist in the navigation of a fractured and probably contradictory, policy landscape (Gruezmacher & Van Assche, 2022; Jessop, 2002; Van Assche et al., 2022). Leadership, moreover, might have to lean on experience elsewhere, or insight gained through learning (from books and by doing) to develop a perspective that is partly the perspective of an outsider, less tied to all assumptions, blind spots and legacies normalized in the community. Good leadership, then, will inherently have some therapeutic function, as it will require a deep understanding of local thinking, but also the conceptual frames to analyze that thinking, see its limitations and the sensibility to confront the community with itself without explosions (Jessop, 2002; Timmermans et al., 2014).

Which, of course, makes leadership very demanding in such circumstances, all the more so if the community is small, if internal divisions are stark and if leadership work is not rewarded. If life is already a struggle and being a local mayor is mostly headaches, if moreover there is little staff and a weak institutional memory within administration, the temptations to stay on the sideline might be strong. The fact that, commonly, leadership under difficult circumstances is more about bad news than good news and comes with little resources that could translate into carrots, so the sticks draw even more attention, adds to the limited attraction to take on such tasks (Gavinson; Jones, 2009). One requires a person or, better, a team with great and diverse skills, a firm belief in the community, a dedication to the common good and, to add a complication, a keen awareness of the uses of power without succumbing to the lure of identification with power. All of this together might bring some communities to the conclusion that they need structural and structuring help from higher level governments, or that they should dissolve into a larger whole, but it might also bring community and leadership alike to a process of self-analysis which then generates a process of strategizing which is seeking, experimenting, adapting and reflecting again (Flyvbjerg, 1998; Gerritsen et al., 2022).

Leadership and the mapping of institutions and power/knowledge

Leadership might also have to play a role in other aspects of mapping, of self-analysis. We discussed in some detail the mapping of narratives as part and parcel of strategy. If we say narratives, we do say power/knowledge, as narratives shape the landscapes of reality and they offer tools to change those landscapes. What looks real is the starting point of strategy and strategy is partly the art of making something look real, while questioning other versions of it (cf. Scott et al., 2012). We know from previous chapters that power/knowledge entwine in complex patterns in governance and that the configurations of narratives in community and governance system affect the choice of institutions, their use, as well as the patterns of inclusion of local and expert knowledges in governance (Seidl & Becker, 2006; Wertsch, 2008).

Mapping all power/knowledge relations in governance is not possible, as not all are visible and as they change all the time. However, in connection with the mapping of narratives, it does make a lot of sense and is entirely realistic to reflect on the connections between those narratives and forms of knowledge included/excluded in governance: how close are actors to a certain narrative, a form of expertise, a version of local knowledge, a way of defining problems and solutions? (Fischer, 2000; Scott et al., 2012; Voss, 2007) How important are certain narratives and their supported knowledge for the understanding of certain institutions and their functioning? Are they directly included, or implicitly relying on certain perspectives?

Selectivity in this sort of mapping is imperative: it can be driven by what the leader, the community, or the external facilitator see as most potential avenues of investigation. Where do we feel we are overusing a particular form of expertise? What do we feel is missing? Are there certain forms of local knowledge, certain understandings of the environment, its potential and scarring, that is systematically omitted? Such choices in the path of investigation, in mapping power/knowledge, can be made more easily when the mapping and unearthing of narratives is under way. Yet, in the other direction, a more technical discussion on the absence or presence of a certain form of knowledge in governance can also lead to a discussion of grounding narratives or embedding ideologies.

We do find similarities here with the discussion of narrative mapping and one can easily recognize that, for the power/knowledge mapping to succeed, a real discussion will be involved, a discussion where truly different perspectives can engage and where complementary angles might be needed, to reconstruct the pattern of inclusion/ exclusion of knowledges in governance (Valentinov et al., 2019). In addition, there can be a discussion on the way that knowledge bestows power on some and how some in power create, use knowledges they believe in and how they succeed or not in encoding this knowledge in institutions (Van Assche et al., 2021). How critical and self-critical this discussion becomes, will have to be managed carefully. One can say in general that the depth of understanding and breadth of perspective required in this aspect of self-analysis do require a group to work on it and that insiders in governance, including leadership, will have to be involved. The workings of power/knowledge can only be revealed through a combination of insiders and outsiders.

Most likely, leadership will also be needed, as well as administrative insiders, for the mapping of institutions and actors. The actor part might be relatively simple, although not all actors are interested in visibility. The institutional part is more complex, as formal and informal institutions always coexist and as not all formal institutions do what they are expected to do (Rosenhead et al., 2019). Recognizing dead institutions, or institutions used for other purposes is a good idea if one aims to change institutions and reconnect them in a new strategy. One aspect, rather technical, of institutional mapping is the search for fragmentation, disconnect and contradiction. Indeed, in most communities, over time such things accumulate, making it hard to coordinate and integrate policy and creating invisible obstacles for a later strategy, as it will be based on flawed assumptions. Diagnosing disconnect and contradiction is helpful in later phases, where the strategists will need to decide how to reconnect, or what to abolish and redefine (see also Chapter 12).

Leadership can be external and temporary at the level of organizations, and the rich experience with consultants and consultants taking over as manager, as well as the literature on interim managers moving around from company to company, or from company to administration, offer valuable lessons. On the positive side, interim managers, or consultants given power, can see and take risk in a new way, they can bring new perspectives to the table, experiences elsewhere, they are not beholden to old masters in the organization, nor to informal rules, traditions and loyalties, and they might see flexibility in organizational identity and diversity in strategy tools where others do not see them. They can shake up organizations and create visions where none existed.

On the other side, there is the risk of lack of interest in and loyalty to the organization, the incentives to come and go quickly, to place private over organizational benefit, short over long term, performance and branding *(of self and organization) over substance, and to copy previous work rather than learn from it and adapt it to new circumstances. There is the drive to come up with strong rhetoric, simple solutions and visible difference with the previous management style or strategy, the suspicion of people and ideas associated with that previous management. There is a real risk of missing risks and imagining opportunities due to lack of knowledge, interest, and short-term perspectives (*Alvesson & Kärreman, 2007; Sturdy, 2011*). Hence the importance of balancing insider and outsider perspectives in governance, and, as we are dealing not with organizations but communities, (*Voß, 2007*) the need for leadership to discern the degree of awareness of path and context already present in the governance system, and which forms of mapping might be necessary, with which levels of participation, in order to revive a process of community strategy.*

The selectivity in self-analysis will also have to come out of the problem at hand and the preliminary explanations of the problem (providing hypotheses), as well as out of the process of self-analysis itself. In the course of discussions on certain narratives, certain aspects of social memory, one might decide to zoom in on certain domains of governance, certain older policies, plans, strategies and look for assumptions, ideologies, connections with certain actors. Just as a therapy cannot be an encyclopedic mapping of a personality or a psyche, a self-analysis in a community has to be driven by what is felt as a problem and hypothetic explanations can be tested and give direction to the self-explanation. We believe that, for our present purposes, the mapping of narratives on past, future and environment can be recommended as a rule of thumb and that some of the more technical explorations can stem from there (Czarniawska, 1997; Jessop, 2002; Uhl-Bien & Arena, 2017).

Thus, we argue for a self-reflection process that is flexible and adaptive, meaning that it can respond to what emerges from the process itself. This should be a process that makes room not only for tough questions and difficult truths that might be uncovered but also that allows for celebration of achievements that have gone unnoticed, discovery of unexpected assets and overall the creative emergence of new narratives (Gunder & Hillier, 2007; Van Assche et al., 2019; Voß et al., 2006). It is a process that cannot be too constricted to a fixed time scale or method. In Chapter 12, we will discuss mapping methods for self-analysis that are able to describe the current context as well as the path that led to it. Now we will revisit and develop our perspective on strategy and what this could mean for resource communities.

Strategy revisited

For the civilizations of antiquity and ever since, it has been clear that strategy is necessary for coordinating large collectives towards shared goods or fencing off threats (Kagan, 2006). Power relations were inherently implicated in strategy as it conceives rearrangements in power and entails the use of power through persuasion or coercion or the use of power to modify perceptions either openly or in the shade (Flyvbjerg, 1998). One of the best-known scholars of strategy is Niccolo Machiavelli who testifies to the role of power dynamics and the entwining of individual, group and communal strategies (Del Lucchese, 2009; Machiavelli et al., 1988). Because of this we take the position that each governance context with its unique path of evolution and particular arrangement of actors, institutions and power structures allows for strategizing in a particular way and at the same time distinctively shapes the effects of strategy.

Many societal and environmental problems in resource communities appear at first to be urgent and requiring short term action; addressing health concerns, cleaning up environmental deterioration, rebuilding or repurposing essential infrastructure. Some of the most difficult challenges stretch over many generations and typically require long-term governance settings and policy solutions (Meadowcroft et al., 2012). Finding sustainable economic alternatives, maintaining viable livelihoods and a healthy environment, for example, are aspects requiring long-term thinking and endurance. It would appear logical then to find ways of linking narratives and ideas about the future with policy tools. The long-term might be the most relevant yet the least knowable and the most difficult to steer towards with existing governance tools.

We understand the narrative side of a strategy as a vision. It is useful now after our discussion of narrative mapping and self-analysis to use a different word and make the distinction between vision and narratives that are already circulating in the community or narratives quietly built into its governance system. A vision we understand to be a narrative that emerges from the discussion and deliberation of other narratives, one unifying narrative that has enough internal cohesion and external support to give direction to the community. Building a vision can thus be understood as an important steppingstone from self-analysis to strategy.

It is worth remembering that visions for the future are not to be equated with predictions. Although a vision should reflect the desires and aspirations of the community it does not guarantee that this goal will be reached or at least not in the precise form it was conceived. A vision will guide and inspire and more likely lead the community to explore different alternatives. In a similar way, a vision should avoid being a fantasy, a decontextualized aspiration (Van Assche et al., 2021). Crafting a vision and a strategy rising from thorough self-analysis should be a way of revealing the limits and possibilities of control within the community.

When referring to a strategy adapted to its context we imply adaptation to the community's governance context, this context we have explained earlier is a reflection of the larger physical and societal context in which it is embedded. A strategy adapted to its governance context will then be able to link visions to existing and possible policies. A precise integration of visions with policy will enable the mobilization of the administrative machinery. While we just called the crafting of a vision a steppingstone towards strategy, from the rest of the book it will be clear that such linearity cannot always hold. Indeed, a deep knowledge of governance will steer the crafting of visions, as some will be understood as impossible, or as relying on tools that do not work or which might not be easy to create in current governance. One of the conclusions can then be abandoning of a certain direction of development, of certain hopes for the future, another conclusion might be that first governance needs to be reformed, after which more potential strategies might become realistic. Coupling vision and policy tools can be considered part and parcel of the articulation of community strategy (Van Assche et al., 2021). Pursuing these couplings is a form of policy coordination and a linking of narrative and institution (Voß & Bornemann, 2011; Wertsch, 2008).

We can make a non-trivial distinction between strategy as the plan or policy itself, strategy preceding the formation of the policy and strategy afterwards, in the implementation process (Pressman & Wildavsky, 1984). As we mentioned earlier the distinction between strategizing and planning is often blurred; making us believe the strategy has been successful when a checklist of tasks has been marked off. Henry Mintzberg (1978) reflected on the relation between strategies understood as plan and strategies as patterns. In the first perspective strategies are seen as purposefully developed sets of actions; the plan. Strategies as patterns emerge from consistent behavior that at some point could be labeled as strategy. The difference between these perspectives lies in the relation between intentions and actions. Intentions are rarely fully known; they can be identified after a certain pattern of actions (Barbuto, 2016; Hax & Majluf, 1988). Actions are different, they can communicate intentions or can deviate from actual intentions, they are easier to recognize and follow. Strategy reflects intentions while a plan focuses on actions.

Systems theory complicates the distinction made by Mintzberg between strategy as plan and emerging strategy, as both dimensions are inextricably part of every set of actions that is considered to be a strategy. From the perspective of social systems theory and organizational theory (Luhmann, 1995; Seidl, 2007; Suddaby et al., 2013) making the distinction between strategy as plan and strategy as pattern is inconsistent with the notion that strategy is *always* a combination of real intention (*a priori*) and ascription of intention (after the facts). In fact, what many present as the same thing (the strategy), is a continuous shifting between original intentions, adapted intentions and ascription of intention. What is recognized in hindsight (ascription) then possibly leads to new strategic episodes and can be a strategy in itself. Strategies can therefore be defined through the distinction between intentions and actions and the further specification of intention as original, adapted and ascribed.

We have discussed how actors, as a collection of individuals with a specific role in governance, each define a particular narrative or set of narratives about the world around them. These narratives can share elements with those of other actors reinforcing their collaboration but they can also discourage collaboration when opposing narratives can't find common ground to deliberate. Narratives that instigate polarization, that are closed to alternative explanations make it difficult for actors in governance to collectively coordinate action. Narratives constitute an actor's identity; at the same time identity shapes narratives. This is continuously happening in governance through the interaction and deliberation between actors and institutions. When narratives and identities become impermeable, when they become fixed and not allow to respond to continuous deliberation, we could say they become entrenched. These entrenched narratives and identities will be mirrored in strategy in a process that will look less like crafting and more like fitting into a predefined mold (Gerritsen et al., 2022; Van Assche et al., 2020).

A strategy, via a vision, can be seen as means to integrate several community narratives. A lack of cohesion among pre-existing narratives is not necessarily a problem. What we can expect in most communities, including prosperous ones, is a situation of multiple narratives and policy tools not entirely synchronized or seamlessly coupled. This multiplicity of tools (policies and plans) reflects the complexity of contemporary governance systems, an array of narratives is an expression of the increasing complexity of human societies (Jessop, 2002). However, a random collection of policy tools will certainly create problems in the overall system, for example overwhelming the legal system and rendering it dysfunctional for society.

A further problem for the formation of strategy is the just mentioned situation where narratives about the future, social memories and identities either reinforce each other to the extent that no change and little critical interrogation is possible (Van Assche et al., 2022). Or, when a crumbling identity is joined by one alternative, in a process of polarization which closes the minds in each of the poles. Both cases, as we know, are common in resource communities, hence the difficulties for strategy, while strategy is more needed than elsewhere. Hence also the need for a possibly therapeutic and most likely tricky process of self-analysis, where gradually the interpretation of self, past and future can be pried open. In such situations of closure (concentration problem) or polarization (trauma, violence and decline), it is imperative that whatever shift in perspective that occurs is attributed to the self not to an outsider, nor to an internal opponent (Figure 10.1).

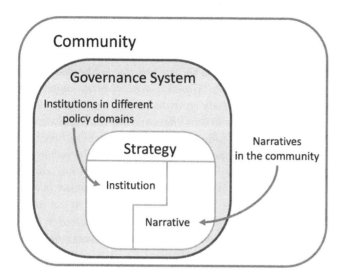

FIGURE 10.1 Strategy as narrative and institution. Community strategy as a narrative and institution in a community will relate with narratives existing in the community as well as with institutions (new and existing) in the community's governance system. For strategy to coordinate futures it will also need to be an institution itself.

*Grande Cache, Alberta was incorporated in 1966, as part of a wave of new town projects in Canada, pushing the resource frontier by means of coordinated strategies (*Robinson, 1979*). Provinces took the lead, yet, aimed at the creation of local governments, and were supported by federal ministries. By the late 80's the trend was over. Grand Cache went through phases of boom and bust, and presently, coal mining resumed, while the town itself was dissolved into the surrounding county in 2018. Older research in Grand Cache (*Skaburskis, 1989*) indicated that locals were proud of not being a company town, but self-organizing, and also co-created by government and company. Even so, the perceived stability due to government planning did not last very long, as population numbers went up and down, together with employment and real estate prices. The provincial government, in the hybrid public-private construction, and with the eye on local government taking over, did not fully invest in recreation, schooling and medical facilities, which reduced the burden initially but made for difficulties later.*

The dependence on coal mining and the power of the companies was never reduced, and, with that, the lack of truly autonomous decision-making, of institutional capacity and of experience with visioning became problematic. When coal went down, buffers and alternatives were scarce, and when coal came back with few jobs, the capacity to strategize wasn't there, and the nearby

Rocky Mountain parks were not utilized as drivers of a new development strategy. Grande Cache is not unique, as it illustrates the dilemmas of many planned resource towns. Initial strategizing, tight integration of policies and coordination of action is easier than elsewhere, yet private, public and mixed models have serious drawbacks, with the Grand Cache hybrid, supposedly overcoming the power concentration of the private model, not really doing so, and supposedly overcoming the rigidity of the governmental option, still suffering from this. In the development stage, provincial planners did not pay attention to the lot servicing, overdeveloped, then caused financial troubles for the new town, which needed an early bail out by the provincial housing corporation, while in 2017, foreign owners of the mining company bailed out on their debt and their responsibilities to the community dependent on them (Van Assche et al., 2022). Which drives home the message that resource town are initially easy places to strategize, yet once they develop, strategy becomes harder because of concentration and other problems.

Reality effect, goal dependencies and strategy

Strategy is enacted in a world that is more complex than the model presumed by the strategy. This is not only because of the continuous evolution taking place in governance, the evolution of actors and institutions and changing power dynamics. Part of the complexity has to do with visualizing the effects of strategy in the present – these effects might only become visible much later in time. We come back here to the concept of reality effects.

This is the idea that communications can change the world around us in two fundamental ways; communications can directly change the physical environment and they can also change the way we understand the world around us. In this way then strategy can have material effects as it can change the physical environment in a community, but it can also change the way the community understands its environment, it can have discursive effects.

Discursive effects and material effects can be intertwined. The way people understand their environment can change because of a physical change in it. For example, a park created in a forgotten wild corner of the community can change the way people appreciate the natural environment around, creating a direct connection between the health of the natural environment and individual wellbeing. A new narrative stemming from the strategy can trigger behavioral changes, the way people navigate the physical environment, revealing elements that might require improvement or change.

While reality effects are the effects of strategy on what is recognized as reality in the community, *goal dependencies* (see above), refer to the effects of the strategy in governance. Reality effects can trigger goal dependencies and vice versa, as changes in governance will affect the community, rather naturally (Bowles & Gintis, 2002). Less obvious might be the diversity of reality effects in the community, which can trigger changes in perception, discourse, evaluation, leading to shifts in public discourse, activism, lobbying, buying, selling, moving, voting. A plan perceived to be a failure or failing to be perceived, will most likely have effects in governance, goal dependencies, which are far from the intentions of the strategists.

In order to optimize reality effects, keep them in line with the intentions of the strategy, a deep understanding of goal dependencies is therefore useful. Which means that the whole set of entwined dependencies in governance needs to be understood, which points back at the utility of governance analysis as an important aspect of self-analysis (Van Assche et al., 2013). Indeed, the mapping of actors, institutions, narratives, of power and knowledge can be carried out through the lens of dependencies in governance evolution, which will give a better idea of what might happen when a new idea, a new big idea, a new strategy is dropped into the machinery of governance.

Careful judgment, accumulated insights and a combination of different methods will yield useful insight in these rigidities in governance. It will be important to conduct historical work at the same time as attempting to understand the current governance arrangements. Tracing dependencies will likely lead to the unveiling of hidden histories, unknown narratives, informal arrangements and persistent power relations. What will ultimately be of use for the community in crafting its strategy will be evidence of how and why persuasive stories changed overtime. Understanding these changes, how they originated and what they led to, will prove to be a powerful part of self-analysis (Aal, 2022; Besio & Pronzini, 2011).

In the German Ruhr area, mentioned in an earlier example as Germany's industrial powerhouse, the coal and steel industries collapse did not trigger the production of a comprehensive regional plan, which could have been expected in a social-democratic country with a strong planning tradition. Initially, private companies and unions of miners and steel workers opposed policies to diversify, yet already in the 1960s the regional government of Nord Rhein Westfalen (NRW) articulated policies to support the redevelopment of the region. Low education levels and the absence of universities in the region were causes for action. A more diversified work force could potentially help some people to move out and for those staying to find or create different jobs. Environmental engineering and consultancy derived from existing engineering knowledge (a cognitive legacy) and new environmental regulation.

Housing stock was diverse but often of low quality and when some villages lost a large part of their population, this set-in motion negative feedback loops leading to the decay of many residential areas, a process exacerbated by the very fragmented spatial structure of the Ruhr. Immigrants who did not feel fully integrated were hesitant to lobby for renovation or rebuilding initiatives. When economic decline continued, many 'guest workers' did not feel very welcome guests anymore.

What slowly emerged and made a real difference on all these fronts was not a plan but a strategy. The Ruhr truly saw a process of emergence and a deliberate refraining from central steering, as concentration of power, of ideas, of skills and industry was understood to be a problem. There was, with governmental actors and advising academics, an early awareness of the concentration problem, and an awareness that an experimental approach should be combined with government investment in social services, education, infrastructure, environmental quality, and overall quality of life, as a set of stabilization measures which could convince people to stay and industries to come. Regional strategies existed but without an overarching or dominant idea and often per policy domain, while still allowing for coordination.

Local initiatives were encouraged and focus points for investment defined. Cooperatives were established to renovate houses as well as to create new universities and later technology and innovation parks. For one of the most problematic areas, near the Emscher tributary, a more design-intensive approach was chosen. This approach still allowed for experimentation: the IBA Emscher, an 'exhibition' which was more than an exhibition, rather a grand experiment including many smaller experiments in reusing old industrial buildings, cleaning up pollution, reinventing residential, commercial and industrial areas. Industrial heritage was preserved but selectively; other buildings were demolished or reused.

Notable is that the state of NRW, the larger region, did adapt its regional strategy continuously, with new funding mechanisms appearing regularly, new forms of collaboration with local governments, NGO's, universities, industries. The goals and methods shifted regularly, as well as the policy tools used. At the same time, the health of the Ruhr was always monitored, always a concern, and collaborative strategizing never ceased.

Observation and self-observation

We have reiterated several times the importance of the quality of self-analysis for strategy. We make a link here with the quality of observation, more specifically with the quality of self-observation or reflexivity (cf. Voß et al., 2006; Voß & Bornemann, 2011). It is relevant here to point out that while every community is capable of some form of observation and reflexivity, there are limits to what a community can observe. From a systems perspective we can refer to different theories highlighting the limits of any system in this case community to observe itself entirely. The categories used by a community to understand itself and its environment, will limit the use of different categories of understanding and interpretation. In Foucaultian terms, each discursive construction renders alternative constructions opaque (Foucault, 2000; Rose et al., 2006; Thomas et al., 2013). We distinguished earlier between discursive identity and autopoietic identity, with the last one being less transparent for the community, in its attempts at self-reflection. This amounts to an argument for slow self-analysis and an argument for a role of outsider perspectives to enrich the analysis.

Each actor in governance associates with a particular collection of narratives, which determine how it understand its environment, including the governance environment. In the whole configuration of actors in governance, certain narratives will dominate in the accepted self-description and self-observation: this selectivity will hinge on what is understood as good governance, on ideology, identity. Discourses structure the selectivity of other discourses, which then lead to a selective interpretation of self, a unique set of limitations on self-observation (Seidl & Becker, 2006). Engineering, law or management perspectives can be more prestigious or dominant in governance, neo-liberal ideologies can limit self-observation, e.g., by reducing the assessment to questions of efficiency in the delivery of a narrow set of services, not to questions of fair procedures of deciding on a shared future and common goods. Ecological or cultural knowledge can be marginalized and the observation of this marginalization can be difficult, because other discourses are dominant and structuring in self-reflection. For resource communities, the use of economic categories to understand self and environment, to structure the self-observation in governance, will limit self-understanding to economic terms and will render it difficult for future strategies to think beyond economic terms. Other understandings of self will become opaque, even if they might be present in the community and in corners of the governance system and such opacity will translate into limits to strategy (Valentinov et al., 2019).

Which then brings us back to the earlier argument that strategy in resource communities under duress will have to rethink governance, as well as choosing a direction for the community. The tools to navigate will have to be partly built during or before the process of navigation. And this requirement will make a deep insight into the evolution of governance, its transformation modes and potential, all the more important. It also brings back another point made earlier, that *after* the articulation and implementation of strategy, so long *after* the possibly therapeutic and confrontational process of self-analysis, new routines of reflexivity might be needed, so the chances of ending up in the same place of opaque problems can be kept low. A third implication of the observations in the previous two sections, on observation, is that, for resource communities and their typical problems, intermediate strategies, might be advisable, strategies aiming at something else than the ultimate goal of community reinvention (Figure 10.2).

Intermediate strategy

Perhaps more often than not crafting strategy will fail to follow a predictable path from self-analysis to visioning to strategy. For some communities the

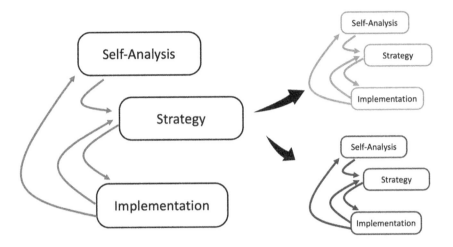

FIGURE 10.2 Adaptive strategy. There is no straight path from strategy to implementation. Strategy is in a continuous process of adaptation where implementation sparks changes in strategy or a process of reflection which in turn can encourage change in strategy as well.

self-reflection process will have depleted energy and resources necessary to continue, in other cases a clear path forward might not be visible. We mention alternative ways of reaching strategizing without necessarily stopping reflection or archiving efforts. In some cases, it will be necessary to think of an intermediate strategy, a temporary form of strategy that enables a longer-term strategy to be crafted. This intermediate strategy can be coupled to a transitional form of organization or transitional governance arrangement that allows for regrouping and gathering whatever elements are thought of as needed for a longer-term strategy.

Transitional governance is a governance arrangement that will allow the community to 'regroup,' to continue taking collectively binding decisions in way that allows for the essential functioning of administration and at the same time opens a space to build assets or capacity necessary for tackling bigger and tougher questions for strategy crafting. We will refer to transitional governance again in Chapter 12. To the concept of transitional governance we can add the idea of transitional leadership. Very much like transitional governance this form of leadership can be meant to stabilize the community, to break dependencies and manage risk (Van Assche et al., 2021). Transitional forms of leadership can act as a controlled disrupter, without having to worry about personal or political favors, it can eventually fade in the background and allow a new arrangement of actors to step into the scene. Leadership in any case will need to keep in mind that while transitioning, a constant self-reflection needs to be maintained (Rosenhead et al., 2019; Uhl-Bien & Arena, 2017).

An intermediate strategy will allow for the building of capacity and assets within this transitional governance arrangement. The goal of an intermediate strategy will be to prepare the community for strategizing. Because strategizing is a context specific process, intermediate strategy will take a different shape for each community, it will need to be adapted to each circumstance. Intermediate strategy could focus on a collection of things like improving infrastructure, acquiring technology, improving internet connectivity, opening access routes or on improving certain skills and expertise. Building assets or capacity for improving the quality and scope of self-analysis will likely yield positive outcomes for the crafting of a vision and strategy. This decision needs to come as a result of an initial attempt at self-analysis and will need to continue to keep as a goal the crafting of a community strategy.

Concluding (for now)

Resource communities desiring transformation will need to begin by uncovering the narratives and legacies that shape their context and their reality. They will need to commit to a self-analysis. This will not be an easy process, it will likely also uncover many troubles, difficult memories and traumas from the past (Brown & Augusta-Scott, 2006; Czarniawska, 1997; Wertsch, 2008). In this process, the role of outsiders might be of value (Caine et al., 2007; Lockhart, 1982). It can also expand, stall, create conflict and question identities and positions of power.

Maintaining a balance between outsider and insider perspectives will be useful throughout self-analysis as well as later in the crafting of a vison and ultimately a strategy for the community. We note that local leadership will play a fundamental role in the whole process and will ideally act as both insider and outsider, guiding and tempering expectations. High-quality self-analysis can produce a high-quality vision, long-term perspective for the community which in turn will be crucial for crafting a high-quality strategy. Often however this will not be a linear process. Crafting strategy will encounter limits and will likely require detours (Van Assche & Verschraegen, 2008).

Limits to strategy come from limits to observation, or rather self-observation. Limits to strategy also come from the inherent dependencies in governance; the path dependencies, interdependencies, goal dependencies and material dependencies that render collective decision-making process rigid (Van Assche et al., 2013). Particularly significant for resource communities are material dependencies. Often difficult to avoid but important to recognize, these dependencies will shape governance arrangements in a community and will also shape the opportunities and obstacles for strategizing, hence the importance in recognizing them. In defining strategy, we discussed its role as both a narrative and an institution, thus serving a function for the community.

References

Aal, E. B. W. (2022). The significance of Luhmann's theory on organisations for project governance. *Project Leadership and Society*, *3*, 100070. 10.1016/j.plas. 2022.100070.

Alvesson, M., & Kärreman, D. (2007). Unraveling HRM: Identity, ceremony, and control in a management consulting firm. *Organization Science*, *18*(4), 711–723.

Alvesson, M., & Sveningsson, S. (2013). Essay: Authentic leadership critically reviewed. In *Authentic leadership*. Edward Elgar Publishing.

Alvesson, M., Bridgman, T., & Willmott, H. (2009). *The Oxford handbook of critical management studies*. Oxford Handbooks.

Barbuto Jr, J. E. (2016). How is strategy formed in organizations? A multi-disciplinary taxonomy of strategy-making approaches. *Journal of Behavioral and Applied Management*, *3*(1), 65–77.

Besio, C., & Pronzini, A. (2011). Inside organizations and out. Methodological tenets for empirical research inspired by systems theory. *Historical Social Research/ Historische Sozialforschung*, *36*(1 (135)), 18–41.

Boje, D. M., Luhman, J. T., & Baack, D. E. (1999). Stories and encounters between storytelling organizations. *Journal of Management Inquiry*, *8*(4), 340–360. 10.1177/ 105649269984002.

Bowles, S., & Gintis, H. (2002). Social capital and community governance. *The Economic Journal*, *112*(483), F419–F436. 10.1111/1468-0297.00077.

Brown, C., & Augusta-Scott, T. (2006). *Narrative therapy: Making meaning, making lives*. SAGE Publications.

Burns, J., & Goldsborough, G. (2012). Roblin city: A gleaming metropolis on Hudson Bay. *Manitoba History*, (68), 40–44.

Caine, K. J., Salomons, M. J., & Simmons, D. (2007). Partnerships for social change in the Canadian North: Revisiting the insider–outsider dialectic. *Development and Change*, *38*(3), 447–471. 10.1111/j.1467-7660.2007.00419.x.

Carter, C., Clegg, S. R., & Kornberger, M. (2008). *A very short, fairly interesting and reasonably cheap book about studying strategy*. SAGE.

Clegg, S. (2006). The bounds of rationality: Power/history/imagination. *Critical Perspectives on Accounting*, *17*(7), 847–863.

Czarniawska, B. (1997). *A narrative approach to organization studies*. SAGE Publications.

Czarniawska, B. (2014). *A theory of organizing*. Edward Elgar Publishing.

Czarniawska, B., & Gagliardi, P. (2003). *Narratives we organize by* (Vol. 11). John Benjamins Publishing.

De Gregori, T. R. (1987). Resources are not; they become: An institutional theory. *Journal of Economic Issues*, *21*(3), 1241–1263.

Del Lucchese, F. (2009). Crisis and power: Economics, politics and conflict in Machiavelli's political thought. *History of Political Thought*, *30*(1), 75–96. JSTOR.

Douglas, M. (1966). *Purity and danger: An analysis of concepts of pollution and taboo.* Routledge.

Douglas, M. (2002). *Purity and danger: An analysis of concept of pollution and taboo* (Vol. 2). Psychology Press.

Fischer, F. (2000). *Citizens, experts, and the environment: The politics of local knowledge.* Duke University Press.

Flyvbjerg, B. (1998). *Rationality and power: Democracy in practice.* University of Chicago press.

Foucault, M. (2000). *Power* (J. D. Faubion, Trans.). New Press.

Gaventa, J. (2004). Representation, community leadership and participation: citizen involvement in neighbourhood renewal and local governance. Report, Neighbourhood Renewal Unit, Office of Deputy Prime Minister, July, 04.

Gerritsen, M., Kooij, H.-J., Groenleer, M., & van der Krabben, E. (2022). To see, or not to see, that is the question: Studying Dutch experimentalist energy transition governance through an evolutionary lens. *Sustainability, 14*(3), 1540. 10.3390/su14031540.

Golsorkhi, D., Rouleau, L., Seidl, D., & Vaara, E. (2010). *Cambridge handbook of strategy as practice.* Cambridge University Press.

Gruezmacher, M., & Van Assche, K. (2022). *Crafting strategies for sustainable local development.* InPlanning.

Gunder, M., & Hillier, J. (2007). Planning as urban therapeutic. *Environment and Planning A: Economy and Space, 39*(2), 467–486. 10.1068/a38236.

Hax, A. C., & Majluf, N. S. (1988). The concept of strategy and the strategy formation process. *Interfaces, 18*(3), 99–109.

Hidle, K., & Normann, R. H. (2013). Who can govern? Comparing network governance leadership in two Norwegian city regions. *European Planning Studies, 21*(2), 115–130. 10.1080/09654313.2012.722924.

Hillier, J. (2002). *Shadows of power: An allegory of prudence in land-use planning.* Routledge.

Jessop, B. (2002). Governance and meta-governance in the face of complexity: On the roles of requisite variety, reflexive observation, and romantic irony in participatory governance. In H. Heinelt, P. Getimis, G. Kafkalas, R. Smith, & E. Swyngedouw (Eds.), *Participatory governance in multi-level context: Concepts and experience* (pp. 33–58). VS Verlag für Sozialwissenschaften. 10.1007/978-3-663-11005-7_2.

Jones, C. O. (2009, April). The legitimacy of inexperience: Leadership from outside. In *The forum* (Vol. 7, No. 1). De Gruyter.

Kagan, K. (2006). Redefining Roman grand strategy. *The Journal of Military History, 70*(2), 333–362.

Kapitan, L., Litell, M., & Torres, A. (2011). Creative art therapy in a community's participatory research and social transformation. *Art Therapy, 28*(2), 64–73.

Kornberger, M. (2022). *Strategies for distributed and collective action connecting the dots.* Oxford University Press USA – OSO. http://public.eblib.com/choice/PublicFullRecord.aspx?p=6836917

Kornberger, M., Meyer, R. E., & Höllerer, M. A. (2021). Exploring the long-term effect of strategy work: The case of Sustainable Sydney 2030. *Urban Studies, 58*(16), 3316–3334.

Lockhart, A. (1982). The insider-outsider dialectic in native socio-economic development: A case study in process understanding. *Canadian Journal of Native Studies, 2*(1), 159–168.

Luhmann, N. (1995). *Social systems* (Vol. 1). Stanford University Press Stanford.

Machiavelli, N., Skinner, Q., Skinner, B. B. P. H. Q., Price, R., & Geuss, R. (1988). *Machiavelli: The prince.* Cambridge University Press.

Martines, L. (1988). *Power and imagination: City-states in Renaissance Italy.* Taylor & Francis.

Meadowcroft, J., Langhelle, O., & Ruud, A. (2012). Governance, democracy and sustainable development: Moving beyond the impasse. In *Governance, democracy and sustainable development* (pp. 1–13). Edward Elgar Publishing. https://www. elgaronline.com/display/edcoll/9781849807562/9781849807562.00009.xml

Meyer, R. E., Kornberger, M., & Höllerer, M. A. (2020). How cities think: Thought style, thought collective, and the impact of strategy. In C. W. J. Steele, T. R. Hannigan, V. L. Glaser, M. Toubiana, & J. Gehman (Eds.), *Macrofoundations: Exploring the institutionally situated nature of activity* (Vol. 68, pp. 185–200). Emerald Publishing Limited.

Mintzberg, H. (1978). Patterns in strategy formation. *Management Science, 24*(9), 934–948. 10.1287/mnsc.24.9.934.

Mintzberg, H. (1987). Crafting strategy.

Mintzberg, H., & Lampel, J. B. (1999). *Reflecting on the strategy process.* MIT Sloan Management Review.

Mintzberg, H., & Waters, J. A. (1985). Of strategies, deliberate and emergent. *Strategic Management Journal, 6*(3), 257–272. 10.1002/smj.4250060306.

Pigg, K. E. (2002). Three faces of empowerment: Expanding the theory of empowerment in community development. *Journal of the Community Development Society, 33*(1), 107–123. 10.1080/15575330209490145.

Pressman, J. L., & Wildavsky, A. (1984). *Implementation: How great expectations in Washington are dashed in Oakland; Or, why it's amazing that federal programs work at all, this being a saga of the economic development administration as told by two sympathetic observers who seek to build morals.* Univ of California Press.

Quigley, T. J., Hambrick, D. C., Misangyi, V. F., & Rizzi, G. A. (2019). CEO selection as risk-taking: A new vantage on the debate about the consequences of insiders versus outsiders. *Strategic Management Journal, 40*(9), 1453–1470. 10.1002/smj.3033.

Robinson, I. (1979). Planning and managing new towns on the resource frontier. *Urban regional planning in a federal state.* Toronto: Mc-Graw-Hill.

Rose, N., O'Malley, P., & Valverde, M. (2006). Governmentality. *Annual Review of Law and Social Science, 2*(1), 83–104. 10.1146/annurev.lawsocsci.2.081805.105900.

Rosenhead, J., Franco, L. A., Grint, K., & Friedland, B. (2019). Complexity theory and leadership practice: A review, a critique, and some recommendations. *The Leadership Quarterly, 30*(5), 101304. 10.1016/j.leaqua.2019.07.002.

Sabapathy, J. (2011). A medieval officer and a modern mentality? Podestà and the quality of accountability. *The Mediaeval Journal, 1*(2), 43–80.

Schuftan, C. (1996). The community development dilemma: What is really empowering? *Community Development Journal, 31*(3), 260–264.

Scott, J. C. (1998). *Seeing like a state: How certain schemes to improve the human condition have failed.* Yale University Press.

Scott, J. C. (2020). *Seeing like a state: How certain schemes to improve the human condition have failed.* Yale University Press.

Scott, J., Carrington, K., & McIntosh, A. (2012). Established-outsider relations and fear of crime in mining towns. *Sociologia Ruralis, 52*(2), 147–169.

Seidl, D. (2007). General strategy concepts and the ecology of strategy discourses: A systemic-discursive perspective. *Organization Studies, 28*(2), 197–218.

Seidl, D., & Becker, K. H. (2006). Organizations as distinction generating and processing systems: Niklas Luhmann's contribution to organization studies. *Organization, 13*(1), 9–35. 10.1177/1350508406059635.

Skaburskis, A. (1989). Options for developing resource towns: The effects of increasing government involvement in new town development. *Journal of Architectural and Planning Research*, 321–343.

Staples, L. H. (2001). Insider/outsider upsides and downsides. *Social Work with Groups, 23*(2), 19–35.

Sturdy, A. (2011). Consultancy's consequences? A critical assessment of management consultancy's impact on management. *British Journal of Management, 22*(3), 517–530.

Suddaby, R., Seidl, D., & Lê, J. K. (2013). Strategy-as-practice meets neo-institutional theory.

Timmermans, J., van der Heiden, S., & Born, M. Ph. (2014). Policy entrepreneurs in sustainability transitions: Their personality and leadership profiles assessed. *Environmental Innovation and Societal Transitions, 13*, 96–108. 10.1016/j.eist. 2014.06.002.

Thomas, P., Wilson, J., & Leeds, O. (2013). Constructing 'the history of strategic management': A critical analysis of the academic discourse. *Business History, 55*(7), 1119–1142. 10.1080/00076791.2013.838039.

Uhl-Bien, M., & Arena, M. (2017). Complexity leadership: Enabling people and organizations for adaptability. *Organizational Dynamics, 46*, 9–20. 10.1016/j.orgdyn. 2016.12.001.

Valentinov, V., Verschraegen, G., & Van Assche, K. (2019). The limits of transparency: A systems theory view. *Systems Research and Behavioral Science, 36*(3), 289–300. 10.1002/sres.2591.

Van Assche, K., & Verschraegen, G. (2008). The limits of planning: Niklas Luhmann's systems theory and the analysis of planning and planning ambitions. *Planning Theory, 7*(3), 263–283.

Van Assche, K., Beunen, R., & Duineveld, M. (2013). *Evolutionary governance theory: An introduction*. Springer.

Van Assche, K., Beunen, R., Gruezmacher, M., & Duineveld, M. (2020). Rethinking strategy in environmental governance. *Journal of Environmental Policy & Planning, 22*(5), 695–708. 10.1080/1523908X.2020.1768834.

Van Assche, K., Birchall, J., & Gruezmacher, M. (2022b). Arctic and northern community governance: The need for local planning and design as resilience strategy. *Land Use Policy, 117*, 106062.

Van Assche, K., Duineveld, M., Gruezmacher, M., & Beunen, R. (2021). Steering as path creation: Leadership and the art of managing dependencies and reality effects. *Politics and Governance, 9*(2), 369–380. 10.17645/pag.v9i2.4027.

Van Assche, K., Gruezmacher, M., & Deacon, L. (2020). Land use tools for tempering boom and bust: Strategy and capacity building in governance. *Land Use Policy, 93*, 103994–103994. 10.1016/j.landusepol.2019.05.013.

Van Assche, K., Gruezmacher, M., & Granzow, M. (2021). From trauma to fantasy and policy. The past in the futures of mining communities; the case of Crowsnest Pass, Alberta. *Resources Policy*, *72*, 102050–102050. 10.1016/j.resourpol.2021. 102050.

Van Assche, K., Gruezmacher, M., Summers, B., Culling, J., Gajjar, S., Granzow, M., ... & Jamwal, A. (2022). Land use policy and community strategy. Factors enabling and hampering integrated local strategy in Alberta, Canada. *Land Use Policy*, *118*, 106101.

Van Assche, K., Verschraegen, G., Valentinov, V., & Gruezmacher, M. (2019). The social, the ecological, and the adaptive. Von Bertalanffy's general systems theory and the adaptive governance of social-ecological systems. *Systems Research and Behavioral Science*, *36*(3), 308–321.

Voß, J. P. (2007). Innovation processes in governance: The development of 'emissions trading'as a new policy instrument. *Science and Public Policy*, *34*(5), 329–343.

Voß, J.-P., & Bornemann, B. (2011). The politics of reflexive governance: Challenges for designing adaptive management and transition management. *Ecology and Society*, *16*(2), 9. [online] URL: http://www.ecologyandsociety.org-9. [online] URL: http://www.ecologyandsociety.org.

Voß, J.-P., Bauknecht, D., & Kemp, R. (2006). *Reflexive governance for sustainable development*. Edward Elgar Publishing.

Wertsch, J. V. (2008). The narrative organization of collective memory. *Ethos*, *36*(1), 120–135.

Whittington, R. (1996). Strategy as practice. *Long Range Planning*, *29*(5), 731–735.

Williamson, O. E. (1999). Strategy research: Governance and competence perspectives. *Strategic Management Journal*, *20*(12), 1087–1108.

11

CONCLUSIONS

Legacies, (in) accessible pasts, and navigating
the futures of resource communities

Introduction: The predicament

In this book, we tried to address the difficult predicament of many resource
communities, across the world. We had in mind and spoke of communities in
the making and communities where resource extraction is a memory – a
powerful one (Antze & Lambek, 2016; Climo & Cattell, 2002). We tried to
answer the question of how resource communities can be shaped by the past
in specific ways and how the past can affect the ways they look at and try to
organize for the future. Finally, we attempted to draw conclusions on ways
to freely look forward, ways to extricate from the past and navigate the
future with more flexibility.

Resource communities, as we diagnosed in this book, are haunted by their
past in myriad ways. We distinguished history, memory and legacies and
discussed different types of legacies. Social memory can be a problem, as a
simplified memory can be tied to a simplified social identity, which underpins
resource extraction and imagined futures revolving around that same extraction (Hinchman & Hinchman, 1997; Perez-Sindin & Van Assche, 2020).
A particular structuring of social memory can be one of the legacies that
causes problems for considering alternative futures, but so can a mono-
functional landscape and infrastructures focused entirely on the resource
extraction. In terms of organizational legacies, one can often recognize a
simplified landscape of organizations, expressing a simplified social and
cultural life and, importantly one can routinely observe legacies in governance, in the system which can take collectively binding decisions (Sinclair,
2008; Van Assche et al., 2020).

DOI: 10.4324/9781003332145-11

Organizations are important in the story, as they can have their own memory, a role in social and economic life and an identity which can be tied or not to dominant identities, social memories and imagined or desired futures (Czarniawska, 1997). They can also associate with versions of the good life, of quality of life, which can make or break the sustainability of the community. Organizations can support narratives about a family friendly community and they can in a practical sense help to make the community livable for families. When families do not settle, or when they do but the next generations leaves, this is a problem. Organizations can be important thus to remind citizen and decision-makers alike that the community is more than a production place and that, in order to be a sustainable production place, it has to offer other things (Seidl, 2016). Furthermore, organizations are tools to bring up and experiment with new ideas and practices, they can start to function as actors in governance and can be ways to open up closed discourses and closed networks (Blaschke et al., 2012).

This is important as homogeneity, simplification and closure are ever present threats for resource communities, leading to what we called *concentration problems,* which can be diagnosed in many resource communities and former communities and which can have a multiplicity of mutually reinforcing effects. The concentration problem points at the tendency to operate on an ever-smaller base of discourses, forms of expertise and fewer actors and institutions to coordinate them (Van Assche et al., 2017). Where tools existed to envision and coordinate towards alternative futures, these tend to atrophy (cf. Wertsch, 2008). In the community at large, a dominant resource identity and linked social memory will not recognize this as a problem and will support this atrophied and rigid governance system because they too, do not see reasons to think of alternatives, or to 'bloat' a little understood governance system.

Identities narrative and autopoietic

We distinguished between discursive and autopoietic identity, as an entry point into the diversity of legacies which might be under the radar, which might be easily observable or understood within the community. As discursive constructs, as entangled narratives of place and group, of past, present, future, discursive identities and their supporting configurations might be relatively easy to unearth. Yet not all aspects will be acknowledged, not all stories that structure the thinking and acting are close to the surface and are reflected upon. We spoke of autopoietic identity, inspired by systems theorist Niklas Luhmann, as the unique form of reproduction of the community, the unique ways it organizes itself and keeps itself alive through actions, decisions, through stories (Bakken & Hernes, 2003; Luhmann, 1995). This autopoietic identity is never entirely clear from within the system, as it would entail a complete understanding of all interactions, structures, elements, semantics, how they evolved and how this unique evolution created a unique pattern of self-reproduction.

In governance, one can locate many aspects of this self-reproduction, as it is through governance that a community shapes itself, consciously and unconsciously. The functioning of governance might be naturalized, understood as a rational, logical way of organizing things but, of course, how governance works is a matter of contingent evolutions (Van Assche et al., 2013). Things could have been different and are different in each community, even if their formal structures are the same. How governance understands itself, how it looks at its own powers, at the community, at possibilities to introduce new narratives, to question existing ones, makes a difference when trying to move out of concentration problems. And these understandings, as well as what governance can actually do in a particular community, emerge from an evolution which is never entirely clear, hence never entirely transparent in its influence on the presence.

To grasp more of the potential and limits of governance under the difficult circumstances many resource communities find themselves in, we resorted to key ideas from evolutionary governance theory (EGT) (Beunen et al., 2014; Van Assche et al., 2013). EGT would argue that no community is completely transparent to itself and that no governance system understands completely how it is shaped by the past when trying to imagine different possible futures and how to organize for that. Routines are needed, productive fictions, master signifiers, black-boxing of complexity is the order of the day. Path creation is possible but the obstacles for this are different in each community, while the degree of awareness of these obstacles also differs.

EGT speaks of different dependencies as ways to understand the rigidities in governance paths. Path dependencies for EGT are legacies from the past, which shape the functioning of governance now, while interdependencies are relations between actors and institutions which tend to keep a configuration in place. Material dependencies, meanwhile, are effects of the environment, usually indirect, on governance and goal dependencies are effects *in governance* of visions for the future. The different dependencies affect each other, as actors and institutions, formal and informal and power and knowledge co-evolve in governance (Van Assche et al., 2022). Indeed, the nature of this co-evolution is unique and this unicity is a marker of autopoietic identity. Path dependencies keep interdependencies in place, while interdependencies modify goal dependencies and material dependencies can underpin inter-dependencies, to mention just one set of possible relations.

EGT thus helped to dissect the pattern of legacies in governance and to link past and future through the concept of goal dependencies. Those connections are also conceptualized in other ways, as narratives on the future are shaped by social memory and identity and as older identities, histories, understandings of the environment, desired futures and ideologies can be built into the policy tools, the institutions that govern the way we try to navigate the future (Hinchman & Hinchman, 1997). The meta-concept in governance, broad ideas on what governance is and should do, can be linked to past realities which are encoded in lingering institutions, procedures, in the structures of governance itself.

Legacies and memories

Legacies thus go far beyond what is remembered yet can extend to legacies in the structuring and functioning of memory itself, in the linking of memory, identity and future (Climo & Cattell, 2002; Lewicka, 2008). For resource communities, social memory and identity can be simplified to the point that they catalyze a reproduction of governance, ideas of limited utility of governance and narratives about the future which repeat the present or go back to the past. Cycles of boom and bust tend to aggravate the process, where shocks do not lead to innovation in governance, but to a low-level functioning of governance, that is, an ossified version where the development of long-term perspectives is not perceived as useful or possible (Van Assche et al., 2021).

When single industry towns exist in the margin of society, in remote, less developed and less integrated areas, the risks are even higher. Local governance tends to be weak, controlled by a few and often at the mercy of private actors, big companies, or higher-level governments. Which means that power-relations are established that are tough to change, with few options for new actors, new perspectives coming in. Underdeveloped checks and balances are a likely feature of governance in such situation, which makes individuals more vulnerable to abuse of power and few guarantees that if an ambitious vision comes up it would truly benefit the community.

In such communities, violence, as in physical violence and symbolic violence, often rears its head and trauma is common. We argued that trauma can be the result of recurrent violence and weak protections of the population but also stem from a history of risky extraction and from closure of an industry which organized everything in the community and was the source of identification as a resource town (Drozdzewski et al., 2016; Gunder & Hillier, 2007; Perez-Sindin & Van Assche, 2020). Repeating of policy mistakes, clinging to the past, or difficulties in recognizing wild policy fantasies as such, can be symptoms of community trauma. Legacies of trauma in governance include the difficulty in assessing past, the self and the environment in different ways, an increased opacity of the community for itself (Saari, 2022; Žižek, 2000). Symbolic violence, too, can make it hard for communities to see the legacies of that violence, of hierarchies which are kept in place even if the initiator of that hierarchy is gone. We used the Lacanian idea of the Big Other to refer to such situations, where, even after the industry is gone, it left as legacy a structure of the symbolic frameworks for identification and justification (Driver, 2009; Zizek, 1992). The master is gone, but one acts as if he is still there and even if the master was a rather terrible figure, finding identifications without reference to that figure and the old order which developed around it, is a tall order (Gunder, 2016).

Legacies of a history of extraction can thus be everywhere and they can be conscious and unconscious, conscious and acknowledged, or less so. They exist with individuals, in the life and imagination of the community and in its governance system. The unacknowledged and invisible legacies in the governance system are especially problematic, as it is in governance that a new path could be articulated and initiated, so if the functioning of governance, its real degree of autonomy, its real powers and weaknesses, is not clear for the governance system itself, let alone for the community, one cannot expect an easy transition process. In our analyses of power/knowledge relations and the concentration problem, we found that legacies in the community and in governance can reinforce each other and that a lack of diverse perspectives in governance and communities aggravates this problem. Using one side to change the other becomes problematic, as they are both marked by the same problems and by the same opacities in self-reflection (cf. Antze & Lambek, 2016; Stirling, 2014; Wertsch, 2008).

Inaccessible pasts and navigating dilemmas

The knots in an inaccessible past which structure behavior in the present, we diagnosed, following Jaques Lacan, as kernels of the Real, while that Real in resource communities was not only such hidden traumatizing memories but also an unacknowledged entwining with and dependence on a material environment that is barely observed (Stavrakakis, 2002; Styhre, 2008). Hence our chapter on tripping over realities and tripping over the Real, as for many resource communities, in the rare cases when ambitious policies for the future come up (either in the embrace of the old industry or rejecting it) they rarely work. We analyzed this at several points in the book in terms of legacies creating difficulties to articulate, implement but also *test,* or assess, potential policies and possible new narratives for the future (cf. Hinchman & Hinchman, 1997; Wertsch, 2008).

Not only are few expertise available, few functioning policy tools, one is likely dealing with a skeleton administration, dominant narratives that ensure the skeleton stays skinny and limited resources, as local governments were in many cases kept poor, even if owners and workers benefited from a resource boom (LUP bbust; LUP AB strateg). Then, there is the common evolution towards de-differentiation and towards a loss of diversity in perspectives in governance. This leads to a lack of counterpressure to functional stupidity, to hegemonic discourse, but also to a lack of creative encounters between perspectives, as it accounts for the weak testing of ideas for the future (Alvesson & Spicer, 2012). If we add part-time politicians and unstable administrations with little institutional memory, tripping over reality starts to look like a logical effect of the combined legacies in governance and community.

What appears as a problem, in governance, the set of possible solutions and the understanding of tools and resources are thoroughly shaped by histories of resource extraction (cf. Wertsch, 2008). In smaller, remote, less integrated, less stable communities, in places marked by weak governance from the start (as a result of intentions with other actors, or neglect), these pressures from the past tend to be worse. Simple references to more extensive engagement or participation in governance are not a solution, as the problems are everywhere and affecting the observation and definition of problems (Sinclair, 2008). Yet, simple references to external experts or higher levels of government offering solutions will probably not work either, as the dissonance with local self-understandings will be too great (Voß et al., 2006).

We encounter, therefore, several dilemma's which require cautious navigation:

- Those communities most in need of a strategy for reinvention are least equipped to recognize this and act on it
- Solutions in closed systems are more likely to emerge where openings already exist
- If new futures come in, they tend to trigger polarization, which undermines governance capacity, rather than increasing it

These dilemmas cannot be ignored when thinking about ways to extricate resource communities from the hold of their past. Broadening observation in governance, widening problem definitions and diversifying possible solutions, will have to start from a base with structural weaknesses, where some issues are not observed, many possible solutions are not recognized and external critiques or alternative interpretations from within the community are either dismissed as unreal or countered as attacks or signs of disloyalty (Van Assche et al., 2020). Ultimately it means that solutions cannot be imposed, either by local leadership or by outsiders and certainly not copied from a playbook based on other places or modernist scenarios expected to be universal (Gunder & Hillier, 2009; Van Assche et al., 2022).

The navigation of these dilemmas is tricky because it means that ways have to be found for the community to shift its interpretations of past, self and environment, in order to make space for new ideas about the future. It means that deep respect for local concerns and narratives must be combined with serious attempts to question the stories about problems and solutions encountered in the community (Czarniawska & Gagliardi, 2003). Leadership, internal opposition and facilitating outsiders can help in such process of gradual opening-up for alternative stories, a most likely slow process of questioning existing interpretations and reinforcing the credibility of alternatives (Nachmias & Greer, 1982).

These principles and these dilemmas will be central in a phase of collective self-analysis we argued for in the previous chapter, a phase of self-examination, possibly with external involvement, where some of the problems discussed in the earlier chapters can be diagnosed. The analysis cannot be outsourced, as this would reduce its connectivity with community and governance, hence its impact and as the self-analysis is not just an exercise in collecting information. Rather and especially in the more difficult cases, the self-analysis will play the role of community therapy, where the therapist is much less important than the opportunity to slowly come to a reinterpretation of self (Gunder & Hillier, 2007; Kinnvall, 2012). From which new perspectives on the future can spring up, through the cracks of a discursive building that requires some renovation.

Guidance and reflexivity

Such a process of self-analysis can require external guidance, or not. Local leadership, or civil society organizations, or local administration supporting a deeply participatory process can structure the self-reflection, help to decide how fast or slow it should be, how far it should go and what to focus on (Clandinin, 2006; Voß et al., 2006). Perceived problems and assets can be a starting point, a mapping of narratives about past, present and future, about self and environment, or, when there is a strong belief that the problems are technical in nature, a mapping of governance paths (Ackerman & Halverson, 2004; Mathie & Cunningham, 2003).

An interrogation of governance, its actors and institutions, power/knowledge interactions, its dependencies, will be helpful in most situations, as most likely, the concentration problem affected not only the world of discourse in the community, but also governance. It most likely shaped the potential and limitations of governance, through a selective use and production of institutions, through pressure on the patterns of inclusion and exclusion of actors and knowledges, through the imbrication of discursive configurations and institutions, together upholding local realities. Stories legitimize policies and vice versa; they naturalize what is contingent and present as immutable what is always in flux (Czarniawska, 1997; Rodríguez et al., 2018; Stirling, 2014).

Self-analysis can sometimes inspire strategy directly, yet in most cases it will have to take a detour, through a process of visioning, where, out of narrative fragments and competing narratives (once a dominant narrative has been dislodged) something new and unifying can be distilled (Fink, 2013;

Hinchman & Hinchman, 1997). This will always be an imperfect representation of what people thought during the process of visioning, yet it can help shaping discourse afterwards, certainly if the community succeeds in turning it into a strategy, which we understood as a process of coupling the new narrative with a set of institutions, some existing and some a product of the same process of strategizing (Kornberger, 2022). If it works, the strategy can itself function as an institution, coordinating collective action.

A period of deep self-reflection as the self-analysis we argued for, is not necessary everywhere but for resource communities in dire straits, we believe it is worth taking the risk and making the effort. Effort and risk are real, as the type of self-reflection that aims to open up the community to a rethink and reinvention, is *per* definition political and will naturally touch many sensitivities in community life (Gruezmacher & Van Assche, 2022; Rodríguez et al., 2018; Stirling, 2014). Identities are taken for granted, power relations exposed, self-imposed limitations exposed as, indeed, self-imposed. Such effort cannot be sustained, it needs to be considered an exception, a transition towards a larger transition. Yet, one objective of any reinvention strategy in (former) resource communities ought to be a permanent increase in reflexivity after implementation. Shifting a community to a different resource or baiting a new 'big fish' mining company can be an answer for the immediate future but if reflexivity is not increased more permanently, if diversity in perspectives is not established and safeguarded, chances are that concentration problems will return.

Certainly, reflexivity has its limits and the story of resource communities is a perfect illustration of this. Reflexivity is not the core of the solution and we know by now it cannot be pursued without restructuring other aspects of governance and without the potentially painful process of self-analysis (as concentration problems reduce reflexivity and hide the problem). However, self-analysis and strategy without attention to new *routines* of reflexivity, risk to squander the gains.

Strategy and diversity

Safeguarding diversity in perspectives, reinforcing checks and balances, maintaining redundancies in governance, multiplying channels of observation for changing environments, enhancing administration and its stability, fostering institutional memory and diverse social memories, creating spaces for ongoing dialog on memory and identity, creating protections for dissenting voices in civil society, all those activities can reinforce each other engendering positive feedback loops and reducing the chances that concentration problems return in one form or the other (Ackerman & Halverson, 2004).

The approach was never intended as a guarantee for success. It is entirely possible that a community does not want to face its problems and it is possible that its problems are insurmountable from their starting position. In such situation, help from the outside, or administrative redefinition of the community can still offer ways out and such avenues might become visible in the process of strategizing. The approach is not a take-it-or-leave-it proposition; self-analysis and strategy can be as elaborate as the community wants, the community must be guided by the problems that it faces and the values and assets it identifies with (cf. Gruezmacher & Van Assche, 2022; Mathie & Cunningham, 2003). It was emphasized before that a re-invention strategy will likely entail a reform of governance, which can be tackled before or in parallel with the substantive strategy, which needs to provide ideas for orientation towards the future. Such reform also must be selective and driven by local circumstances and the outcomes of self-analysis. Thus, one town might focus there on fostering institutional memory and stabilizing administration, while elsewhere, failing checks and balances need restoration.

In Chapter 12, these principles will be translated into a flexible methodology for self-analysis and strategy, tailored for resource communities not finding themselves in the most promising circumstances. This methodology explicitly aims to provide many pathways for analysis and strategy and does not assume that going through all steps is possible, desirable or necessary. It does offer a structure for self-guidance, points to stop and reflect, to draw partial conclusions and diagnose issues. What the end of the therapy will be, when it will be a good moment, an acceptable or desirable result, is entirely up to the community itself.

References

Ackerman, M. S., & Halverson, C. (2004). Organizational memory as objects, processes, and trajectories: An examination of organizational memory in use. *Computer Supported Cooperative Work (CSCW)*, *13*, 155–189.

Alvesson, M., & Spicer, A. (2012). A stupidity-based theory of organizations. *Journal of Management Studies*, *49*(7), 1194–1220. 10.1111/j.1467-6486.2012.01072.x.

Antze, P., & Lambek, M. (Eds.). (2016). *Tense past* (0 ed.). Routledge. 10.4324/9781315022222.

Bakken, T., & Hernes, T. (2003). *Autopoietic organization theory: Drawing on Niklas Luhmann's social systems perspective*. Copenhagen Business School Press. https://research.cbs.dk/en/publications/autopoietic-organization-theory-drawing-on-niklas-luhmanns-social.

Beunen, R., Van Assche, K., & Duineveld, M. (2014). *Evolutionary governance theory*. Springer.

Blaschke, S., Schoeneborn, D., & Seidl, D. (2012). Organizations as networks of communication episodes: Turning the network perspective inside out. *Organization Studies*, *33*(7), 879–906. 10.1177/0170840612443459.

Clandinin, D. J. (2006). *Handbook of narrative inquiry: Mapping a methodology*. SAGE Publications.

Climo, J. J., & Cattell, M. G. (2002). *Social memory and history: Anthropological perspectives*. Rowman Altamira.

Czarniawska, B. (1997). *A narrative approach to organization studies*. SAGE Publications.

Czarniawska, B., & Gagliardi, P. (2003). *Narratives we organize by* (Vol. 11). John Benjamins Publishing.

Driver, M. (2009). Struggling with Lack: A Lacanian perspective on organizational identity. *Organization Studies*, *30*(1), 55–72. 10.1177/0170840608100516.

Drozdzewski, D., De Nardi, S., & Waterton, E. (2016). Geographies of memory, place and identity: Intersections in remembering war and conflict. *Geography Compass*, *10*(11), 447–456. 10.1111/gec3.12296.

EXTRA

Fink, B. (2013). *Against understanding, volume 2: Cases and commentary in a Lacanian key*. Routledge.

Gruezmacher, M., & Van Assche, K. (2022). Crafting strategies for sustainable local development.

Gunder, M. (2016). Planning's "failure" to ensure efficient market delivery: A Lacanian deconstruction of this neoliberal scapegoating fantasy. *European Planning Studies*, *24*(1), 21–38. 10.1080/09654313.2015.1067291.

Gunder, M., & Hillier, J. (2007). Planning as urban therapeutic. *Environment and Planning A: Economy and Space*, *39*(2), 467–486. 10.1068/a38236.

Gunder, M., & Hillier, J. (2009). *Planning in ten words or less: A Lacanian entanglement with spatial planning*. Ashgate Publishing, Ltd.

Hinchman, L. P., & Hinchman, S. (1997). *Memory, identity, community: The idea of narrative in the human sciences*. SUNY Press.

Kinnvall, C. (2012). European trauma: Governance and the psychological moment. *Alternatives*, *37*(3), 266–281. 10.1177/0304375412452050.

Kornberger, M. (2022). *Strategies for distributed and collective action: Connecting the dots*. Oxford University Press.

Lewicka, M. (2008). Place attachment, place identity, and place memory: Restoring the forgotten city past. *Journal of Environmental Psychology*, *28*(3), 209–231. 10.1016/j.jenvp.2008.02.001.

Luhmann, N. (1995). *Social systems*. Stanford University Press.

Mathie, A., & Cunningham, G. (2003). From clients to citizens: Asset-based community development as a strategy for community-driven development. *Development in Practice*, *13*(5), 474–486.

Nachmias, D., & Greer, A. L. (1982). Governance dilemmas in an age of ambiguous authority. *Policy Sciences*, *14*(2), 105–116. 10.1007/BF00137112.

Perez-Sindin, X., & Van Assche, K. (2020). *From coal not to ashes but to what? As Pontes, social memory and the concentration problem*. The Extractive Industries and Society. 10.1016/j.exis.2020.07.016.

Rodríguez, I., Sletto, B., Bilbao, B., Sánchez-Rose, I., & Leal, A. (2018). Speaking of fire: reflexive governance in landscapes of social change and shifting local identities. *Journal of Environmental Policy & Planning*, *20*(6), 689–703.

Saari, A. (2022). Topologies of desire: Fantasies and their symptoms in educational policy futures. *European Educational Research Journal*, *21*(6), 883–899. 10.1177/1474904120988389.

Seidl, D. (2016). *Organisational identity and self-transformation: An autopoietic perspective*. Routledge.

Sinclair, S. (2008). Dilemmas of community planning: Lessons from Scotland. *Public Policy and Administration, 23*(4), 373–390. 10.1177/0952076708093250.

Stavrakakis, Y. (2002). *Lacan and the political*. Routledge.

Stirling, A. (2014). From sustainability to transformation: Dynamics and diversity in reflexive governance of vulnerability. *Vulnerability in Technological Cultures: New Directions in Research and Governance*, 305–332.

Styhre, A. (2008). Management control in bureaucratic and postbureaucratic organizations: A Lacanian perspective. *Group & Organization Management, 33*(6), 635–656. 10.1177/1059601108325697.

Van Assche, K., Beunen, R., & Duineveld, M. (2013). *Evolutionary governance theory: An introduction*. Springer.

Van Assche, K., Deacon, L., Gruezmacher, M., Summers, R., Lavoie, S., Jones, K., Granzow, M., Hallstrom, L., & Parkins, J. (2017). *Boom & Bust. Local strategy for big events. A community survival guide to turbulent times*. Groningen/Edmonton, Alberta: InPlanning and University of Alberta, Faculty of Extension.

Van Assche, K., Gruezmacher, M., & Beunen, R. (2022). Shock and conflict in social-ecological systems: Implications for environmental governance. *Sustainability, 14*(2), 610. 10.3390/su14020610.

Van Assche, K., Gruezmacher, M., & Deacon, L. (2020). Land use tools for tempering boom and bust: Strategy and capacity building in governance. *Land Use Policy, 93*, 103994–103994. 10.1016/j.landusepol.2019.05.013.

Van Assche, K., Gruezmacher, M., & Granzow, M. (2021). From trauma to fantasy and policy. The past in the futures of mining communities; the case of Crowsnest Pass, Alberta. *Resources Policy, 72*, 102050–102050. 10.1016/j.resourpol.2021.102050.

Van Assche, K., Hornidge, A.-K., Schlüter, A., & Vaidianu, N. (2020). Governance and the coastal condition: Towards new modes of observation, adaptation and integration. *Marine Policy, 112*. 10.1016/j.marpol.2019.01.002

Voß, J.-P., Bauknecht, D., & Kemp, R. (2006). *Reflexive governance for sustainable development*. Edward Elgar Publishing.

Wertsch, J. V. (2008). Collective memory and narrative templates. *Social Research: An International Quarterly, 75*(1), 133–156.

Zizek, S. (1992). *Looking Awry: An introduction to Jacques Lacan through popular culture*. MIT Press.

Žižek, S. (2000). Melancholy and the act. *Critical Inquiry, 26*(4), 657–681. 10.1086/448987.

12

A PRACTICAL METHODOLOGY

Self-analysis and strategy in resource communities

Introduction: Forms and trajectories

Henry Minztberg coined the term 'crafting' strategy to circumvent the mainstream assumptions and depict strategizing closer to how it is experienced by those involved: building skills as you go, learning from past mistakes, constantly adapting and engaging with the materials and capacities at hand (Mintzberg, 1987). It's never a predictable process, always a continuous learning cycle that leads to outcomes often unexpected. Embarking on the crafting of strategy will often lead to a journey with unknown destinations. In this process, procedure becomes less important and capacity to steer, no matter what the circumstances, becomes fundamental. Much like navigating rough waters, strategizing is a constant process of reconsidering and rethinking the initial itinerary based on what has been experienced and learned.

The journey must begin with self-analysis. For resource communities with complicated relationships with the past, self-analysis will likely have the feeling of a therapeutical exercise. It will likely require guidance since difficult discussions bring up memories and trauma of the past. As we have discussed in Chapter 10 strategy it is a process in which many resources communities will likely need assistance and different kinds of support from outsiders at different points in the process. Tempering the depth of self-analysis regularly might help decide whether it is necessary to dig deeper or if digging in the past has revealed enough to move forward.

Figure 12.1 below gives an overall impression of possible trajectories, starting from self-analysis. As standard procedure, we propose a succession of mapping, to visioning, next articulation of a strategy. Mapping can take different forms and can have different functions, which were hinted at earlier

DOI: 10.4324/9781003332145-12

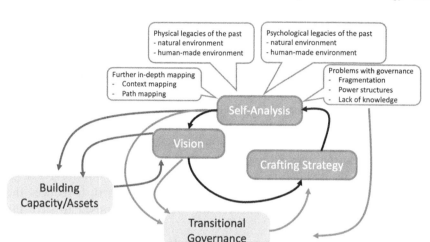

FIGURE 12.1 Strategy in communities as a continuous self-reflection.

and will be further explained below. Visioning is the crafting of a narrative for the future which can find enough local support and strategy is then the vision which is equipped with the necessary institutions, policy tools, to make it happen and which might be transformed in that process. Yet, as the diagram shows, there is no standard procedure and different points can serve to stop the process or move it in a different direction. This can mean that the direction of the strategy is adjusted, but it can also mean that a community jumps from an early stage of self-analysis to vision, or to strategy.

Pathways and inflection points

We will speak of *inflection points* and *reflection points*, where the process goes in a certain direction and where time is taken to think about the process and adapt (cf Gruezmacher & Van Assche, 2022; Kornberger, 2022; Van Assche & Gruezmacher, 2022). A reflection point can become a stop, it can become an inflection point if a step is taken or direction is changed and it can simply be a pause used to reduce chances that blind spots are reproduced. In the next paragraphs, we identify a few possible pathways through the process which skip steps and involve noteworthy inflection points, which, we argue, should be reflection points.

1 As the diagram points out, it is possible that a form of transitional governance will be constructed, a form of governance which is intended as temporary and focuses on the building of capacity, networks, assets, on reinforcing checks and balances, if this is understood as necessary before a proper process of visioning and strategizing can be started. When the conditions are not there and/or the future is entirely opaque or suspiciously

transparent and simple (perhaps someone points at that), then transitional governance can be an option.

2 It is also possible to focus on capacity building, checks and balances and asset building within the current governance arrangement. This could be an option when there is an agreement that the governance system overall functions, is trusted and that it is clear just a few things need to happen before proper strategizing can be embarked upon. Of course, this assumes a thorough self-analysis, which tackles both opacity and false transparency (things seem all too clear and simple). All too often self-analysis skips steps, is not deep enough, does not observe, e.g., concentration problems are not observed and this in turn reduces the strategy to one project or intervention which is supposed to save the community.

3 Self-analysis can, in some cases reveal a unity in future narratives, an easy consensus, or can produce a series of elements of a community future which can easily be assembled. In that case, a jump from self-analysis to strategy can be made, as the assemblage of the narrative can happen while considering the connection with institutions, new or old, towards implementation. An extreme situation could come up where a widely supported narrative even after self-analysis remains highly supported. From that stage, one can jump from self-analysis to strategy.

4 Even more radical yet risky is the idea of skipping self-analysis altogether and trying to turn an existing and supported future narrative into a strategy by tying it to institutions. The process can then focus on identifying institutions which might be repurposed and on gaps where new institutions (policies, plans, bylaws, regulations) might be needed. This is risky as the absence of self-analysis is also the absence of a diagnosis of the series of possible problems which were presented as very common for resource communities in the previous chapters.

5 In some cases, there is already a strategy which is still supported, yet does not work. In those cases, the analysis of the failure will trigger a targeted self-analysis based on the reflection of the implementation failure. This reflection can later be broaden to include a diagnosis of underlying issues in governance, the community or the environment which created the implementation obstacles.

Given the particular situation of resource communities, analyzed in previous chapters, we cannot recommend skipping self-analysis, recognizing that such process can be difficult and even potentially trigger conflict. The main reason why self-analysis cannot be avoided is that the many issues brewing in resource communities cannot be diagnosed without such self-analysis and therefore solutions for those issues cannot be identified. We refer here to versions of the concentration problem, trauma, histories of violence (symbolic and otherwise), polarization, legacies of shock and conflict, fragmentation of institutions, problematic patterns of dependencies in governance and overall weak governance.

Self-analysis

Self-analysis can be fast and slow, deep and shallow, driven entirely by insiders or with the help of outsiders and spearheaded by local leadership or in a more participatory manner. All those options can work; however, what might be truly 'local' needs to be clear; otherwise, the conclusions drawn might be immediately rejected because they are perceived as imposed by outsiders. As self-analysis has no natural limits. The limits as well as the direction of self-analysis need to be established by the community partly before the process and in partly as emerging from the process (Feindt & Weiland, 2018).

To set parameters, as initial limits, a community can decide to articulate steps, to limit time, resources, participation, or topics in a process of self-analysis. It can start from a perceived problem or a goal or an image of a desirable future. It can focus on one domain of policy or more. Self-analysis can predefine roles, for insiders and outsiders, or do this only for a first phase. To emphasize the variation in form and duration of self-analysis, we will speak of mapping.

Some parts of self-analysis we can call *mappings*. Just as a map can help us navigate a physical environment by providing information about different features of the landscape, community mapping exercises will be able to reveal features of the community that can help it in navigating paths towards an improved future. A map is a representation, selection of information that allows us to navigate, to reach a destination, to avoid disastrous decisions. It cannot guarantee that we will reach our destination or how exactly that will be done but we would certainly not embark on a long journey through unknown territories without some sort of map.

Mapping exercises are a way of self-analysis they are an opportunity to ask basic questions. They can be useful for strategizing if they are able to illustrate the links between long-term perspectives or narratives about the future, the institutions and the broader plans or strategies currently in place (Alcorn, 2000). Mapping exercises can be useful as part of a continuous process of self-analysis, a constant adaptation of strategy, not only as a starting point. Mapping exercises can combine well with both academic and more participatory methods to collect, process and share information (Hatleskog & Samuel, 2021; Jakes et al., 2015). We begin by discussing mapping in self-analysis and later we will present more specific methods of mapping that can be useful at different points in the entire process.

The aim of the *first mapping* should be to reveal an initial story of the current situation of the community including that of its governance system.

It should be evident from a first mapping who are the main actors in the collective decision-making process and what institutions mediate their interactions. Some of the main struggles in the system and in the community at broad should also be part of this narrative. An important challenge at this point is to keep in mind the invisibility of certain local problems and issues, the fact that there might be actors influencing collective decisions that are in the background or there might be tacit rules that arbitrate interactions between actors. This invisibility might be the result of a series or combination of problems in the current governance arrangement.

First mapping: Starting from narratives

For a *first mapping* and, with all the caveats about context-sensitivity, we would recommend a focus on *narrative mapping* first. Narratives which deserve special attention are:

- Identity narratives
- Narratives on the past, social memories
- Narratives on the future
- Narratives on assets
- Narratives on problems

The starting point and the focus can depend on the context. Here, the mapping cannot be just a collection of stories. The diversity of stories, common traits and differences, polarities and cleavages, as well as coagulations of stories into discursive configurations which harden the perceived truth or natural character of stories. Especially the connections between stories on past, self and futures deserve attention (Czarniawska, 1997).

The narratives then need to be interrogated, starting with the question where they came from. One can also try to discover, in discussion, blind spots and possibilities to overcome cleavages and polarities. The interrogation is an ongoing process, as a shifts in the interpretation of social memory and identity are the most important goals of the whole process of self-analysis, as they will create space for new futures, which can then form the basis of new strategies (Lowery et al., 2020; Van Assche et al., 2021). Other questions which could come have to do with identifying who benefited from that particular version of the story, which effects does that story have on the environment and whether those stories make other futures impossible right away.

This approach can lead into a questioning of patterns of inclusion and exclusion, in governance and in the stories. Do the stories make certain people, ideas invisible? Are those people also invisible in governance? (Maron & Benish, 2022; Van Assche et al., 2011) One can make a distinction here between inclusion and participation. Actors that do not have the means to participate in governance are being *excluded* (intentionally or not) and even if they were to be encouraged to participate, they are unable to do so because certain barriers prevent them from doing so. When there is a problem of *participation*, we should assume all actors have the means to be part of the collective decision-making process but for some reason are unwilling to do so. The reasons or motivations for lack of participation may point at troubles of the past, misinformation about their participation in governance, etc. Yet another issue is that of *representation* where actors or narratives can participate in governance, they have the means to do so but are not represented in the decisions that are taken (Beunen et al., 2022). This is a situation where vote but not voice is granted in the governance arrangement; their narratives remain absent.

Thus, a mapping and first interrogation of key narratives and patterns of inclusion and exclusion can be a good starting point of self-analysis. The idea of interrogation is important because a substantial part of the effort of self-analysis is diagnosis of problems and for resource communities, this is largely an unveiling of features of memory, identity and governance which are not immediately visible to the community.

Some considerations that can assist the flow and direction of the first mapping include (Gruezmacher & Van Assche, 2022; Van Assche et al. 2020, 2022):

1 The role and involvement of outsiders and leaders. To tackle some of the most difficult issues, the community will need the assistance of a politically neutral actor, possibly a trustworthy outsider that is able to tap into these topics fully being aware of their sensitivity. As we have mentioned, outsiders are also able to ask difficult questions and confront troublesome ideas within the community, trying to avoid oversimplifications of the situation. Sometimes, local leaders can play a role as facilitator and guide, as discussed in Chapter 11.

2 Build in safeguards against false certainties blueprints and over-simplifications. Both outsiders and insiders will need to be aware of the ineffectiveness of following recipes and 'copy-paste' approaches and signal them out. Similarly, when certainty about the future prevails, this is reason for suspicion. Simplification of the problems and issues of the community is also a dangerous trap, equivalent to stating that the rupture in the hull of the Titanic was a mere scratch.

3 Anonymization of voices. Depending on the context, for example, whether the community has access to internet or not, it will be important to consider ways to collect entirely anonymous information from the community and within local administration in a secure manner. People need to feel safe to disclose issues of corruption, coercion, abuse, and they need to have the option to choose whether the information they are disclosing will be made public or not. Perhaps everyone knows there is only one person who could

know of such a problem so even if the identity of the informant is not disclosed the nature of the information reveals their identity.

4 Temporality. Some stories and memories will take time to come to the surface and some only come up at certain points in the analysis, in the conversations or discussions. Either the group or the facilitator will need to discern such points, where new narratives, new shades of interpretation, new affects come to the surface. Trust is of the essence here and if people do not identify with the process, this is a problem. If people do not, honestly, see a future for the community, that is not necessarily a problem, but something that ideally should be brought up in the process, as something that can be worked with.

5 Pressure and decision-making. If the self-analysis is presented as a technical exercise, where information is collected and where a strategy *has* to be produced, as a 'deliverable,' it will not work as self-analysis. A therapeutic, revealing function, will not emerge, as the pressure from decision-making and the lack of pressure coming from the idea of information gathering work together to *misdirect* the analytic effort.

In parallel, or beforehand, a more elementary collection and presentation of information can take place and can involve surveys, interviews, basic historical work, local exhibits, newspaper article series. In addition, a careful collection of old and new documents which were supposed to function as strategy can be collected, summarized and shared. They can be discussed as part of the self-analysis.

If these points are taken into consideration, it is possible that a *diagnosis* of some of the potential problems of resource communities can occur. Is there a version of the concentration problem that occurs? Are we suspecting a deeper trauma? Is there a problem of weak governance which already becomes clear in this kind of mapping? Yet, it is also imaginable that diagnosis is not possible yet, while the presence of some problems is detected in a general sense.

Building-in enough *reflection points* in early self-analysis can help to shorten the analysis, by revealing earlier some of the latent issues in the community, some of the connections routinely not made, some of the hidden memories, closed identities (Meadowcroft, 2007; Melin & Nordqvist, 2007). Cracks in the certainties on past, present and future can bring up elements of the repressed Real. Reflection points can become inflection points if they enable a shift from self-analysis to something else, but also if the analysis moves into new territory, in a new direction. Reflection points can come up naturally, where in the process it becomes clear that something that seemed normal or good before, now starts to look different. Or they can be catalyzed by leadership or facilitator, when they can confront the group with internal contradictions, omissions, alternative perspectives, or questions which did not come up organically.

Reflection is important for resource communities because, as we discussed in earlier chapters, self-observation is a problem, trauma can be a problem, symbolic violence, hidden power relations, material dependencies, all tend to have a latent existence. If problems are deep, more analysis is needed along with more work to unearth what is latent. The partly invisible legacies in resource communities extend to the functioning of governance as well and to the capacity to observe these legacies in governance. As we discussed, working through governance, possibly restructuring governance, will be necessary for a successful strategy (Alvesson & Sköldberg, 2017; Suddaby et al., 2013; Van Assche et al., 2020).

Second mapping: Introduction

A *second mapping* therefore will likely include a detailed *path mapping of governance*. It will certainly be contentious and politically sensitive, nonetheless fundamental to address. Polarization can show-up in governance and leave legacies there, as will trauma, concentration problems and all other troubles mentions above. In some cases, self-analysis might leave spirits down, morale weak and endurance reduced-especially after confronting difficult memories or bringing up troubles of the past, time to regroup might be needed. After a first phase of self-analysis, the path forward will be determined by the answers to a set of questions.

1 A first question would be whether the community is still believing in the need to craft an entirely new strategy. A conclusion can be that the existing narratives, strategies, institutions, general shape of governance are ok for now, that not much else is possible or desirable. If the community comes to such conclusion quickly a serious reflection point can be recommended, where there is a serious scrutiny of processes of exclusion, where dissenting voices, diverging external perspectives are sought, even invited.
2 If the need for a new strategy becomes clear and self-analysis of the preceding sort is deemed enough, one can move to a process of visioning, or to a continuation of analysis with a limited focus, trying to discern what did not work in the old strategy and why.
3 It is possible after initial analysis to realize that a rethinking and nuancing an existing strategy might be the best path forwards. After this, visioning becomes possible and/or a limited further analysis, with again a focus on a further exploration for the reasons the previous strategy failed to be implemented.
4 Possibly, initial analysis reveals that changes to the institutional landscape might be needed, as in changes in the toolset of institutions available for the implementation of an old strategy.

5 In many cases, more serious problems can emerge which require further diagnosis and then working through. A restructuring of social memory and a reinterpretation of identity might be needed, a re-introduction of diversity, a working through fantasy, or dislodging of concentration problems.
6 More diagnosis can be required, a deeper self-analysis which then finds that articulating a direction, a narrative is not possible yet but working on an improvement of governance, or on transitional governance might be feasible. This might be accompanied with a further, slow breaking open of old narratives and weakening of hegemonic power relations. Temporality might be the key.

Often, difficulties in self-analysis will trigger calls for stopping, archiving the self-analysis, with vague promises to return to it later. The long term then becomes not a guiding point for actions in the present, or a future driving visioning but a closet where everything can be hidden and where no implications for the present should be expected. This is not the same as a reflection point; it does not help with rendering transparent what is opaque and it does not help in managing temporality, i.e., finding better occasions to push the analysis further. What *is* often helpful, in managing conflict and complexity, in managing temporality is creating a time and space to *regroup*.

This can be a pause in the process, a shift to easier questions, a slight reorganization of the process, possibly with different actors taking the lead, or a different form of participation taking over for a moment in order to create a breathing space, to simply calm down, to slowly restart from a slightly different angle (Dittrich et al., 2011). *Transitional governance* can function as an extended regrouping, to assemble strength, address some pressing issues and building governance capacity and reflexivity in governance. This can work as a regrouping as long as the intention of self-analysis is not forgotten, as long as there is a remaining awareness that issues in identity and social memory have to be addressed at some point (Van Assche et al. 2020, 2022).

We can say therefore that initial self-analysis can launch several different courses of action. As we discussed before, it can lead to more analysis, different analysis, to visioning, crafting strategy, to a simple return to old routines, or an old strategy, to transitional governance forms, or to a narrow focus on a project, building an asset, or a particular capacity. We would like to emphasize that *self-analysis should be allowed to resume at any point,* as, with sufficient reflexivity, it can appear at any point in visioning or strategizing, or after everything went back to normal, that legacies from the past are causing problems, or are becoming more transparent and susceptible to discussion (Kornberger, 2022). Reflection points, a regrouping and sometimes a hiatus cannot be avoided.

A few implications of our approach become clear at this point and distinguish it from many other perspectives on governance, public management and planning:

- Efficiency cannot be a driving force or central value.
- Fixed goals or expectations of finished products cannot constrain the process.
- Information is not the same as insight.
- Many legacies which need to be addressed are initially not transparent.
- Visions do not emerge from deliberation starting from opinions which are not questioned.

In resource communities, when an awareness is growing as a result of an initial self-analysis the legacies of extraction histories appear more diverse, opaque and constraining than initially thought in both governance and in the community. The community might to come to the realization that more self-analysis is needed, but of a different sort.

Second mapping: Path mapping and context mapping

More in-depth mapping exercises are *context mapping and a path mapping*. These methods are focused on the governance system but they can generate findings which can restart the reflection on narratives, memories, identities and legacies in the community at large (Green & Haines, 2015). As the explanation of some findings in governance can be found in the discursive configurations in the community and in anxieties, hopes, traumas, symbolic violence, master signifiers or unnoticed aspects of the concentration problem existing far beyond the sphere of governance.

Path mapping is essentially a reconstruction of the governance path or trajectory of the community. It necessarily implies looking back in time and relying on those more senior members of the community involved in local decision-making, as well as local histories, media archives and old policy documents and other administrative archives. Context mapping is a broader look at the context affecting governance at the scale observed (Van Assche et al. 2020, 2022). These elements might already become obvious and apparent during the first mapping. In the first mapping, aspects of path and context mapping might have occurred already.

Context mapping is not an encyclopedic exercise, as not all policies at higher levels must be mentioned, not all actors, private and public, which could in theory have an effect on what happens locally. The idea is more to work your way up selectively, from the analysis of local governance paths. As soon as higher levels of governance, or external private actors show up, lobby or constrain what happens locally, they can be included in context mapping. Later, this can serve also in the articulation and assessment of strategy, to refer back to such enabling or constraining influences, or to continue the context mapping at that point (to see who could help for strategy a or b).

Where to draw a boundary or where to stop drawing connections might not be as straightforward as it appears, as the real influence of external actors might be invisible, forgotten, veiled. Some current actors might not be interested in revealing the actual role of outside actors in governance, either now, or in the past. The reasons can be manifold. Also, the influence of stories, fashions, anxieties, obsessions and ideologies from the outside can be accepted but not necessarily acknowledged (Feindt & Weiland, 2018; Gunder & Hillier, 2009). As with other aspects of analysis which are likely to unveil uncomfortable truths, the focus cannot be on maximizing the reveals. The discovery must be a self-discovery, which then can be accepted more easily and can hopefully have consequences for collective action. Thus, individuals, insiders or outsiders, who tackle this work as investigative journalists, can be very important but can also cause great trouble, as they can upset the process of trust-building and self-examination taking place. The process, as we know, is also more complex than for individuals, as here, we need individuals (or organizations) to accept a revelation, after which the revelation needs to be accepted in the community at large (with likely a step in between, of increased awareness and acceptance in the network de facto tasked with the self-analysis).

Questions worth asking in context analysis thus try to identify higher level actors directly or indirectly interacting with or constraining local governance, in a way that is important enough to make them necessary for understanding local governance paths. Additional questions need to address traveling discourses, imposed discourse and affects shared in larger community. One can add questions regarding the material context which can shape the way decisions are made locally or have shaped the course of the governance path.

Path mapping inevitably starts in the initial mapping but cannot be carried out comprehensively there. The first mapping will reveal actors and institutions in the present which associate with dominant narratives, problem definitions, etc, yet almost always some reference to the past will sneak in. Reconstructing the circumstances that led to the arrangements in governance today will enhance the understanding of the possibilities for a change and the options for steering. This exercise will require detective work involving a variety of methods. Patterns of inclusion and exclusion of actors, of emerging, vanishing, transforming actors, of informal actors becoming formally visible and active and the other way around, will need to be established not just through consulting the various institutional memories but also through a careful and cautious tracing of influences, triangulating many sources of information.

How certain important institutions for current and potential strategies came about, which actors were behind them, which other institutions were supporting and supported by it, is indeed serious investigation. Which brings us to the point of limitations in time, resources, patience, interest and understanding, which have to be respected, but to come back to the warning made above, this cannot be an exercise felt as alien or alienating or else it will reduce its impact. Which might them mean that different versions of the path analysis can coexist and second, that it can happen in phases, digging deeper when necessary, zooming in on certain aspects of the governance evolution, on questions which arise in the first steps of path mapping or earlier, in initial self-analysis.

In Chapter 11, we also drew attention to the need for selectivity in mapping power/knowledge interactions and configurations. We mentioned there that the focus, the selectivity can emerge naturally out of previous steps of self-analysis and often from problem definitions: what is perceived as a problem can be traced back to not all but some presences/absences of certain forms of knowledge in governance, certain forms of expertise, narratives, ideologies, forms of local knowledge. It leads back to not all but some power relations, to certain forms of persuasion, some entrenched discourses and forms of expertise in particular policies and in the structure of administration (Carter, 2010; Hendry, 1995b).

In the self-analysis, problem definitions will (hopefully) shift, so new trails of investigation in power/knowledge interactions can follow. So, a question why an existing strategy does not work can lead to questions about a local weakness in governance which can then be traced to the dominance of one ideology in council, to a powerful chief of administration and his preferred expertise, to a legal specialist who used to occupy a position as *de facto* chief strategist and left organizational and cognitive legacies which were never really questioned and only partly observed (Shaw, 2008). When it dawns on a collective mandated with leading the self-analysis that the same ideas seem to come up all the time and hit the same obstacles, this can bring them to take a closer look at both the repetitive nature of ideas underlying strategy, or the repetition of generic arguments against strategy and at the nature of the obstacles.

As actors privilege certain forms of knowledge, institutions entrench further and erode, resulting in the embedding of certain perspectives. Knowledges of different forms and different generalities reinforce each other in governance, work to push people to do something, steering governance in a direction and thus changing the realities of both the people strategizing and those subjected to strategy (Meadowcroft et al., 2012; Rhodes, 1997). Power/knowledge configurations are never stable, although they can contribute to the stabilization of governance configurations and the realities they assume and create. Of course, power/knowledge is not only involved in creating the impression of timeless truths and eternally stable communities; they are also responsible for creating conflict and competition and representing situations as such. In resource communities trapped in concentration problems, the overriding problems of rigidity, stability and simplification in governance do not change the volatility in power/knowledge configurations: slight differences in the perspective can have substantial power implications and can make a big difference in politics and administration. Take the case of a community, or part of it, in search of closure and taking the position of representing and knowing the 'real' version of the identity, this will most likely have an influence in power relations and therefore politics and administration.

Questions worth asking in path mapping thus involve the identification of formal and informal actors; how the configuration have evolved over time. This will help to understand how the configuration could be changed in the future. Identifying real influence versus paper roles is of the essence. So is identifying differences in influence, keeping in mind that quantification is not a goal here. Further, for resource communities, it is helpful to identify which actors, institutions, forms of knowledge mediate the relationship with the natural environment (Roseland, 2000). Who established and maintained the centrality of extraction and of resource identities and futures in governance as well as which relations, institutions and power/knowledge relations did they maintain? Further questions can focus on the narratives and futures promoted by actors (Miller et al., 2015). Narratives on institutions and the actors they connect and they divide, the knowledge they promote or exclude. Informal institutions can be guiding the relation between some actors but not all or can be guiding governance more broadly but only for selected topics (Paschen & Ison, 2014).

Many other questions can be derived from or can be part of path mapping. The analysis must structure itself at some point around the insights gained in a previous step defining the focus of the next step in investigation. One can speak of an adaptive methodology, where no need for comprehensive mapping should be postulated, but also nothing can be considered irrelevant *a priori* (van Assche et al., 2021). It might be revealed that overly expensive utilities make certain strategies improbable, which then directs the path mapping to an earlier time and to actors in governance not considered before. It could transpire that community design is entirely absent as a tool and a form of knowing in local governance and that after some prodding, old-timers with governance experience admit they all hate it. This in turn can point the path mapping towards an old plan which was considered an absolute failure or proposed by ideologues now completely discredited. The trail of investigation in path mapping is thus different from a careful mapping of a murder scene. The trail can be the investigation of a murder, why something did not work, but also the investigation of why something did work and how certain ideas on present and past were inscribed in governance (Alcorn, 2000; Van Assche et al., 2021). Who made concentration problems worse? The murder analogy does show that, before clues that give direction appear, some general mapping does need to take place, in this case, a general understanding of governance and its evolution.

Second mapping: Assets and asset mapping

Asset mapping is a third entry to more detailed self-analysis. Here the focus is not on problems and perceived problems but on the more positive aspects of the community. This can be fundamental for crafting strategy, if such strategy is to be more than tackling problems, assuaging fears, or trying to extend the present into the future. Asset mapping can take place in self-analysis, both first and second mappings and it can take place in visioning and again strategizing. This is the case because evolving ideas on community, past and future also entail evolving ideas on what counts as an asset (Broadley, 2021). One can also present asset mapping as an innocuous and incontrovertibly useful way of opening discussion that can later enable debating more difficult topics as mentioned earlier (Green & Haines, 2015; Jakes et al., 2015).

What appears as an asset, hinges on what is seen as valuable and what is of value emerges from within a particular context. What is of value amidst the tropical rainforest might not appear as valuable in a temperate urban setting and vice versa. For this reason, we talk about asset mapping being contextual, meaning it requires defining and delineating within the relevant context. The boundary of that context will ensure a limit to the exercise, preventing a situation where everything is defined as an asset.

Assets can be defined differently for different futures and for that reason we believe asset mapping should also be understood as virtual. A new vision can be built around existing assets which are recognized, or not recognized yet, while they can also aim at the creation of new assets, which might sense in the overall future narrative, or a new interpretation of self and environment which can create openings for such creation of new assets. Recognizing assets in old futures, in old ideas about the future, both in stories and as encoded in policies, plans strategies, can be useful in evidencing what happened to that virtuality: was an initially identified asset later still recognized as asset? Did collective action follow? What were the reality effects and how were they assessed? Did this lead to a reinterpretation of the asset, or to other changes, which left the asset unquestioned or unchanged?

As communities and their governance systems change, asset definitions evolve as well. This can be mapped and inspire new reflection on old, new and future assets. Such reflection can connect self-analysis and visioning. Changes in the physical as well as discursive environment can lead to shifts in asset definition and valuation, changes in governance and community (Green & Haines, 2015; Mathie & Cunningham, 2003). New technologies, climate change, new infrastructures, new national policies, new people moving in with new lifestyle ideas, can alter assets, can change the way a place assigns value and connects this to collective action. Cultural change, slowly shifting ideas on democracy, rights, about the good community, the role of politics and administration, environmental quality and quality of life, can all contribute to changing understandings of what constitutes an asset and what not. A landscape might exist as a backdrop for resource extraction, largely invisible except as obstacle and later take center stage, either negatively as polluted place, or positively as an asset which can support attractive lifestyles and a variety of new activities (Hatleskog & Samuel, 2021).

Asset mapping, path mapping and context mapping, as we mentioned, draw the focus on the smaller world of governance and its evolution. This is useful as it can explain the present better, how it can be transformed and why older futures did or did not have much impact. Yet, as we mentioned before, this might have to be interrupted when trauma erupts, when scars are opened and when the process is felt as meddling with memories that belong to an uncomfortable or distressing past. It might be useful to make a shift, inflect the process, bring in an outsider, move back to initial self-analysis or move the focus away from governance itself (Van Assche & Gruezmacher, 2022). Expertise in the field of social work, community healing, community psychology can be called upon but trusted locals, leaders or other community members (or organizers) recognized as wise and impartial can be preferable when outsiders are not trusted or experts are recognized only in a technical sense (Hendry, 1995a).

We would like to recall that the goal is not to establish goals or force the enactment of a strategy, for many resource communities certainly the goal is to shift discourse on memory and identity after which new futures might surface or could be constructed with less resistance. That shift could require working through of fantasy, dislodging concentration problems, addressing a history of violence and a gradual rethinking of the past. The different forms of secondary mapping can be helpful but at the same time can also draw the attention away from the problems stemming from opaque legacies. Path mapping and other mappings will prove useful connections to visioning and strategy. These types of mappings, if they do take place, can elucidate the way narratives and institutions might be connected and could help illustrate the way certain futures are likely to play out (Alcorn, 2000).

Visioning

Visioning is not always clearly demarcated from the other stages and not always necessary, as we have already mentioned. We draw attention to it, as a possibly important inflection point which requires ample reflection and assessment of possible alternatives. We also bring it up to emphasize that strategy cannot be based on a narrative that is assembled in a technical or non-participatory manner and that if a strategy exists based on a narrative for the future this does not mean that the narrative finds support in the community (Elkins et al., 2009).

Visioning itself, the creation of a unified narrative for the future to feature in a new strategy can start from:

- an existing strategy and its future narrative,
- from existing narratives encoded in other policy documents,
- from a more or less unified identity narrative already existing, or
- from a diversity of stories which can overlap, compete, contradict.

Hence, the narrative mapping discussed above is immediately useful for visioning and doing it can already productively question old dominant narratives, or narratives already built into policy and strategy (Lowery et al., 2020; Sandercock, 2003). Although a good strategy is informed by a good analysis this does not necessarily mean that analysis translates directly into strategy; visioning can be necessary and not a waste of time.

External expertise, in substance or in organizing processes of visioning and strategizing can come in handy but as mentioned before, it cannot replace local knowledge or ignore local sensibilities nor simply assemble existing narratives. A common practice is to derive vision and then strategy from scenarios. Those scenarios can then be informed by projections of key indicators in the future, sometimes by local narratives, sometimes by existing or anticipated local policies (which could be strategy options). The openness for and connectivity of expert-driven scenarios towards what exists and what is hoped for in the community can thus vary widely. Although working with scenarios could certainly be used in visioning exercises a vision should not be limited to a few scenarios or predictions of the future and should certainly not be an artifact huddled by an expert (Hendry, 1995a).

A vision then must be a participatory exercise where the many stories and images of the future of a community must be forged into one. If this construction is not a collective effort, it will lie far from the hearts of the people, likely to be an imperfect synthesis and won't hold for a very long time in the collective mind (Sandercock, 2003; Wates, 2014). Self-analysis of a participatory kind, even in diffuse forms such as a phase of more intensive reflection in local media, politics, cultural associations, on local identity, social memory and resource futures, can nonetheless help to embed visioning in a collective process, increasing chances that a vision will connect to the broad collective. In addition, the self-analysis, in many cases already offers elements of a shared vision, shared ideas on past, future, on identity and environment, shared affects.

Moreover, the appearance of diverse pasts and futures in self-analysis starts the discussion on different options for the future, as a vision underpinning a strategy needs to be both desirable for the community and deemed realistic (Newig et al., 2007). Of course, the testing of what is desirable and realistic will continue during the process of strategy building, when links with institutions and resources are envisioned. It will continue during implementation as well but the strategy will stand a better chance if such testing already started during self-analysis and big question like what are different ideas on what the community wants and what they believe is realistic or what suits their environment and identity will have already been initially tackled. In visioning, something needs to happen – choices need to be made and the result can be:

- An entirely new narrative
- An assemblage of elements of existing narratives
- An assemblage of existing narrative fragments and expert input
- An old narrative

The difference between types of scenarios mentioned above can be invoked again here as a difference between scenario and vision or as a difference between prediction and vision. This difference is important because ignoring it makes it difficult to truly strategize as community but also because the way a community ignores or understands this difference is telling about its self-image. This self-image is important for the self-analysis and the strategy process itself. In practice, many communities do not have a realistic understanding of their own degree of autonomy, their potential to intervene in trends they see unfolding, in realities they see as hard (Jakes et al., 2015; Meadowcroft et al., 2012). They either underestimate or overestimate their own power and autonomy. These misconceptions can be associated with concentration problems, trauma, symbolic violence, with ruling ideologies and master signifiers, with neglect of administration and lack of diverse perspectives in governance to the extent that blind spots multiply and become harder to diagnose.

Reflection points or pauses might have to be built in, especially if the self-analysis has glossed over some of the underlying problems and conflict is erupting. Even if the self-diagnosis was honest enough, conflict can remain and come to the surface in the visioning process. Reflection points can then be moments to:

- Continue self-analysis
- Remind the visioning group or the community at large of insights from the self-analysis
- Bring in, change, or remove external advisors or leadership roles in visioning

- Shift the form of participation in visioning
- Either zoom in or take a step away from the knottiest conflict
- Try new methods, new media
- Bring in new information or new people when comparing and thinking through different visions, possibly bracketing part of the problem and projecting competing ideas into the future to identify consequences, future differences and overlaps

What counts in the literature as visioning methods can all be considered, yet we add a word of caution in the sense that no method on offer can cover the diversity of situations and phases in a process. In other words, crafting methods based on existing ones is perfectly fine, shifting methods and combining them, moving from structured visioning and intense participation to more diffuse processes of discussing possible futures can all be recommended (Van Assche & Gruezmacher, 2022). Some of the methods used in self-analysis can come in handy during visioning as well (see the toolbox glossary), e.g., charrettes, discussion based on exhibits, after cultural events, workshops, meetings, focus groups, formation of committees and councils with a limited time span.

Sometimes, the problems diagnosed during self-analysis will make it difficult to embark on a productive visioning process, that is, a process that does reproduce existing blind spots and forms of closure, exclusion and disconnect. In such case, a form of transitional governance can be devised aiming at the increase of diversity of perspectives at the table (nr34). This could be in governance itself, in the short-term governance of the network thinking about the future or maybe, in the community as such. This is a dilemma, mentioned earlier, since concentration problems in governance and community can reinforce each other, the effort to diversify perspectives in the community (and them being heard in governance) can encounter obstacles in terms of perceived legitimacy.

Diversity will tend to prompt deliberation ensuring a kind of 'quality-control,' another way to avoid one sided perspectives or oversimplifications and, ensuring the vision is shaped by both its strengths and weaknesses (Voß et al., 2022). Debates during the process will help pointing out at its flaws as well as its advantages. In the end, if the overall story is persuasive for the community, then the process could be considered constructive and will probably be useful (Lowery et al., 2020). It might be possibly to assuage part of the concentration problem and diversify perspectives during the process of visioning itself, without taking a detour through transitional governance. This might make the process of visioning more palatable to the community but requires a double effort on the part of the organizers of the process (Sandercock, 2003).

Crafting strategy

Shaping the community's vision into a strategy, articulating narrative and connecting them to institutions will be a process requiring constant reflexivity and creativity. In practice, the strategizing process will be a back and forth between open spaces for participation and deliberation and less open spaces (Van Assche & Gruezmacher, 2022). The crafting itself will not be entirely participative, it will require smaller circles of deliberation, among experts in administration or consultants, in well-informed networks of politicians and public and private sector experts. This is especially true for larger communities where complexity of issues will require delegation of tasks. In smaller communities more active forms of participation are possible. However, as we mentioned already, systems of governance in complex societies are unable to run on participation alone. The balance between open and closed spaces for deliberation as well as the balance between local and external participants will change throughout the process and will need to be evaluated continuously.

Strategy is more art than science, it is always crafted. Community strategies are per definition the product of politics and no doubt more complex than strategies for an organization. In our perspective, they should be the product of politics in the broad sense, in other words the product of governance. The expertise of politicians and administrative staff is essential as is participation of the broader community. Strategy must begin with a thorough self-analysis which will yield elements useful *throughout* the process of strategizing (nr 17; and Kornberger, 2022). There is no straightforward path from self-analysis to strategy, in practice there will be detours and hiatuses. In the journey taken by the community, reflexivity should be a constant. Enhanced reflexivity post-strategizing in normal governance routines, will be very useful for the implementation and adaptation of strategy. It is important to keep in mind that strategy should be understood as a function; bringing together narratives and institutions and becoming an institution itself (Van Assche et al., 2022).

Thus, the process must be structured in a way that makes sense for the community and adjust to insights from self-analysis, visioning and previous steps in strategizing. Various methods mentioned above (and below, see toolbox) can be used, participation methods can change and expert, facilitator and leadership roles can vary. However, some questions and some points of advice can be generalized.

1 Strategy (this cannot be stressed enough) cannot be seen as the goal in itself and that goal cannot be reduced to a paper document (Carter et al., 2008; Golsorkhi et al., 2010). Strategizing is a function of governance implying it might not be possible or in some cases advisable to reach it from just any point in the evolution of a community's governance. Certainly, in resource

communities where, initially, many things which could or should influence strategy are not observed or acknowledged, one cannot jump to strategy.

2 One can ask which form the strategy will take. This question can be answered at the outset, after self-analysis, or during the process of visioning and strategy. It has to be kept in mind that strategy can take many forms, with the more elaborate formal versions not necessarily the most effective. Strategies can be openly comprehensive and ambitious, aiming to coordinate large number of policy domains, or be constructed around one policy domain, or one area (a downtown or former mining site) which is expected to be a catalyst of change (Kornberger, 2012). It can be short or long, even informal, yet leading to the creation of new institutions. It can be short because it is most about new forms of coordination between what exists, or because of a very general direction and substantial goal, with a few indications regarding policy coordination or integration. It can be short yet very ambitious. Or long and not truly ambitious.

3 One can ask whether, on the institutional side, the focus is on the coordination of existing institutions, their integration maybe, or on the production of new institutions. Recognizing gaps in the existing institutional fabric can only happen after visioning, when it becomes clear what is absent that would enable that particular vision. It can entail a recognition that certain policy tools are there, but not working (dead institutions), which then triggers an inquiry as to the why. And it can involve an effort to discover how existing institutions might be fragmented, contradict each other, resist coordination.

4 From the perspective of assets, the focus can be on finding synergies between existing assets, or on redefine assets in the new perspective of the vision. Or, in ambitious strategies, there can be a strong interest in the creation of new assets (Mathie & Cunningham, 2003).

5 A distance has to be defined from the initial problem and asset definitions. If during the strategy process, it is discovered that these remained the same, it is advisable to introduce a reflection moment, as it can indicate that not all problems have been diagnosed in self-analysis.

6 Someone needs to be responsible for the implementation of the strategy and this choice will have significant effects. If too many people or departments are made responsible this can effectively mean nobody feels responsible. If too few, are tasked or if a department with narrow focus is tasked it can mean that the strategy will be marginalized in politics and administration (Carter et al., 2008; Kornberger, 2012). Chances are that this small group will become a minor actor in governance and except when backed by leadership and officially mandated to coordinate it will become an afterthought; implementation will become scattershot. On the other hand, if a focus on one policy domain makes sense and that domain is

allowed to coordinate the others then it can be housed there (think economic development, or tourism, or natural resources, or 'diversification').

7 An important decision to take is whether the community strategy also involves a restructuring of governance. For many resource communities, self-analysis will hint at problems with current governance, if certain desirable futures are to be realized. The conclusion can then be to change the vision or to not even start visioning. It is also possible to consider a strategy of reform of governance which can precede the other steps in strategy implementation or take place simultaneously.

Many of these points can be addressed early on, some will return a few times during the process. Some issues are more technical and can be reflected early on, in general terms but are best addressed when other decisions have been taken already. We are thinking now of questions such as the following:

- Which existing policies and other institutions will need to be coordinated through this strategy? Are there some dead institutions?
- Which forms of policy fragmentation and contradiction need to be resolved to allow for coordination or integration?
- Which goals in the vision require new institutions? Who can most easily recognize those gaps and do we have procedures to fill the gaps?
- Are we missing basic information, even after analysis and visioning, regarding the community or regarding the requirements for or implications of certain goals and aspects of the vision? What is missing and who can help quickly?
- How will goals, elements, steps in the strategy be linked to each other and to the narrative? How can we assess before and after enacting the strategy that it does function as one thing, as one institution and not as a paper frame around a list of goals, a few departments, a series of policies and plans? One can consider goals as links between narrative and policy (or other institutions). This can work but one needs to avoid then that the strategy is not turning into a checklist of goals to be achieved.
- To what extent can we predefine subtopics, groups, steps and phases, low-hanging motivational fruit, without losing the coherence in the strategy without losing sight of the idea that a community strategy is meant to foster coordination, not specialization or compartmentalization.

In the process of strategizing, it will be easy and seductive to forget about the seemingly elusive problems discussed earlier in this book and the often-prickly process of tackling them. Yet, if self-analysis did not bring to light concentration problems and other issues mentioned before and if they have not been worked through; if the process of visioning and strategizing were not helpful and if the resulting strategy did not start from a point of sufficient transparency and distance from these problems of closure, rigidity and self-deceit, then the strategy will have little chance of success (Van Assche et al., 2022). Nevertheless, one needs to recognize the real difficulties of resource communities to climb out of a pit that was often dug by others, out of problems created by others; one aspect of the strategy will have to be the continuation of work on those problems.

Governance reform

If we say that for many resource communities, strategy will have to be, in part, aiming at reform of governance itself because, as we know, the toolbox of governance tends to be insufficient and a history of extraction tends to leave other undesirable and opaque legacies in governance (Van Assche et al., 2021; Voß & Bornemann, 2011). Coming back to the understanding that each governance configuration has its own deficiencies, in relation to what the community aspires to, there are a few things that often reappear as goals of governance reform and which make sense given the typical issues of resource communities:

- *Enhancing reflexivity* post-strategy can be helpful to prevent a return of the concentration problem or other issues. It can help to make dependencies more transparent, possibly reduce them and make them more manageable, enhancing the steering capacity in local governance. This can be approached from different angles. It can include building in routines of self-interrogation: why are we doing this? Is this what we wanted? Who told us this? Does this reflect the way we want to go? How does this relate to other policies? Does this contribute to a larger goal? Is that goal still supported? Citizens, politicians, administration can do this, formally and informally and it is easier when media, public discourse are vibrant and critical and when diverse perspectives are still (or again) present in community, politics and administration (Feindt & Weiland, 2018; Voß & Bornemann, 2011).
- *Maintaining and restoring diversity* in governance and community, by not only tolerating but encouraging diverse perspectives and giving them a position in governance, therefore helps with reflexivity. And it helps with the prevention of concentration and other problems, as once diverse perspectives are established, that diversity is easier to maintain. Restoring diversity is not a technical matter alone and we know it can be the result of thorough self-analysis, since it can slowly open perspectives and allow either existing diversity to be revealed and voiced or new diversity, including reinterpretations of social memory and identity, to emerge in the process (Wates, 2014).
- *Checks and balances* in resource communities tend to be affected and restoring diversity, plus institutional reform can slowly make a difference. Working on checks and balances, on diversity and (in self-analysis)

social memory means that positions of power must be questioned and seemingly evident truths need to be dislodged. This is not a simple matter yet working on several of the points in this list at the same time can offer several openings for change, while the quality of self-analysis can make a difference. Simpler measures can include term limits, public debate, re-balancing the power between politics and administration, between departments in administration, stabilizing administration (Green & Haines, 2015; Kelly, 2012).

- *Enhancing institutional memory and transparency* can help in all other efforts, in working on checks and balances, enhancing diversity and reflexivity (Rhodes, 1997). If stability in administration is fostered, operational transparency in politics and administration are improved and institutional memory preserved and easily mobilized, then it is easier for citizens and staff to form a counter-weight to dominant politicians. A new style of politicians can more easily find arguments, allies and procedures in trying to pry open hegemonic stories and closed networks.
- *Autonomy* of the community to shape its future is something that is not a given. It can be developed by understanding and using the existing tools of governance better and by strategically developing new tools, new assets and resources. The formal powers of a community do not have to be altered by higher-level governments to achieve this. Increased autonomy means increased agency and this can, together with a process of self-analysis and visioning, allow for a diversity of possible futures. An intermediate strategy of increasing autonomy of local governance will need a starting point in mapping, careful mapping of the actual and paper powers available, the tools that work and do not work and the narratives about the actual and desirable powers of local governance (Sandercock, 2003).
- *Weak governance* can therefore, in almost every case, be transformed and increasing autonomy is one of the paths. Building expertise, enhancing reflexivity, working on checks and balances, stimulating diversity and recognizing de-differentiation can all be part of a strengthening of governance capacity (Jakes et al., 2015). Building assets, finding resources, expanding networks, lobbying, courting if necessary might all be useful (Hatleskog & Samuel, 2021). Yet, we believe most useful of all in this long-term effort is creating a situation where it is easier to distance reflectively, from dominant identity narratives and social memories without repercussions.

Memory and identity might be the most elusive of concepts for many people interested in community development, in policy, planning and administration, yet, for an understanding of the actions of resource communities, an understanding of the myriad legacies a history of resource extraction, resource dependence and resource identification, they are essential. One can argue that the case of resource communities demonstrates more clearly what is also present deeper under the surface in all other communities. Many of the limitations in the reinvention of resource communities are self-limitations but one cannot point the finger at the people and their representatives, as the self is not entirely self-aware and the limits to self-observation and understanding largely stem from the same history of resource dependence they are trying to escape or perpetuate (Van Assche et al., 2021). Chances are that neither of those options is the best one and that many others might be available, but hard to imagine and organize from the vantage point they find themselves.

Opening alternative possible futures for the community thus means making the community more transparent for itself. This will, in all likelihood, involve a slow and painful process of self-analysis to dislodge concentration problems, become aware of the legacies of violence, symbolic violence and trauma, to recognize legacies and break dependencies (Jakes et al., 2015). Nothing less than a restructuring of social memory and identity is at stake, but this cannot be directly aimed at; it can come about slowly through self-analysis, visioning and strategizing, which will likely entail the partial rebuilding of the tools the community has to shape itself, to imagine its future and navigate in the desired direction. If outsiders try to do this, certainly if they aim too directly at issues of identity and memory, this will not work (Hendry, 1995a).

Analysis must be self-analysis and strategizing must be perceived as an activity *for* the community that is recognized and supported *by* the community. At the same time, people in the community, in leadership, in civil society organizations, in administration, in the private sector, can all play the role of quasi-outsider and help prying open closed perspectives and bringing about diversity (Hughes et al., 2021; Kelly, 2012). Actual outsiders can be helpful in defined roles that are not leadership roles. A new generation or a new dialog between generations can also be helpful to break open the stories which make it difficult to see how the past is constraining the future (Van Assche et al., 2017; Wates, 2014).

References

Alcorn, J. B. (2000). *Borders, rules and governance: Mapping to catalyse changes in policy and management*. International Institute for Environment and Development.

Alvesson, M., & Sköldberg, K. (2017). *Reflexive methodology: New vistas for qualitative research*. SAGE.

Beunen, R., Van Assche, K., & Gruezmacher, M. (2022). Evolutionary perspectives on environmental governance: Strategy and the co-construction of governance, community and environment. *Sustainabilty, this issue* (14).

Broadley, C. (2021). Advancing asset-based practice: Engagement, ownership, and outcomes in participatory design. *The Design Journal*, 24(2), 253–275.

Carter, C. (2010). *Re-framing strategy: Power, politics and accounting*. Emerald Group Publishing Limited.

Carter, C., Clegg, S. R., & Kornberger, M. (2008). *A very short, fairly interesting and reasonably cheap book about studying strategy*. SAGE.

Czarniawska, B. (Ed.). (1997). *A narrative approach to organization studies*. Sage Publications.

Dittrich, K., Guerard, S., & Seidl, D. N. (2011, January). Meetings in the strategy process: Toward an integrative framework. In *Academy of Management Proceedings* (Vol. 2011, No. 1, pp. 1–6). Briarcliff Manor, NY: Academy of Management.

Elkins, L. A., Bivins, D., & Holbrook, L. (2009). Community visioning process: A tool for successful planning. *Journal of Higher Education Outreach and Engagement*, *13*(4), 75–84.

Feindt, P. H., & Weiland, S. (2018). Reflexive governance: Exploring the concept and assessing its critical potential for sustainable development. Introduction to the special issue. *Journal of Environmental Policy & Planning*, *20*(6), 661–674.

Golsorkhi, D., Rouleau, L., Seidl, D., & Vaara, E. (2010). *Cambridge handbook of strategy as practice*. Cambridge University Press.

Green, G. P., & Haines, A. (2015). *Asset building & community development*. SAGE Publications.

Gruezmacher, M., & Van Assche, K. (2022). *Crafting strategies for sustainable local development*. Groningen: InPlanning.

Gunder, M., & Hillier, J. (2009). *Planning in ten words or less: A Lacanian entanglement with spatial planning*. Ashgate Publishing, Ltd.

Hatleskog, E., & Samuel, F. (2021). Mapping as a strategic tool for evidencing social values and supporting joined-up decision making in Reading, England. *Journal of Urban Design*, *26*(5), 591–612. 10.1080/13574809.2021.1890555.

Hendry, J. (1995a). Culture, community and networks: The hidden cost of outsourcing. *European Management Journal*, *13*(2), 193–200. 10.1016/0263-2373(95)00007-8.

Hendry, J. (1995b). Strategy formation and the policy context. *Journal of General Management*, *20*(4), 54–64. 10.1177/030630709502000404.

Hughes, J., Kornberger, M., MacKay, B., O'Brien, P., & Reddy, S. (2021). Organizational strategy and its implications for strategic studies: A review essay. *Journal of Strategic Studies*, *0*(0), 1–24. 10.1080/01402390.2021.1994950.

Jakes, S., Hardison-Moody, A., Bowen, S., & Blevins, J. (2015). Engaging community change: The critical role of values in asset mapping. *Community Development*, *46*(4), 392–406.

Kelly, E. D. (2012). *Community planning: An introduction to the comprehensive plan*. Island Press.

Kornberger, M. (2012). Governing the city: From planning to urban strategy. *Theory, Culture & Society*, *29*(2), 84–106. 10.1177/0263276411426158.

Kornberger, M. (2022). *Strategies for distributed and collective action: Connecting the dots*. Oxford University Press.

Lowery, B., Dagevos, J., Chuenpagdee, R., & Vodden, K. (2020). Storytelling for sustainable development in rural communities: An alternative approach. *Sustainable Development*, *28*(6), 1813–1826. 10.1002/sd.2124.

Maron, A., & Benish, A. (2022). Power and conflict in network governance: Exclusive and inclusive forms of network administrative organizations. *Public Management Review*, *24*(11), 1758–1778.

Mathie, A., & Cunningham, G. (2003). From clients to citizens: Asset-based community development as a strategy for community-driven development. *Development in Practice, 13*(5), 474–486.

Meadowcroft, J. (2007). National sustainable development strategies: Features, challenges and reflexivity. *European Environment, 17*(3), 152–163.

Meadowcroft, J., Langhelle, O., & Ruud, A. (2012). Governance, democracy and sustainable development: Moving beyond the impasse. In *Governance, democracy and sustainable development* (pp. 1–13). Edward Elgar Publishing. https://www. elgaronline.com/display/edcoll/9781849807562/9781849807562.00009.xml.

Melin, L., & Nordqvist, M. (2007). The reflexive dynamics of institutionalization: The case of the family business. *Strategic Organization, 5*(3), 321–333.

Miller, C. A., O'Leary, J., Graffy, E., Stechel, E. B., & Dirks, G. (2015). Narrative futures and the governance of energy transitions. *Futures, 70*, 65–74. 10.1016/ j.futures.2014.12.001.

Mintzberg, H. (1987, July 1). Crafting Strategy. Harvard Business Review. https:// hbr.org/1987/07/crafting-strategy

Newig, J., Voss, J. P., & Monstadt, J. (2007). Governance for sustainable development in the face of ambivalence, uncertainty and distributed power: An introduction. *Journal of Environmental Policy & Planning, 9*(3–4), 185–192.

Paschen, J.-A., & Ison, R. (2014). Narrative research in climate change adaptation—Exploring a complementary paradigm for research and governance. *Research Policy, 43*(6), 1083–1092. 10.1016/j.respol.2013.12.006.

Rhodes, R. A. W. (1997). *Understanding governance: Policy networks, governance, reflexivity, and accountability.* Open University Press.

Roseland, M. (2000). Sustainable community development: Integrating environmental, economic, and social objectives. *Progress in Planning, 54*(2), 73–132. 10.1016/S0305-9006(00)00003-9.

Sandercock, L. (2003). Out of the closet: The importance of stories and storytelling in planning practice. *Planning Theory & Practice, 4*(1), 11–28.

Shaw, M. (2008). Community development and the politics of community. *Community Development Journal, 43*(1), 24–36. 10.1093/cdj/bsl035.

Suddaby, R., Seidl, D., & Lê, J. K. (2013). Strategy-as-practice meets neo-institutional theory.

Van Assche, K., & Gruezmacher, M. (2022). Asset mapping 2.0; contextual, iterative, and virtual mapping for community development. *Community Development*, 1–16. 10.1080/15575330.2022.2131861.

Van Assche, K., Beunen, R., Duineveld, M., & Gruezmacher, M. (2021). Adaptive methodology. *Topic, theory, method and data in ongoing conversation. International Journal of Social Research Methodology*, 1–15. 10.1080/13645579.2021.1964858.

Van Assche, K., Beunen, R., Gruezmacher, M., & Duineveld, M. (2020). Rethinking strategy in environmental governance. *Journal of Environmental Policy & Planning, 22*(5), 695–708. 10.1080/1523908X.2020.1768834.

Van Assche, K., Deacon, L., Gruezmacher, M., Summers, R., Lavoie, S., Jones, K., Granzow, M., Hallstrom, L., & Parkins, J. (2017). *Boom & Bust. Local strategy for big events. A community survival guide to turbulent times.* Groningen/Edmonton, Alberta: InPlanning and University of Alberta, Faculty of Extension.

244 A practical methodology

Van Assche, K., Duineveld, M., Beunen, R., & Teampau, P. (2011). Delineating locals: transformations of knowledge/power and the governance of the Danube Delta. *Journal of Environmental Policy & Planning, 13*(1), 1–21.

Van Assche, K., Duineveld, M., Gruezmacher, M., & Beunen, R. (2021). Steering as path creation: Leadership and the art of managing dependencies and reality effects. *Politics and Governance, 9*(2), 369–380. 10.17645/pag.v9i2.4027.

Van Assche, K., Gruezmacher, M., Summers, B., Culling, J., Gajjar, S., Granzow, M., Lowerre, A., Deacon, L., Candlish, J., & Jamwal, A. (2022). Land use policy and community strategy. Factors enabling and hampering integrated local strategy in Alberta, Canada. *Land Use Policy, 118*, 106101. 10.1016/j.landusepol.2022. 106101.

Van Assche, K., Verschraegen, G., & Gruezmacher, M. (2021). Strategy for collectives and common goods: Coordinating strategy, long-term perspectives and policy domains in governance. *Futures, 128*, 102716. 10.1016/j.futures.2021.102716.

Voß, J. P., Schritt, J., & Sayman, V. (2022). Politics at a distance: Infrastructuring knowledge flows for democratic innovation. *Social Studies of Science, 52*(1), 106–126.

Voß, J.-P., & Bornemann, B. (2011). The politics of reflexive governance: Challenges for designing adaptive management and transition management. *Ecology and Society, 16*(2), 9. [online] URL: http://www.ecologyandsociety.org-9. [online] URL: http://www.ecologyandsociety.org.

Wates, N. (2014). *The community planning handbook: How people can shape their cities, towns and villages in any part of the world.* Routledge.

INDEX

For Product Safety Concerns and Information please contact our EU representative GPSR@taylorandfrancis.com Taylor & Francis Verlag GmbH, Kaufingerstraße 24, 80331 München, Germany

Printed and bound by CPI Group (UK) Ltd, Croydon, CR0 4YY

01/05/2025

01858406-0001